Where's The EQ?
Race and Policing Up Close

By

B. Bernard Ferguson, Ph.D.

Foreword by J.W. Wiley

Published by

EQ Perspective

B. Bernard Ferguson, Ph.D.

Las Vegas, Nevada

ISBN 978-0-9978651-0-3 (Ebook)

ISBN 978-0-9978651-9-6 (Paperback)

Acknowledgments

This book was not written in a vacuum and could have not have been accomplished without the help of many individuals in my life, starting with my wonderful wife, Diane, and my children, JaRon and JaNae. I want to thank each of you for providing me with the type of support that allowed me to balance the demands of having a career in law enforcement while at the same time attending to my responsibilities as a husband and father. Your love and understanding has made all of this possible, enabling me to string together the thoughts occupying space within my mind relative to the role race plays within American policing. Being able to *see* the police profession through your eyes allowed me to write more openly, as opposed to how I initially began this literary journey, where I was merely circling the wagons when addressing some of the tough issues involving engagements between police officers and the African American community. I love each of you more than words could ever express, and I want you to know just how much I value your perspective and appreciate you always being in my corner.

To my dad, Buford Douglas Ferguson, thank you for sharing with me your positive and not-so-positive experiences with police officers and for ensuring that, although I had joined the ranks of policing, I would never turn a blind eye to the critical work that needs to be done in bridging the relationship gap between police officers and private citizens. Our conversations served as motivation for me taking on a project such as writing this book, and I thank you for them.

To my mom, Narsis Reese Ferguson, you still, and always will, inspire me through your spirit. Not a day goes by without me wishing that you were alive to witness the completion of this book; however, because I feel your presence, I know that you are aware of my every achievement. Thank you for the painstaking effort you devoted to my early learning, which created the foundation from which I write today. May you rest in peace.

To my younger brother, Don, thank you for providing me with a first-hand account of some of the struggles faced by newly hired police officers seemingly caught between wanting to fit in with fellow officers, while at the same time experiencing difficulty with supporting observed inappropriate behavior. Your input provided me with a perspective that, while not personally encountered during my law enforcement career, was invaluable to me while piecing together my thoughts for this book.

Thanks to two of my former colleagues (you know who you are) for enhancing the content of my book through the input you provided based on your respective law enforcement experiences. I particularly appreciate your candor when providing your thoughts surrounding some of the more volatile encounters we have witnessed between police officers and the public in quite some time. Your input not only gives readers a glimpse into the thinking of a police officer faced with such an encounter, but also showed that at times, there are no clear-cut answers when it comes to determining what exactly constitutes an *appropriate* police response. Your contributions serve as excellent examples relative to the impact of perceptions on one's thinking, but more importantly, they indicate that the thinking of police officers is often guided by the perceptions they hold, just like any other member of society.

Thanks to my long-time friends who are as close to me as brothers, Alan Zinsmeister and Wes Smith, for pouring your all into my manuscript and providing suggestions relative to content, tone, and style. The dialogue the three of us have had surrounding engagements between police officers and the African American community did not begin with the writing of this book, but rather has been a continuous conversation that began long ago. Thanks to both of you for contributing to that discussion, and know that you have inspired and enriched my thinking, for which I am eternally grateful.

Thanks to Ginny Glass at WordSugar Designs, for creating an awesome book cover following our many conversations surrounding the image I hoped the cover would convey. My desire was to show a linkage through graphic illustration, the relationship between emotional intelligence (EQ), race, and policing. The verdict is in, and you nailed it!

I owe a debt of gratitude to my editor, Toni Williams. I truly appreciate your support on this book project, and the guidance you provided me along the way. The enthusiasm you expressed when I first brought this project to your attention was more encouraging to me than you will ever know, and for that, I thank you.

Finally, a special thanks to my friend, colleague, and brother, Dr. J. W. Wiley. For the past several months while writing this book, you have been there in the trenches, inspiring and encouraging me. Your immense knowledge of social justice continues to point me in directions I had not intended to travel when I began writing this book. I am eternally grateful for our friendship, and sincerely thank you for those long conversations. Above all, thank you for providing me with that space, where I was able to splice all that I had learned through growing up in the inner city, my law enforcement experience, and my doctoral research, to come up with what I truly believe will provide insight for a better understanding of the impact of race on policing.

Table of Contents

Acknowledgments i

Prologue viii

Foreword xxvi

Introduction 1

1   We Act In Accordance With Our Thoughts 17

2   An In-Depth Look At Policing 87

3   Why The Need For Change? 101

4   EQ And American Policing 205

5   Bridging The Gap Between Police And

    Communities 258

Epilogue 290

Bibliography 297

Index 312

Prologue

On the morning of January 17, 2009, our plane had taken off and I was well into my typical routine of relaxing with some easy reading material selected specifically for this trip. About 30 minutes into our flight, a voice came over the loudspeaker advising passengers that due to a mechanical malfunction, our plane would be returning to the airport. Well, that is not exactly how it happened.

In a near state of panic, the flight attendant rushed feverishly through the aisles yelling "get in your seats, this is a directive, we are returning to the airport!" Then, when a visibly nervous passenger asked if we were going to make it back, to my surprise, and I am sure the dismay of other passengers, the flight attendant said, "I don't know—this has never happened before." So much for composure, not to mention keeping passengers calm during an emergency. Although this was not the first time a plane on which I was a passenger was forced to divert due to mechanical problems, I had never experienced returning to the airport midflight and observing emergency vehicles lining the runway on standby and then speeding after our plane with flashing lights as we slowed to a stop.

After about an hour of what mimicked being held hostage in our seats without any apparent solution in sight, we were suddenly told to collect our belongings, disembark the aircraft, and head for the terminal to be reassigned to another flight. Delays aside, because I had vowed that barring things totally beyond my control, nothing would stand in the way of my trip from Los Angeles to Washington, DC, not even my shaken nerves were capable of dampening my spirits on that day. The next day, there I was, standing among the estimated 400,000 people in front of the Lincoln Memorial and listening to Bettye LaVette and Jon Bon Jovi singing their rendition of "A Change is Gonna Come," a song by American recording artist Sam Cooke.

I can vividly recall having to temper my emotions while listening to the song as I reflected about its origin. Perhaps I was just caught up in the moment, but I remember thinking, "This is really going to happen," and although I had heard the song on more than a few occasions over the years, the words took on considerably more significance at that moment. The song was inspired by some of the struggles experienced by Cooke, including a time in 1963 when he and his band were turned away from a Holiday Inn in

Shreveport, Louisiana, because of the color of his skin. With the song having morphed into somewhat of an anthem symbolic of the Civil Rights Movement, I couldn't help but think of how much society has changed over the years, in spite of the amount of work that still needed to be done.

Still, I was attending my first presidential inauguration and about to witness history. Although the temperature outside hovered around 28° F at the time of the inauguration ceremony on January 20, standing alongside my son and friends Wes and Brenda, there was nothing cold about the moment, as together we witnessed Barack H. Obama being sworn into office as the 44th president of the United States using the same Bible used by President Abraham Lincoln at his presidential inauguration. The inaugural theme, "A New Birth of Freedom," a phrase from the Gettysburg Address, was in commemoration of the 200th anniversary of Abraham Lincoln's birth. And while the words spoken by President Obama during his inaugural speech to the crowd often referred to ideals expressed by Lincoln relative to renewal, continuity, and national unity, his words, "We are a nation of Christians and Muslims, Jews and Hindus, and nonbelievers. We are shaped by every language and culture, drawn from every end of this Earth," told me that we had a president who believed in celebrating the differences among people within the depths of his soul.

With the inaugural ceremonies behind us, I left Washington feeling hopeful and that one more barrier standing in the way of racial harmony was finally breached. I also thought that perhaps we were now at that point in time so eloquently described by Dr. Martin Luther King, Jr. in his "I Have A Dream" speech, when he said, "I have a dream that my four little children will one day live in a nation where they will not be judged by the color of their skin but by the content of their character." Things are far better than the days when my family moved into what I considered a very nice area of town, only to witness the demographics change over time, leaving only African Americans living in my neighborhood. But we are still only speaking of societal improvement in degrees and circumstances, because while things are unquestionably better on many levels, much work remains to be done, as we are often reminded during challenging times.

American voters had elected an African American man to the highest office in the land. Note that I did not say "the most powerful position." That distinction is actually much better suited for individuals who wear a badge—yes, police officers. There is no other position within our society where someone has the power to command another person to stop whatever it is that they are doing and comply or risk the consequences.

The outcome of confrontations between police officers and African Americans indicates that, in many instances, less emphasis was placed on the content of an individual's character than on skin color, which appears to have edged into some of these engagements, if only subliminally. Something that we must never lose sight of is that a select number of officers who fall short of upholding their oath are in no way representative of the entire police profession. This brings me to the compelling reason why I took on the challenge of writing this book.

After spending several years in law enforcement and having an in-depth understanding of the critical role police officers play within our society, it pains me to hear about incidents involving police officers conducting themselves in an unprofessional manner, particularly when it diminishes the reputation of the good officers who are out there every day trying to make a difference. My goal here is to frame a conversation on some of the issues I believe are separating police officers from the communities they are sworn to protect and to serve within the context of emotional intelligence (EI). Approaching our conversation in such a manner will hopefully lead to a broader understanding of the perspectives of both police officers and private citizens leading up to, during, and particularly after these types of engagements take place.

The topic of law enforcement typically evokes strong feelings within individuals that are either positive or negative, depending on their perspective and personal experiences with police officers, which makes it virtually impossible to write a book that everyone will agree with. While portions of this book might be perceived as contrary to prevailing group think in accordance with whatever position one might hold, the issues that are standing in the way of cohesion between police and communities must be addressed in a way that leaves everyone whole to the greatest extent possible. This book therefore represents an attempt to assess the impact of EI in confronting some of the difficult issues that have transpired between police officers and private citizens, while at the same time making the case that such encounters might not always be as they first appear.

During the 21 years I spent as a federal law enforcement officer, I arrested a number of lawbreakers, but I also witnessed countless other arrests. Although I carried out my job responsibilities in accordance with agency policy, I often questioned whether there was a better way of effecting arrests without degrading suspects. At the time, I was oblivious to the fact that I possessed higher than average levels of EI that I would not become aware of until being tested after my 16th year in federal law enforcement during my doctoral research. The one thing that remained on my mind during my entire career was the fact that not even joining the ranks of law enforcement would be enough to shield me from many of the same negative encounters that sometimes surface during engagements between police officers and African Americans.

Take, for example, one day early in my career while driving my unmarked police vehicle in South Central Los Angeles, when I was stopped at a signal light on Central Avenue. I happened to look across the street at the facing traffic and noticed a police vehicle with two officers, and I caught the eye of the driver. After the signal light turned green, I proceeded north on Central Avenue, and I noticed the police vehicle make a U-turn and turn on the red lights, signaling for me to pull over, which I did. What happened next caught me off guard. Both officers opened their car doors and pointed their firearms at me while I sat in my vehicle, while the driver issued commands over the loudspeaker. Having intimate knowledge of the dangers associated with not complying with orders issued by police officers, I placed both hands out of the driver-side window as instructed. It was not until the officer approach the window of my vehicle and heard the squelching of my police scanner that he realized I was a law enforcement officer, at which point he immediately deescalated his tone. He asked,

"Hey man, who are you with?" I will finish the rest of this story later.

The very nature of law enforcement dictates that there will be times when an individual's compliance is only obtained subsequent to a law enforcement officer having to resort to vulgarities and sometimes hands-on actions. Nonetheless, there is a level of engagement that, once breached, transcends into what society might categorize as abuse. Consider the deaths of Michael Brown and Eric Garner resulting from encounters with law enforcement, both of which erupted into massive public debate questioning the use-of-force policies by law enforcement agencies. What goes through an officer's mind at that critical moment when a decision must be made relative to interacting with people on the streets? The officer's thoughts might traverse a continuum ranging from upholding the law at one end to self-preservation at the other. The decision the officer makes at that time will not only have an impact on public perception of law enforcement, but will also set in motion every judicial action that ensues thereafter. We are well aware of countless incidents of alleged misconduct by police officers, and while some cases make it difficult for the law enforcement community to defend an officer's actions, there are many other situations where the public's perception of police officers was tainted well before the facts of the case were known.

When addressing the thoughts that go through an individual's mind, consider the daily emotions law enforcement officers and their families must engage in knowing that saying goodbye might mean just that. Of course private citizens are subjected to societal circumstances that might place their personal safety in jeopardy, but for those who have taken an oath to protect and to serve, encountering harm is a daily routine. Consider for a moment the response you would receive from most individuals who were asked what they would do if they observed shots being fired. The logical answer would be something to the effect of "take cover" or even "run," which is by no means abnormal. Still, as a result of training, regimentation, or simply dedication to duty, a sworn officer's initial instinct is to confront the threat, even if that means advancing toward the very hazards from which others are attempting to escape. Such decisions place the officer's life in danger and may be detrimental to the emotional and financial well-being of the officer's family.

On a personal note, I would like to share an excerpt taken from the Officer Down Memorial Page involving the untimely death of a former coworker of mine, Kim Tonahill, who lost her life within months of joining the police ranks. Kim was killed in the line of duty, and prior to beginning her career with the San Diego Police Department, I had the pleasure of working with her when the two of us were directory assistance operators at Pacific Bell. The following is a recap of the tragic incident:

Patrolman Kimberly Sue Tonahill

San Diego Police Department, California

End of Watch: Friday, September 14, 1984

Patrolman Kimberly Tonahill and Patrolman Timothy Ruopp were shot and killed by an armed suspect at the Grape Street Park. The officers had located a vehicle in the park that contained two underage females and two males. While Patrolman Ruopp was writing a citation to one male for contributing to the delinquency of minors, Patrolman Tonahill was questioning the other male. It was unknown to Patrolman Tonahill that the male she was questioning had a handgun concealed on his person.

This male suddenly produced his handgun when Patrolman Tonahill began to search him. Patrolman Tonahill was shot in the side in an area where her vest did not protect. Immediately after shooting Patrolman Tonahill, the suspect then fired at Patrolman Ruopp. Patrolman Ruopp was struck in the leg and knocked down. The suspect then ran up to Patrolman Ruopp and shot him in the head.

A third officer then arrived at the park as a matter of routine cover. The officer had heard what sounded like gunshots about a block away from the park. The officer located the victim officers' patrol vehicles, but did not see the officers. When this officer was investigating the situation, the hidden suspect fired at him. Though the officer was slightly wounded, he succeeded in wounding the suspect.

The suspect escaped and made his way deeper into the park as arriving police units surrounded the location. When daylight appeared, the suspect was located and arrested for the murders of Patrolman Tonahill and Patrolman Ruopp. The suspect was tried and convicted of two counts of first degree murder. He was sentenced to death, and while incarcerated at San Quentin's death row, the suspect hung himself several years after the incident.

Patrolman Tonahill had served with the San Diego Police Department for 9 months. She was survived by her parents, and it is that word, *survived*, that I would like to reflect upon. Just as what occurred with the untimely death of Patrolman Tonahill, the loss of every police officer killed in the line of duty creates a vacuum in the hearts of those they leave behind, no different from what each of us experiences with the loss of a loved one.

Still, in spite of the many hazards faced by these sons and daughters, mothers and fathers, and brothers and sisters on a daily basis, the expectation is that police officers carry out their law enforcement responsibilities in accordance with their position description, regardless of problems they might be experiencing either personally or professionally. This means being able to use tact in the face of adversity while deescalating volatile situations, even when the person they are dealing with is displaying conduct that conflicts with that of a law-abiding citizen. With missteps by law enforcement officers resulting in exponentially worse consequences when things go wrong compared to most other professions, such expectations appear to be fair when taken in context. Possessing an emotional compass that alerts us not only to what we are feeling, but also provides us insight into the feelings of others, is foundational to EQ, which is particularly important for police officers who are often in situations where the ability to deescalate situations can dictate the outcome of the engagements between themselves and citizens.

Although debate continues relative to defining viable correlations between EI and organizational effectiveness, studies have overwhelmingly shown the impact of an individual's emotional status on the outcome of interactions between humans. Daniel Goleman popularized the concept by defining EI or EQ as an individual's ability to understand his or her own feelings, as well as the feelings of others, and to use that knowledge in facilitating effective relationships. Further, EQ has been defined as the ability to identify, understand, and manage emotions in positive ways to relieve stress, communicate effectively, empathize with others, and diffuse challenges. Most writers use the terms interchangeably when describing emotional intelligence. For consistency, I will only use EQ for the remainder of this book when describing emotional intelligence.

As part of the requirement for completing my doctoral degree, my dissertation was a quantitative study titled, *The relationship between emotional intelligence and leadership styles of African American law enforcement executives* (Ferguson, 2014), which aside from assessing the EQ level among law enforcement executives, sought to determine whether there were any differences in EQ when comparing assessment results of African American and Caucasian police executives. The population sample used in my study consisted of African American police officers who were members of the National Organization of Black Law Enforcement Executives (NOBLE). To compare EQ levels of police executives along racial lines, I compared my results to a similar study that included Caucasian police executives who were members of the International Association of Chiefs of Police (IACP) as its population sample (Campbell, 2012).

One of the interesting findings of my study was a result that supported prior research showing African Americans scoring higher than Whites on EQ assessments, where noted variances were believed to be linked to cultural differences. African Americans in the United States tend to align with the collectivist society where individuals feel more comfortable thinking and acting in groups, and the use of emotion is customary when interacting with others. In contrast, Caucasians in the United States typically learn to be more individualistic, rather than identify with a group mentality, and may not be in agreement emotionally as much as other ethnic groups. Studies have pointed to factors associated with the cultural norms of these two groups as primarily creating the variance in EQ assessment scores.

Although my research study focused on the thinking patterns of police executives, leaders typically come from the same employee pool as other police officers. Along those lines, a case may be made that supports the idea that EQ assessment scores would likely follow a similar racial pattern, irrespective of the position held by officers within the organization. This is something to be mindful of during our quest to make sense of the high number of officer-involved shootings in which White police officers kill African Americans.

Although there are as many claims as there are defenses regarding whether such incidents are racially motivated, the relationship between EQ and human behavior cannot be disputed, nor can we afford to overlook the potential correlation between a police officer's EQ level and the decision to use deadly force. Working on the supposition that an individual's perception of reality occasionally interferes with the acceptance of another person's point of view, this book explores the potential benefits of police organizations using EQ as both a leadership platform and a bridge to effective relationships between police officers and the communities they serve.

Now to finish my earlier story relating to my encounter with the police officers who pulled their guns on me during a traffic stop while I was driving my unmarked police vehicle in South Central Los Angeles. Well, my reply to the officer who asked me which agency I work for was simply,

"Your actions make all law enforcement officers look bad in the public's eye, and you know the reason for me being pulled over was not because of any crimes that I had committed, but merely because I had looked in your direction."

Coincidentally, the officer giving the orders to me on that day over the loudspeaker was African American. Some of you are likely to be surprised, as you had already formed an opinion that what I described was simply another case of a White police officer pulling over an African American, which is understandable based on widely held perceptions. Still, albeit perhaps associated with the time I spent within the law enforcement community, my thinking surrounding this incident is that it further underscores the need to assess the prevailing cultural norms that continue to plague American policing as it pertains to the treatment of private citizens by police officers.

References

Campbell, G., Jr. (2012). *The relationship among emotional intelligence and leadership styles of law enforcement executives* (Doctoral dissertation). Available from ProQuest Dissertations and Theses database. (UMI No. 3505907)

Ferguson, B. (2014). *The relationship between emotional intelligence and leadership styles of African American law enforcement executives* (Doctoral dissertation). Available from ProQuest Dissertations and Theses database. (UMI No. 3615140)

Goleman, D. (1995). *Emotional intelligence.* New York, NY: Bantam Books.

King, M. L., Jr. (1963, August 28). I have a dream [Audio file]. Retrieved from http://www.americanrhetoric.com /speeches/mlkihaveadream.htm

Officer Down Memorial Page. (n.d.). Retrieved from https://www.odmp.org/

Foreword

Why didn't the police officer who choked and ultimately killed Eric Garner choose another approach to engage him? Why did the episode that led to the arrest of Sandra Bland escalate beyond a traffic ticket? Could the shooting of Mike Brown in Ferguson, Missouri, have been avoided?

Dr. B. Bernard Ferguson, recently retired inspector in charge of the Los Angeles Division of the U.S. Postal Inspection Service presents compelling arguments that unabashedly suggest alternatives to the actual actions that were taken. Using Daniel Goleman's theory of emotional intelligence (EQ) to deconstruct all of the above law enforcement scenarios (and many more), Dr. Ferguson provides insight into these highly problematic scenarios.

Dr. Ferguson also uses some cutting-edge scholarship to unravel the complexities of race relations in ways that serve as supplements, if not complements, to Goleman's theory. Dr. Ferguson uses Joy Leary's book *Post Traumatic Slave Syndrome: America's Legacy of Enduring Injury and Healing* to provide the reader with an articulation of the multigenerational trauma experienced by African Americans from the historical scars of slavery and systemic and structural racism. Dr. Ferguson further accentuates his academic interrogation of law enforcement's ways of seeing African Americans by applying J. W. Wiley's theory of biased perceptions of different people as especially problematic to law enforcement, exacerbated through the unceasing use of dysfunctional language in his book, *The Nigger in You: Challenging Dysfunctional Language, Engaging Leadership Moments*. Dr. Ferguson also uses Michelle Alexander's book, *The New Jim Crow: Mass Incarceration in the Age of Colorblindness*, to address how mass incarceration practices are a perpetuation of pre-Civil War slavery and post-Civil War Jim Crow laws to maintain a racial caste system. Dr. Ferguson accomplishes this through his exploration of Alexander's interpretation of the criminal justice system's war on drugs.

Years of experience rising through the ranks from adolescent in a gang-infested neighborhood, to street agent, to executive manager—coupled with the reality of growing up Black in America—equipped Dr. Ferguson with insight into many of these controversial situations.

As chief diversity officer for SUNY Plattsburgh and director of its Center for Diversity, Pluralism, & Inclusion for nearly two decades, as well as having clientele that include law enforcement and military clients, I am responsible for the education of both the campus and community in terms of diversity and social justice. With the racial tensions that have recently erupted on the streets of major cities—as well as university campuses across the country—understanding and unpacking the problematic proclivities that far too often are portrayed as standard practices in policing are essential in rebuilding communities' confidence in fair policing. Having known Dr. Ferguson since our teenage years when we attended high school in Los Angeles County, I can't imagine anyone more capable of articulating the phenomenon of capturing and framing the complexities of policing amid the advent of social media and vulnerability of citizens who are disenfranchised far too often.

In Dr. Ferguson's provocative book, he urges and models Goleman to better engage the subtleties of crime, criminals, xenophobia, irrational fear that goes unchecked, and misguided perceptions due to inadequate exposure and insight into diverse communities using the tools of emotional intelligence. If you are interested in adding more depth to your analysis of law enforcement practices and procedures in these difficult times, especially in the context of racial policing, this book will serve as a map that situates you for what will be a far less complicated journey.

J. W. Wiley

Introduction

Due to the changing dynamics of the work environment resulting from globalization, leadership in the 21st century requires individuals who possess strategic vision, are aware of their internal and external surroundings, and are capable of adapting to the many uncertainties confronting organizations. Consider the changes in the expectations of employees relative to their desires for increased involvement in workplace decisions that affect their lives, where employees are sometimes resistant to simply following through on orders put forth by their supervisors. The possibility of such resistance further emphasizes the need for individuals leading organizations to possess leadership competencies suitable for garnering the support of followers and to influence those they lead toward achieving organizational objectives.

Whereas the mechanistic work environments of the past may have realized certain aspects of success in terms of goal attainment under a command-and-control form of leadership, the intricacies of contemporary organizations require leaders to have the ability to inspire others through facilitating work environments conducive to followers feeling valued for their contributions and consequently accepting larger roles to ensure organizational success. Although persons in leadership roles are capable of using the perceived power in their position to ensure employees perform at minimum standards, inspiring organizational commitment requires a form of leadership that connects with employees' emotions to the point where employees willingly support the strategic vision of organizational leaders. Thus, leaders can reasonably expect employees to do whatever is required in their job, but getting employees to perform beyond the tasks articulated in their job description requires transformational leadership that is both inspirational and highly capable of garnering the full support of the workforce.

Transformational leaders use emotional support to motivate followers. Transformational leaders also use nonverbal tools to be effective and charismatic, and they consequently benefit from the emotional commitment of followers. A requisite of organizational effectiveness is for leaders to possess four basic levels of emotional abilities: the ability to recognize and interpret facial expressions of others, the ability to weigh conflicting emotion against each other and determine the best course of action, the ability to understand the relationships associated with shifts in one's emotion, and the ability to regulate emotion in oneself and others. Within this context, emotions are a mental state, and even more broadly, emotions are an impulse in response to a sudden physiological change that prepares our bodies for action (Nelson & Low, 2011). The key is being able to channel unexpected impulses in a manner that fosters positive relationships in both private and professional relationships.

Popularized by Goleman (1995), emotional intelligence (EQ) relates to individuals being able to manage not only their own emotions, but also the emotions of others with whom they interact. Before delving any further into the EQ construct, we will spend a little time addressing the elephant in the room, which in this case refers to the use of the word intelligence outside of the realm of the intelligence quotient (IQ). As is commonly known, IQ refers to an individual's performance on a standardized intelligence test relative to the average performance of like-aged individuals to assess human intellect in accordance with the barometer set forth by society for projecting one's propensity for achievement. Through simple extrapolation, a high IQ should virtually ensure organizational success, but that would be far too easy, and there are extensive accounts where this has been shown not to be the case. There are many reasons why some very intelligent individuals do not fare very well once organizational success becomes dependent upon the work of others, where the discretionary effort of employees is a by-product of the leader's ability to influence the workforce. Each of us can think of someone who is intellectually brilliant and highly capable of solving complex mathematical equations, but who cannot seem to get along with people. The following backdrop on early attempts at defining human intelligence will hopefully lend itself to a better articulation of human intelligence, as well as shed some light on why there is occasionally a disconnect between high IQ and organizational effectiveness.

Since the early 1900s, scholars in the field of psychology have debated the nature and impact of human intelligence, with much of the controversy surrounding attempts at defining criteria suitable for deciphering intellectual differences among individuals. For example, some researchers believed that a single unitary quality within the human brain generated intelligent behavior, and as such, individuals scoring well on tests designed to measure intellect would be expected to perform equally well on other tests containing similar content or processes. Other researchers contradicted such claims by contending that standardized intelligence tests only accounted for abstract intelligence and were therefore incapable of measuring human intelligence due to its complex nature. The inability of earlier researchers to substantiate a correlation between performing a particular task and intellect rendered the tests used to assess an individual's level of intelligence inadequate and added to the debate surrounding what constituted human intelligence. Researchers who opposed the theory of general intelligence believed that individuals do not possess just a single form of intelligence, but instead have multiple intelligences that correlate with their life experiences. This understanding leads to a question regarding whether intelligence is a reflection of one's genes or the result of knowledge acquired throughout one's life experience.

Contemporary researchers have found common ground as it pertains to the components of human intelligence, which was later suggested as encompassing both mechanical intelligence, described as the ability to visualize relationships among objects and to understand how the physical world worked, and social intelligence, described as the ability to function successfully in social relationships. In the scientific community, this concept is commonly known as the theory of multiple intelligences, which consists of linguistic, logical-mathematical, musical, spatial, bodily-kinesthetic, naturalistic, interpersonal, intrapersonal, and existential intelligence (Gardner, 1983). Under this supposition, although standard intelligence tests might be useful in measuring for specific competencies, attempting to assess intelligence by a single score also renders the tests vulnerable to omitting critical information relative to the manner in which individuals differ in intelligence because individuals are complex in nature.

In accordance with this theory, it is apparent how an individual might be strong in mechanical intelligence (IQ), where they would be considered highly intelligent, but this individual might experience difficulties interacting with people due to possessing poor social skills if he or she lacked social intelligence; hence, the individual scores off the charts in IQ, but is sorely lacking in relationship management skills. Now we are ready to revisit the EQ construct to both differentiate it from traditional IQ, as well as explore its usefulness for police leaders in confronting 21st-century law enforcement challenges that at times involve the manner in which police officers engage the public. Researchers have defined EQ as the ability to identify, understand, and manage emotions in positive ways to relieve stress, communicate effectively, empathize with others, and diffuse challenges.

When analyzing this construct from the perspective of the many obstacles associated with interactions between police officers and private citizens, the significance of EQ becomes obvious, particularly during potentially volatile situations. Think about two individuals, where one or perhaps both are having a bad day. Should the engagement between these same individuals become confrontational, the conversation would likely quickly deteriorate. If the scenario just described involves a confrontation between a private citizen and a police officer, the stakes are exponentially higher. Although the expectation is that law enforcement officers should at all times conduct themselves above reproach, it is important to be mindful that these individuals possess the same human frailties and are susceptible to becoming entangled in conflicts like anyone else. Like other humans experiencing personal problems with no apparent nexus to the individual's employment, without adequate coping skills, these problems can permeate the walls of the job and consequently affect the employee's ability to perform well. A situation can become exceedingly more complex if a law enforcement officer is armed, which only heightens the stakes for a very bad situation should the officer not be able to manage his or her emotions effectively, and such feelings can be played out during confrontations with the public.

Although there is no fail-proof mechanism for guarding against every potential negative encounter between law enforcement and society, creating an organizational culture that facilitates respect of all citizens begins and ends at the top with those individuals entrusted to lead. It is therefore vital for leaders of police organizations to establish the right organizational culture so that employees placed in positions of having to make critical decisions without the benefit of first consulting with management do so in a manner that upholds the highest standards of the police profession. Only then will the law enforcement community and private citizens forge a true partnership, where police organizations receive the full support of the citizens they are sworn to protect and to serve.

In laying the foundation for writing this book, the most appropriate starting point to begin a discussion relating to my experience within the law enforcement profession is to begin with my development as a child at a time when the thought of a career in law enforcement never crossed my mind. Before we were moved near what was then known as Sportsman Park, as a young child, my family lived in Compton, California, at a home located at 1408 W. Caldwell Street. And although I first became aware of gangs during the time we lived in Compton, it was not until we moved to Los Angeles that I experienced the devastation caused by gang violence. While I was fortunate enough to grow up in a part of the city that provided an opportunity to acquire a decent education, there was no escaping the criminal element that plagued the streets of a metropolis such as Los Angeles.

Although I knew early on that joining a street gang was not for me, several of the kids in the neighborhood where I grew up decided to take that route, and similar to oil and water, with our interests being so different, we never mixed. But not even my attempts at placing distance between the dangers of the streets and me could fully protect me from many of the same disparities faced by individuals who grew up in my neighborhood. Being far too young to understand the plight of African Americans resulting from the impact of housing, education, employment, and political discrimination, I was certainly at an age where I understood that the images aired over the local news covering the Watts riots meant that African Americans were not satisfied with circumstances as they currently stood.

In addition to images of burning buildings, looting, and skirmishes between law enforcement and the public, I can still remember the National Guard vehicles rolling down our street and my parents requiring me and my siblings to sleep on the floor out of fear that a bullet from a firearm would inadvertently find its way through one of our street-facing windows. Such fears were not out of paranoia but instead from experience stemming from the time a stray bullet penetrated our home and lodged in a wall about 4 feet above my father's head while he lay sleeping in bed. I also recall the enormity of the tension that burdened our neighbors due to the riots that were taking place only a few miles from where we lived.

Although at the time of the riots I had no real conception of what started the uprising, I later learned that local community members became angry and began taking out their frustration on law enforcement after word had spread that two White officers attempted to effect an arrest of an African American motorist suspected of drunk driving, believing such actions were racially motivated. The riot consumed a 50-square-mile area of South Central Los Angeles, during which time individuals fired gun shots at police officers and firemen, engaged in looting, set fire to buildings, and physically assaulted anyone who was not an ethnic minority until the city solicited the assistance of thousands of National Guardsmen to restore order. By the time the curfew was lifted, 5 days of violence resulted in 34 deaths, 1,032 injuries, nearly 4,000 arrests, and property damage totaling approximately $40 million (Queally, 2015).

I recall at one point during the riots when nearly every neighbor within the general vicinity of where I stood was fixated on the sky above as a sky-writer etched the letters

B-L-A-C-K, which had everyone's attention for obvious reasons. Each of us stood there somewhat captivated on the writing as we hung on every letter of the next word that when finished spelled out Magic, which we all knew was the name of a hairspray designed to give all textures of hair a lustrous and lasting sheen. When the word "Black" first appeared, no one knew for certain whether this was an attempt to communicate with African Americans who could see the sky. Even today, some 50 years later, when I discuss that particular incident of aerial advertising with my friends who grew up in Los Angeles at that time, the jury is still out as to whether it was just a coincidence that hairspray was being advertised at that time, or perhaps something far more covert.

My first real exposure to law enforcement outside of what I saw portrayed on television was being stopped for no apparent reason by Los Angeles Police Department (LAPD) officers whether I was walking down the street or traveling in a car with my friends. The instructions I received from my parents were to be respectful of law enforcement and do as I was told. Those types of rules of engagement were the marching orders me and my buddies lived by, and although carpooling would have certainly saved on fuel costs between destinations, we often made the decision not to pile four deep in a vehicle for reasons related to self-

11

preservation or just wanting to arrive at our destination without being pulled over for looking suspicious.

Two weeks after graduating from high school, I enlisted in the U.S. Navy, and each time I think back on that decision, I wholeheartedly believe it was by the grace of God that I was able to get off the streets when I did. When I was in boot camp, my mother wrote to me to relay that my childhood friends were involved in an altercation while attending a party where someone was shot and killed by one of my friends. Those who grew up in my old neighborhood know the incident I am referring to, as well as the individuals involved. They also know that were I not in the military at the time of the incident, I would have been right there with my friends. I often wonder the path my life would have taken had I not made the decision to separate myself from the criminal element I fought hard to maneuver around throughout my childhood. Attending the funerals of individuals I used to pal around with helped to reaffirm my belief that there was no future for me in the streets.

Following my stint in the military and a few jobs here and there, I could not shake my belief that change is effected from within, nor could I deny that I was being drawn toward a career that involved the law. I initially thought about being an attorney before deciding that law enforcement was the ideal fit for me and was how I wanted to spend my immediate future. During conversations with some of my closest friends after I secured my position as a federal law enforcement officer, and largely due to them not having a clear understanding of what transpired behind the scenes of police work, some would tell me how they envisioned me in a similar context to Laurence Fishburne's character "Stevens" in the 1992 motion picture film *Deep Cover*, who was also a street kid who ended up landing a job in law enforcement. Granted, and luckily for me, I did not experience the same upbringing as Stevens, who was the son of a drug-addicted, alcoholic father, whereas my parents provided for us and ensured that spirituality was instrumental in our rearing. Still, opportunities existed for me to make decisions that would have likely resulted in my life turning out differently and would have disqualified me from securing a career in law enforcement. While the comparison of my law enforcement experiences to that of the *Deep Cover* character is not a carbon copy, there were times during my career where I would marvel at the opportunity placed before me to see behind the scenes of police work, and while my undercover capacity primarily involved working narcotics investigations, working within the law enforcement community allowed me access to places where I was able to often see the best, but also the "less than best," of police work.

Although it was disciplinary in nature and had nothing to do with police corruption, I would be remiss if I did not address one situation involving the disgraceful conduct of an employee fresh out of the academy due to its relevance to the context of this book. As a senior executive, one of my duties entailed serving as the deciding official for employee administrative proceedings. During one such incident, an agent only months out of basic training continually used racial slurs in his descriptions of minorities. An audio recording of the employee's inflammatory language was produced, which eliminated any chances of denial and ultimately led to the employee's termination. Beyond the insensitive nature of the language used by the employee, what is even more troubling relates to the perceptions individuals bring with them to the police ranks.

For example, the young agent under discussion was in his twenties when he entered the academy and was likely already jaded by whatever environmental exposure was present during his formative years, which means there is no way a 14-week training academy focused on academics, firearms, physical fitness, and defensive tactics was going to undo whatever beliefs he masked during the recruitment process. The issue was not racism, or an insinuation that the young agent was a racist (because I do not know whether he was), but it did have to do with someone new to the police ranks thinking it was acceptable to use racist remarks toward minorities in the presence of coworkers he barely knew. It also adds to the discussion surrounding the havoc caused to society when police officers holding similar beliefs as this young agent go undetected or when organizational leaders know individuals exhibit such behavior, but do not properly deal with the issue.

Each of us can probably think of someone we would absolutely dread if that person ever made it onto the police ranks. Our reasons might be the result of having intimate knowledge of the person's character and believing that individual would be incapable of handling the type of authority given police officers without abusing it. What about people labeled nerds at high school, who were good at neither athletics nor attracting a mate? How do you think these people might conduct themselves if ever given the power to command others to obey, particularly if they had spent years believing that others viewed them as an outcast? As we continue to search for EQ, try to identify and learn from situations where perceptions appear to have detracted from engagements between police officers and private citizens.

References

Gardner, H. (1983). *Frames of mind: The theory of multiple intelligences.* New York, NY: Basic Books.

Goleman, D. (1995). *Emotional intelligence.* New York, NY: Bantam Books.

Nelson, D., & Low, G. (2011). *Emotional intelligence: Achieving academic and career excellence* (2nd ed.). Upper Saddle River, NJ: Prentice Hall.

Queally, J. (2015, July 29). Watts riots: Traffic stop was the spark that ignited days of destruction in L.A. *Los Angeles Times.* Retrieved from http://www.latimes.com

1

We Act In Accordance With Our Thoughts

If your emotional abilities aren't in hand, if you are not able to manage your distressing emotions, if you can't have empathy and have effective relationships, then no matter how smart you are, you are not going to get very far

—Daniel Goleman

The Role of Psychology

With its focus on mental and behavioral processes, the field of psychology is situated at the center of what makes humans tick. Granted, being well-versed in psychology would simplify the ability to make a correlation between our thoughts and our actions, but as our journey unfolds, it will become evident that possessing such knowledge is not a requisite to understanding how our thought processes anchor much of what we do. In accordance with the belong-

17

ingness theory, psychologists Roy Baumeister and Mark Leary suggested that humans possess an innate drive for a minimum number of lasting interpersonal relationships.

To associate this concept with the police profession, we will begin with the Law Enforcement Oath of Honor police officers take at the beginning of their careers. Although the specific oath might vary according to the organization, typically it will state the following:

> On my honor, I will never betray my badge, my integrity, my character, or the public trust. I will always have the courage to hold myself and others accountable for our actions. I will always uphold the constitution, my community, and the agency I serve.

Although the recruits are just getting started on a career in law enforcement, the initial seeds of officer derailment are already lurking in the background. The need for interpersonal attachment creates what will likely develop as a thought crisis for new recruits the first time they face having to decide between upholding their oath and doing whatever is required to gain the trust and respect of fellow officers, even though such actions might clash with their normal behavior. The decisions made by recruits when faced with these types of dilemmas reflect their character and serve as components of their reputation that may follow them throughout their career.

Continuing to show the manner in which humans have a need to belong, I will now talk briefly about the concept of group dynamics, which is described as a system of behaviors and psychological processes occurring within a social group (Asch, 1955). The hope is that by examining rules associated with the nature of group conformance, a clearer picture of what is at stake both for the police profession and for society in general surfaces in our quest to fit in. One of the rules pertains to what we discussed earlier relating to our desire to be associated with a social group. Belonging to a group provides a social identity, which also shapes our sense of who we are. There is also a rule pertaining to initiation rites that individuals desiring to join the group are expected to perform to gain the confidence of other group members. Another rule involves the requirement to conform to group norms by adhering to the behavior of the group, and while individuals might see themselves as independent thinkers, research has shown that group norms have a way of causing individuals to act out of character.

For example, Solomon Asch conducted an experiment to investigate the extent to which individuals would conform to social pressure from a majority group, even when they believed other group members were incorrect. For his experiment, Asch had participants sit among a group of other people and judge which of the lines found on the two cards placed before them were of the same length. Unbeknownst to the real participant, all the other members of the group had been told to lie about which line was longer. Research results showed that 75 percent of participants discounted what they truly believed at least once and conformed to the group. When asked why they went against their own judgment at the conclusion of the experiment, the reason participants gave most often was fear of ridicule or being perceived as peculiar, which is plausible when considering another rule of group dynamics that requires members to adhere to specific group norms or face ostracism. This is particularly important when taking into account the internal strife some officers must experience when having to choose between going public or maintaining their silence on issues of wrongdoing in support of the established camaraderie among police officers.

For the next layer of our discussion on what occurs when individuals conform to group norms, we add a concept known in social psychology as deindividuation, which refers to a tendency of individuals within groups to lose some of their own self-awareness and self-restraint to the point of becoming less of an individual and more anonymous. Acting under the group, individuals may be more inclined to commit acts they otherwise would not because they feel less responsible for their actions, such as a case with a shy boy who garners the nerve to propel rocks through his neighbor's window along with his group of friends just because they are doing so. We have observed these types of scenarios in the case of private citizens becoming so hyped up during riots that they decide to join in on the burning of buildings and looting, as well as during egregious actions on the part of officers, such as alleged instances of police brutality where otherwise good officers become active participants in the wrongdoing.

When Emotions Interfere With Our Thinking and Subsequent Actions

While some people routinely evaluate evidence and make decisions through a structured, logical process, others tend to rely more on their values and emotions to guide their actions. Having strong emotions sometimes creates problems for some individuals, particularly when the emotions interfere with balanced and realistic thought processes that lead to distorted views of situations and relationships. Among the attributes individuals seeking employment with police organizations are expected to possess is the ability to use tact and diplomacy to accomplish their goals while interfacing with individuals from diverse backgrounds.

Prospective officers must be able to work autonomously or within teams and must demonstrate respect for others, as well as the ability to elicit cooperation from the public. Some of the desired behaviors police organizations look for in new hires include the following:

- Understanding the impact of words and behaviors on others and modifying one's own behavior, comments, or course of action accordingly.

- Concern for the feelings and perspectives of others.

- Demonstration of impartiality involving issues related to age, gender, sexual orientation, race or ethnicity, religion, and cultural diversity.

Because of the powers given to police officers, beginning with the authority to confront, question, detain, and search and ending with the authority to use deadly force when deemed justifiable, officers must be able to assess their environment objectively and exercise sound judgment in the performance of their duties. Prospective police officers do not enter the academy without preconceived ideas, and like the rest of us, these individuals have been exposed to environmental factors that have shaped their thought processes and therefore their foundation from which they will interact with the public.

At one point or another, if you have not done so already, you are likely to come across a quote that has been attributed to Roman emperor Marcus Aurelius, which reads, "Everything we hear is an opinion, not a fact. Everything we see is a perspective, not the truth." Even if one day it turns out that Emperor Aurelius' words were not exactly as they appear in the quote, my guess is that we will only be dealing with semantics as best. I particularly like the quote the way it is written here.

Think back to the last time you were among individuals who looked at the same situation and perceived things differently. For me, some of the most gratifying conversations I have had with individuals involving the subject of cultural diversity occur when I ask people to articulate their understanding of what differentiates one individual from another. More times than not, at least one person will mention race or ethnicity.

My general response is typically that "individuals can look the same, or might actually be identical twins, but in accordance with how each perceives the world around them, may draw polar opposite conclusions about the same event based solely on differences of thought." Following a brief moment of silence while that statement is pondered, the conversation usually transitions to a much deeper discussion on diversity, and it is refreshing anytime I am in the presence of someone who broadens his or her thinking on differences among people and the values those differences bring to our society. But why do we continue to struggle with understanding the thinking of individuals who may not see things exactly like us?

Chris Argyris's (1990) ladder of inference may lead to a better understanding of how individuals' perceptions might have a significant influence on their actions. The bottom rung of the ladder represent real data and experiences. Similar to images captured through a camera lens, this information is composed of what individuals might experience from the world around them or simply through interactions with others.

The next rung traveling upward on the ladder represents the selected data and experience. While individuals might encounter a number of experiences during a prescribed time frame, only selected data are focused on and retained in memory for whatever reason. The third rung up the ladder is where individuals translate the experience into their own terms and affix meaning to the selected data.

24

Still traveling upward, the fourth rung is where individuals explain the data to themselves and make assumptions relative to the data. While on the fifth rung, individuals draw conclusions based on those previously made assumptions. On the sixth rung of the ladder, individuals begin to form beliefs based upon their ascension up the ladder, and once they reach the seventh and final rung, individuals' actions are a reflection of what they have been exposed to throughout their life.

The events that help shape our experiences and ultimately our beliefs or biases can be positive or negative. For example, should the positive stimulation we experience be associated with a particular event, person, or group of people, the chances are that, over time, we would develop an affinity toward whatever is believed to be responsible for generating those positive experiences. The same holds true when assessing negative experiences that we encounter from time to time. If we reverse the previous example, rather than experiencing positive stimulation, we will associate negative feelings with our interactions with a particular event, person, or group of people. Argyris described the process of solidifying our belief system as the *reflexive loop*, where based on our experiences, subsequent exposure to similar stimuli will result in selecting only those data that serve to reinforce that which we already believe (Senge, 1990).

25

Thus, if we believe a particular person or group of people are a certain way, our mental model of them is continually reinforced by us focusing only on those things that serve to keep our thinking in balance as we have defined it.

Taking a closer look at the thought processes of humans in the context of how individuals might assign meaning to differences they perceive in others highlights some of the problems our society continues to experience with cultural diversity and social justice. Our thinking becomes particularly problematic when, because of our experiences, rational thought is short-circuited in a manner that leads us to react to situations based on our beliefs rather than what is real. An in-depth discussion on how this occurs appears later in this chapter under the section titled Losing Control of Our Emotions. Such mental transactions take milliseconds to occur and are taking place all day long during our interactions with others or while performing seemingly benign routines such as watching the news. We are likely unaware that our beliefs are assigned meaning based on only a portion of the data available to us. But the real problem relates to the inability of others to visualize our thought processes or to know the stages we have gone through to reach our conclusions. Other people can only experience our actions that create the pool of data from which they will draw in forming their beliefs and subsequent reactions to us.

It is important to interject the topics of prejudice and discrimination into the conversation by first differentiating between the two. Whereas prejudice refers to a preconceived opinion toward certain people that is not based on reason or actual experience, discrimination refers to unjust treatment of different categories of people that may be on the grounds of race, age, or sex (Merton, 1949a). While often thought to be the same, Merton demonstrated four distinct ways individuals might combine prejudice and discrimination:

- *The Unprejudiced Nondiscriminator (All-Weather Liberals)*—These individuals accept others for whatever racial or ethnic belief they might hold. They adhere to the ideal of equal opportunity for all, and they are neither prejudiced, nor do they discriminate against others.

- *The Unprejudiced Discriminator (Fair-Weather Liberals)*—These individuals are free of prejudice, but under certain circumstances, such as when it is profitable or otherwise seems justifiable, they may discriminate against others.

- *The Prejudiced Nondiscriminator (Fair-Weather Bigots)*—These individuals do not believe in the notion of equality of opportunity for

27

all and hold many prejudices toward racial and ethnic groups; however, they do not discriminate because they fear the consequences.

- *The Prejudiced Discriminator (All-Weather Bigots)*—These individuals are unashamed bigots who do not believe in the notion of equality of opportunity for all, which leads to them translating those sentiments into the unequal treatment of certain groups of people.

Because race is often a factor that dictates the outcome of engagements between police officers and private citizens, it is important to frame racism within this context. On a very high level, racism can be described as the practice of treating people of other races or groups in a prejudicial manner based on feelings of superiority of one's own race and culture. This is particularly important for a couple of reasons. Although perceptions of racism reflect the thinking of countless African Americans in relation to their dealings with police officers, a greater concern pertains to the noted differences in some of the sentences handed out to offenders and to whether racism is at the core of such disparities.

To continue our discussion on how exposure to certain life events shapes our belief system, we will revisit the March 3, 1991, beating of Rodney King by members of the Los

Angeles Police Department (LAPD) following a high-speed car chase. Video footage of the incident recorded by a witness and sent to a local news station showed several police officers indiscriminately striking King with their batons. Although the nature of police officers gaining control during volatile arrest situations is not something one would expect to be serene, the number of baton strikes doled out during the King incident placed police tactics under the microscope.

With several years having passed since the occurrence of the infamous arrest, I decided to take another look at one of the videos posted on the Internet for a brief review and found that I had either forgotten about or never really paid attention to the number of police officers who were on the scene and just stood by watching their fellow officers literally beating the hell out of King. Upon seeing the manner in which the officers hit King with their batons, regardless of whether he crawled along the ground or stopped moving altogether, I recalled the whippings I got as a kid for something I had done wrong, and if I cried, my dad would say something like, "I'll give you something to cry about," and hit me a few more times. Likewise, if I tried to suppress my tears during the administering of punishment, my dad would continue to apply the belt until it became evident that his point was getting through. Reminiscing on the time when the preamble to discipline were the words, "This is going to hurt me more than you," I guess that was my first real introduction to the saying, "Damned if you do, damned if you don't," which may have been some of the same thoughts running through King's mind between baton strikes.

The senseless beatings by LAPD officers do not absolve King of the crimes he committed during the encounter. King was suspected of driving under the influence, which prompted the car chase. Something not routinely discussed is a time during the arrest attempt when King is reported to have raised up off the ground and charged at one of the police officers in an aggressive manner, upon which the officer, acting in self-defense, struck King with his baton. A major sticking point of the King incident is that there came a time during the arrest situation where the dynamics changed from police officers having to defend themselves against King's aggression to becoming the aggressors themselves.

I will now use my law enforcement experience from a time when circumstances warranted the use of my baton to gain compliance of a suspect in a narcotics investigation. A videotape of that incident would have showed me striking the individual three to four times with my baton before he decided he had enough and complied with my orders to get down on the ground. Had the only portion of the video made public been the point where I hit the suspect, someone viewing the video would have considered my actions to be abusive. The information they would have been missing is that prior to resorting to my baton, the suspect was not only physically resisting arrest, but was swinging wildly at my partner and I before attempting to flee the scene where he continued the fight once we caught up with him. Bearing in mind that police officers are permitted to use a degree of force that is reasonably necessary to accomplish their lawful objectives and to overcome any unlawful resistance, there are stark differences between the incident just described and what occurred during the King incident—namely, once the suspect complied and was on the ground, all baton strikes ceased, handcuffs were placed on him, and emergency medical services was called to the scene to ensure we were not transporting someone to jail who needed medical attention.

Police officers, as well as suspects, experience an adrenalin rush during these types of arrest situations, but even that is not an excuse for the apparent loss of control on the part of the police officers in the King incident who were videotaped swinging their batons time and time again while their comrades stood around and watched. These actions resulted in outrage in neighborhoods where there was long-standing racial tension and public concern stemming from perceptions of wrongdoing by police officers against African Americans. The tension reached its boiling point following the jury verdicts acquitting three of the officers of all charges. The fourth officer was also acquitted of the charge of assault with a deadly weapon but the jury failed to reach a verdict on the use of excessive force.

Although I do not remember verbatim the content of the conversations I had with my friends during the jury trial for the police officers, I do recall feeling somewhat uneasy, as the trial took place around the time I was undergoing a background check and anticipating an appointment to the academy to begin my career in federal law enforcement, which was something I wanted more than anything else at the time. The greatest contributor to my apprehension was the fact that the neighborhood where I grew up was ground zero for the King incident, and taking into account my personal experience with local law enforcement, I believed the police officers had acted inappropriately.

With the heightened sensitivity surrounding race relations between police officers and individuals residing in and around the nearly 51-square-mile region of Los Angeles County known as South Central Los Angeles, classifying the announcement that jurors failed to convict the officers in the King trial as not going over well among the African American community was an understatement. What ensued after the acquittals were the 1992 Los Angeles riots that broke out across the city and resulted in more than 1,000 buildings being burned to the ground at an estimated cost of about $1 billion dollars, 53 deaths, and more than 2,000 injuries. All four officers eventually went on trial in federal court, where two of the officers were found guilty and subsequently imprisoned, while the other two were acquitted once again.

The top rung of the ladder of inference displays the words "take action," and if we focus solely on the perceptions held by individuals living within the inner-city of Los Angeles during the time of the Rodney King beating, chances are we would find that the belief system of many who lived through the incident either was already, or was in the process of being, shaped in response to engagements between themselves and the police officers who patrolled their neighborhoods. Keep the words "take action" in mind as we work through our next case, *People of the State of California v. Orenthal James Simpson*, as they will bring clarity to understanding how the conclusions made by individuals are impacted by their perceptions.

While my formative years may have been filled with a love of football, including an admiration of the on-the-field prowess of football superstars such as The Juice," I was skeptical of Simpson's denial of his involvement in the crime for various reasons from the very beginning but decided to temper my judgment out of fairness and because, under the Fourteenth Amendment, a person is considered innocent until proven guilty. At the time of the deaths of Nicole Brown Simpson and Ronald Goldman, I had already joined the ranks of law enforcement, and as you might imagine, there was plenty of watercooler talk and opinions swirling around the office.

Simpson was being tried on two counts of murder involving the 1994 murders of his ex-wife Nicole and a waiter named Ronald Goldman. His defense team was initially led by Robert Shapiro and later spearheaded by Johnnie Cochran, a flamboyant attorney known for taking on cases involving questionable police practices against African Americans. Other high-profile attorneys on the defense team included F. Lee Bailey, Alan Dershowitz, Robert Kardashian, Gerald Uelmen, John Yahoe, and Carl E. Douglas and DNA specialists Barry Scheck and Peter Neufeld.

During the trial, Simpson's defense team was able to persuade jurors that there was reasonable doubt involving the prosecution's DNA evidence, including allegations that blood samples had been mishandled by lab scientists and technicians. There were also allegations of police misconduct, including a discovery that Detective Mark Fuhrman had made racist remarks about African Americans, including the N-word. Further complicating the prosecution's case was the introduction of an audio tape where the detective was heard using the inflammatory language on numerous accounts in his description of African Americans, which was a point successfully emphasized multiple times by both Cochran and Scheck during closing statements. By the time the defense team wrapped up its case, the mental model in the minds of jurors was an evocative image depicting the thought processes of Detective Fuhrman and Adolf Hitler as being interchangeable.

The censure of Detective Fuhrman in front of the jury relative to his repeated use of the N-word was not simply a ploy by the Simpson defense team to play the race card. Consider the closing arguments of Deputy District Attorney Marcia Clark, who, in what appeared to be a desperate attempt to salvage the prosecution's case, faced the jurors and said the following:

Let me come back to Mark Fuhrman for a minute, just so it's clear. Did he lie when he testified here in this courtroom saying that he did not use racial epithets in the last 10 years? Yes. Is he a racist? Yes. Is he the worst LAPD has to offer? Yes. Do we wish that this person was never hired by LAPD? Yes. Should LAPD have ever hired him? No. Should such a person be a police officer? No. In fact, do we wish there were no such person on the planet? Yes. But the fact that Mark Fuhrman is a racist and lied about it on the witness stand does not mean that we haven't proven the defendant guilty beyond a reasonable doubt. And it would be a tragedy if, with such overwhelming evidence, ladies and gentlemen, as we have presented to you, you found the defendant not guilty in spite of all that because of the racist attitudes of one police officer.

Still, on October 3, 1995, in spite of what was commonly described as a mountain of evidence, the jury turned in a not-guilty verdict that acquitted Simpson of murder charges in the killing of his ex-wife and Ronald Goldman in a decision that according to national polls was split along racial lines in terms of thoughts pertaining to Simpson's guilt or innocence. As we take a closer look at the case evidence presented during the trial, be mindful of the words "take action" I mentioned earlier as being key to understanding the link between an individual's actions and what they perceive to be true. The following are important evidentiary points:

- The prosecution presented documentation that showed a series of 911 calls from the Simpson residence to local law enforcement as well as a history of domestic violence committed by Simpson against Nicole.

- There was hair evidence found on a cap at the Bundy residence and on Ron Goldman's shirt consistent with Simpson's.

- There were cotton fibers consistent with the carpet in the Bronco found on both the glove at Rockingham and on the cap at the Bundy residence.

- DNA evidence linking blood found near shoe prints at Bundy was the same type as Simpson's and would only be a match for about 0.5 percent of the population.

- Simpson had fresh cuts on his left hand on the day after the murder.

- Blood was found in Simpson's home, in the Bronco, on his driveway, and on socks found within his home that matched Nicole's.

- There was a left glove found at Bundy, and a matching right glove found at Simpson's residence that was the same type as the gloves purchased by Nicole in 1990 at Bloomingdale's. Evidence also showed that Simpson wore the same type of gloves between 1990 and 1994.

- There were shoe prints found at Bundy from a size 12 Bruno Magli shoe, as well as a bloody shoe impression on the carpet of the Bronco consistent with a Bruno Magli shoe. Simpson's shoe size was 12.

I remember the malicious name-calling aimed at the jurors began almost immediately after the reading of the verdicts, when people started referring to them as dumb, stupid, idiots, and even retards, but let us not forget the public outrage at the conclusion of the Rodney King case, where the public also questioned the fairness of the justice system and we experienced similar name calling lodged against the jurors in that trial. So how could the jury not convict Simpson with such compelling evidence?

Although the Simpson murder trial has long since passed, the conversations I continue to have with individuals within the African American community about that case have remained almost the same. I realized early on that the trial was far greater than Simpson's guilt or innocence, and I found myself in somewhat of a predicament, as I was fairly new to the law enforcement community where, because of my training, I assessed a person's guilt or innocence based solely on the evidence. At the same time however, because I too had come from the inner city, not only did I understand the potential problems associated with negative encounters between police officers and the public relative to perceptions, I also understood that, because of human nature, perceptions might have a bleed-over effect during jury deliberations.

So was this a case of the jurors *taking action*, where perceptions of an unfair criminal justice system had simply found their way to the top rung of the ladder of inference? Now that time has passed since the acquittal, African Americans do not speak with one voice with a blanket endorsement of Simpson's innocence. I discovered that when I ask someone to focus on the evidence presented during the trial, many people believe that he simply got off. There are others who continue to proclaim that Simpson is innocent and was framed by the LAPD.

The 2015 biopic *Straight Outta Compton* showed not only one example of how belief systems might be formed, but also how the life experiences of inner-city youth affect their progression along the various rungs of the ladder of inference. Whereas the film was promoted as revolving around the rise and fall of the Compton hip-hop group N.W.A., the subtext of the film is a stark reminder of the dynamics between local communities and police officers that have played a role in sculpting the most negative views held by African American men toward law enforcement in general, many of which are expressed through the lyrics to N.W.A.'s "Fuck Tha Police."

Whether you are a fan of rap or are convinced that lyrics in such raw form instigate gang violence, listening intently to the message conveyed through those particular lyrics provides otherwise unattainable insight into the realities from the perspectives of those who have witnessed up close the perceived unjust treatment of local citizens. Such sentiments continue to plague inner-city neighborhoods across the country, in spite of the oversimplified suggestion by some individuals that we now live in a color-blind society. Dr. Ben Carson, the accomplished neurosurgeon and only African American candidate (formally) seeking the bid for the White House in 2016, who when asked by Megyn Kelly during the August 6, 2015, Fox News GOP debate what he would do to help race relations in the United States if he was elected president, responded, "I was asked by an NPR reporter once, why don't I talk about race that often." He continued,

> I said it's because I'm a neurosurgeon. And she thought that was a strange response. And I said, you see, when I take someone to the operating room, I'm actually operating on the thing that makes them who they are. The skin doesn't make them who they are. The hair doesn't make them who they are. And it's time for us to move beyond that.

Although I do not believe that solving race relations in America is as simplistic as telling everyone to just get over it, which based on my conversations with others following the debate was how many interpreted Dr. Carson's words, I do feel compelled to defend Dr. Carson, at least in part. The backlash that ensued almost immediately after his comments were, in my opinion, unfairly critical of Dr. Carson, whereby he was called almost every demeaning name one could think of, including being labeled an Uncle Tom. What we observed during the debate was that, just like the rest of us, Dr. Carson speaks from his position of reality, which means, the divergent thinking surrounding race relations stems from the beliefs each of us hold, where one's concept of reality is merely a manifestation of the manner in which each of us processes the data collected through our unique life experiences.

Three examples of equal positions of reality were observed during Kendrick Lamar's 2015 BET Awards performance of "Alright" on top of a police car, Beyoncé's tribute to the Black Panthers during her 2016 Super Bowl half-time performance, and actor Jesse Williams' acceptance speech for the Humanitarian Award during the 2016 BET Awards, during which he addressed various aspects of race inequality. And, while in some circles the performances were labeled as being either antipolice or racist, the African American community overwhelmingly viewed the actions of these celebrities as nothing more than lights being cast upon the perceptions of an unjust society. The backlash from each of the expressions once again placed the divergent thoughts surrounding race relations in America, and the difficulty some people continue to experience addressing this touchy subject, in the spotlight.

While petitions were being circulated calling for Mr. Williams to be fired from his spot on *Grey's Anatomy* for his BET Awards comments, the type of disparate treatment of African American men by police officers that he so eloquently spoke of happened again 9 days after his speech, this time in Baton Rouge, Louisiana. The video that surfaced showed that on the morning of July 5, 2016, two police officers issued orders for a man, later identified as Alton Sterling, to get on the ground, and after he failed to comply, a struggle ensued where the officers are seen on the video tackling Sterling to the ground. Although he was not handcuffed at the time, the police officers still appeared to have the upper hand, as Sterling was lying on his back with the two police officers on top trying to subdue him (Solis, 2016).

Shortly thereafter, one of the officers shouted, "He's got a gun," at which time the other officer drew his weapon and after a short pause where he is heard on the video telling Sterling, "Hey bro, if you fucking move, I swear to God," he fired multiple rounds mortally wounding Sterling. Preliminary autopsy reports showed that Sterling was struck multiple times in the chest and back (Solis, 2016). The owner of the convenience store where the incident occurred, who was also a witness, said that he had given Sterling permission to sell CDs at that location, and that at the time of the incident, he did not see Sterling causing a commotion of any kind (Solis, 2016).

The store owner also said that during the time Sterling was on the ground and being told by police officers not to

43

move, all he was asking of the officers was for an explanation of what he had done wrong. A subsequent video taken from a different location showed police officers removing what appeared to be a gun from Sterling's right-side pants pocket after he had been shot. The second video also appeared to show that police officers had him fairly restrained. That being said, and to be fair, although it appears that Sterling was pinned to the ground and not in a position to use his weapon against the police officers, what was difficult to determine from either video released on social media is whether there were events taking place in close quarters and out of view of the camera that may have led to the officers believing deadly force was the appropriate response.

So, the perceived reality of many within the African American community relative to unjust treatment by police officers was reinforced once again, stemming from the death of Alton Sterling at the hands of police officers in July 2016. Some surely believe that had Sterling simply complied in the first place, none of this would have occurred. However, the other side of this scenario relates to whether it was even necessary for the police officers to put Sterling in a positon of having to get on the ground, when, based on witness accounts, it did not appear that he had done anything warranting such treatment, and this is where the ability (or willingness) to deescalate encounters before they become volatile is necessary for police officers.

Police officers received an anonymous call reporting that a man had threatened someone with a gun; however, video of the incident showed that Sterling did not have a gun in his hand when police officers arrived on the scene. As Louisiana is one of the most lenient states regarding gun ownership, where approximately 50 percent of households own firearms (Crawford, 2016), and based on the ease of acquiring a carry permit, I question police officers' rationale behind assuming that Sterling had committed a crime. What had he done that police officers felt ordering him to the ground was necessary, particularly in light of multiple witness accounts confirming that Sterling had not exhibited, and was not exhibiting, disruptive behavior toward anyone.

This is the question my son and I were on the phone discussing late on the evening of July 6, 2016, when he suddenly exclaimed, "I don't believe it! They did it again!" when he learned about the shooting death of Philando Castile by a police officer in a suburb outside St. Paul, Minnesota. I immediately turned on the television and caught a glimpse of the horrific video broadcast over the media. What I saw was heart wrenching and actually sickened me at a level I had not experienced before; after all, I was a member of the law enforcement community for over 21 years, and although there is unquestionably a brotherhood among fellow officers, at some point, police officers are going to have to stand up and say, "Enough is enough."

It is a common practice for organizations to take into account input from the public when they want to reinvent themselves. What makes law enforcement any different? There have been far too many deadly engagements between police officers and members of the African American community. Every time a member of the African American community stands up and attempts to bring the problems to the forefront for anyone truly interested to see, they are somehow labeled as a racist for pointing out such injustices.

The graphic images showing how police treated Alton Sterling and Philando Castile are what create perceptions. These are the images cataloged within the minds of not only African American adults, but also African American children, who have been unable to escape the rage understandably consuming African American households following the deaths of these two individuals at the hands of police officers. And while the courts will ultimately decide what is appropriate in terms of justice, if the past handling of these types of incidents is any indication, once the police

46

officers involved in both the Sterling and Castile encounters utter the words, "I feared for my life," there is a very good chance their actions will be deemed justifiable due to the difficulty disputing one's mental state.

Using our respective life experiences as a point of reference, when assessing belief systems from the vantage point of interactions between police officers and the public, the picture begins to take shape relative to the potential dangers of perceptions. Protests and other expressions of outrage by community members against perceived police brutality leave little doubt when it comes to the perceptions within the minds of many within the African American community, particularly when police shootings like the kind that resulted in the death of Philando Castile occur, where based on witness accounts, Castile did everything right.

Consider this. There are often attempts made to justify the actions of police officers by making a point that the individual being engaged by the officer failed to comply, such as some of the statements following the death of Alton Sterling. But, if the statements provided by Castile's fiancée, Diamond Reynolds, regarding what occurred just prior to the shooting are to be believed, and she certainly sounds credible, Castile had advised the officer that he was armed and that he had a carry permit, which is protocol when those licensed to carry firearms are stopped for traffic violations.

She further stated that Castile was reaching for his wallet, only after advised to do so by the police officer, when the same police officer who had given him the instruction suddenly shot him multiple times. Again, the only video of the incident that has surfaced thus far begins at the point after the actual shooting, and although the final investigation of the incident has yet to be completed, enough material was contained on the video footage to affect the perceptions of those holding onto long-held beliefs of police brutality. But what about the perceptions held by police officers relative to the community members who reside within the neighborhoods they patrol?

Police officers have the law on their side. But what if officers somehow become jaded by negative experiences with individuals that are of a race or background different from their own? Can you see the potential problems that might arise if those in a position of power such as police officers develop, already have negative feelings, or, even worse, bring negative experiences associated with diversity with them to the job that somehow interfere with their ability to perform their jobs in a manner that also respects the rights of others? What if those negative feelings somehow develop into actual fears on the part of police officers when it comes to engaging African American men? The short answer is that such fears can facilitate police behavior that leads to disparate treatment of African Americans, but in its worst form may be perceived by some as indistinguishable from racism.

Theoretical Foundation and Evolution of EQ

As a forewarning, this section gets a bit technical; however, I assure you that jumping directly into a discussion on EQ without first explaining the early works associated with cognitive thinking is akin to telling only half of the story. My hope is that reading through the next several pages will better prepare you for not only making a contrast between EQ and IQ, but more importantly, enhancing your understanding of why there is so much excitement surrounding studies on emotional competence. Scholars in the field of psychology have debated the nature and impact of human intelligence for several years, with much of the controversy surrounding attempts at defining criteria suitable for deciphering differences among individuals.

For example, Spearman (1904) proposed that a single, unitary quality within the human brain generated intelligent behavior, and as such, human intelligence was capable of being measured by a general factor of g (general intelligence), which Spearman believed to be a common element present among diverse measures of intellect that form a positive manifold. Spearman contended that as long as the criteria measured were somehow correlated, an individual who performed well on one of the tests should perform equally well on other tests containing similar content or processes. Further, Spearman believed that it was possible to measure and express intelligence by a single number such as an IQ score, and although researchers no longer use such procedures, the process involved dividing an individual's suggested mental age by a chronological age to determine a score.

Such prevailing thought contrasted with descriptions of intelligence proposed by Thorndike (1920), who believed that intellectual development was multifactored and that researchers were incapable of measuring it with standard intelligence tests that only accounted for abstract intelligence. For example, Thorndike suggested that part of the difficulty in assessing levels of intelligence is due to the halo effect, where a marked tendency of the rater to think of the individual in general as good or inferior often affects the ratings an individual receives, which ultimately leads to a general feeling becoming the basis of the rating. Thorndike further suggested that although early researchers made improvements to rating instruments, three fundamental defects remained: ambiguity in content, arbitrariness in units, and ambiguity in significance.

Early instruments such as the Stanford Binet, the Army Alpha, and the National Intelligence Test contained a series of tasks linked to words, numbers, space relations, pictures, facts of home life, puzzles, or informational depictions, where some researchers gauged intelligence by an individual's ability to accomplish more tasks at a faster pace. Thorndike contended that intelligence tests lack validity due to the nonexistence of an inventory of the tasks, no prior determination of correlations between the tasks and intellect, no determination of an adequate battery of tasks to gauge intellect, and no meaningful weights associated with the tasks. The inability of the tests to show a correlation between someone's demonstrated ability and intelligence level rendered them inadequate.

Scales used to measure intellect did not contain zero or numbers representing increasing amounts by constant differences. The problem with this was that researchers could not take the scores derived from using the instruments to assess intellect at face value because there was no methodology to determine the impact represented by the differences between the various scores. Thus, due to the inherent flaws in the scales, scoring twice as high as another on a particular measure does not equate to being twice as smart. Rather than being a reflection of the subject's intellect, the scores contained so much subjectivity that they were ultimately a mere reflection of the rater's impression of the subject's performance. In essence, the faults surrounding such methodologies for measuring intellect stemmed from the inability to draw correlations between a person's actual level of intellect and that reported by the instrument, thus leaving such conclusions to the rater's perception.

Thorndike (1920) also suggested that individuals do not possess merely a single form of intelligence, but instead, multiple intelligences that vary in correlation with an individual's life experiences. In distinguishing between three broad classes of intelligence, while supporting Spearman's concept of abstract intelligence as it relates to one's ability to manage ideas, Thorndike contended that mechanical intelligence, described as the ability to visualize relationships among objects and understand how the physical world worked, and social intelligence, described as the ability to function successfully in social relationships, were equally important components of human intelligence. Social intelligence is "the ability to understand and manage men and women, boys and girls—to act wisely in human relations" (Thorndike, 1920, p. 228), and although the underpinning of the EQ construct goes back to Thorndike's theory of social intelligence, its origin is also firmly rooted in Gardner's (1983) theory of multiple intelligences.

While not disparaging the definitions of intelligence proposed by earlier theorists, contemporary definitions widely seem to oppose the contentions that human intelligence is a phenomenon capable of accurate assessment using instruments that assign scores to individuals in accordance with an intelligence scale created with a mean of 100 and a standard deviation of 15, where Gardner (1983) contended that 95 percent of the population falls within two standard deviations of the mean. For example, Gardner suggested that intelligence was multifaceted and significantly broader in scope than the concepts proposed by earlier theorists whose findings aligned with the psychometric approach, which defined intelligence from the perspective of emanating from a singular source. Gardner further suggested that intelligence competence must entail problem-solving skills that enable individuals to resolve genuine problems or feasible difficulties.

Similar to Thorndike's (1920) position, Gardner (1983) believed that individuals possess a myriad of intelligences that simultaneously interact with one another to produce different outcomes, and he described multiple intelligences theory as consisting of linguistic, logical-mathematical, musical, spatial, bodily-kinesthetic, naturalistic, interpersonal, intrapersonal, and existential intelligence. Gardner viewed intelligence as being "a biopsychological potential to process information that can be activated in a cultural setting to solve problems or create products that are of value to culture" (p. 34). Gardner theorized that although standard intelligence tests might be useful in measuring for specific competencies, because individuals are complex in nature, attempting to assess intelligence by a single score also renders the test vulnerable to omitting critical information relative to the manner in which individuals differ in intelligence. Moreover, individuals who experience numerical challenges but are strong musically will more than likely develop numerical skills through a reliance on their musical strengths as opposed to an immersion process focusing solely on numbers.

Along those lines, Gardner (1983) believed that rather than allowing intelligence test scores to define a person, at least two types of intelligences can better assess that person's true success in life. Among those types is interpersonal intelligence, which allows individuals to understand the intentions, motivations, and desires of other people and to work effectively with others, and intrapersonal intelligence, described as self-understanding, where individuals are cognizant of their own desires, fears, and capacities and are therefore able to use such information to regulate their own life (Gardner, 1983). Gardner contended that the interplay between independent intelligences provides the best understanding of the variety and scope of human cognition, which mirrors Thorndike's (1920) position regarding the interaction between the variety of intelligences possessed by humans and subsequent outcomes. Two of the types of intelligences proposed by Gardner became foundational elements of early EQ constructs: interpersonal and intrapersonal.

Drawing from the early work of Thorndike (1920) and influences based on Gardner's (1983) principles of intrapersonal (emotional) and interpersonal (social) intelligences, Bar-On (2006) developed a construct referred to as emotional-social intelligence. Bar-On described emotional-social intelligence as a compilation of interrelated emotional and social competencies, skills, and facilitators that influence an individual's ability to adapt to environmental demands and pressures. Under this concept, individuals categorized as being emotionally and socially intelligent are aware of not only their strengths and weaknesses but also others' emotions and are able to make effective use of this knowledge in relating to others and expressing their thoughts and feelings in a nondestructive manner. The five components of Bar-On's mixed model are (a) intrapersonal skills, (b) interpersonal skills, (c) adaptability skills, (d) stress management, and (e) general mood, each of which is part of the self-report Emotional Quotient Inventory (EQ-i) instrument.

Credited with first coining the term EQ, Salovey and Mayer (1990) used prior research on social intelligence to under-pin their EQ ability model in which they proposed a four-branch measure of EI known as the Mayer-Salovey-Caruso Emotional Intelligence Test (MSCEIT). This self-report EQ ability model correlates more with cognitive abilities than with personality traits and is reflective of an individual's ability to perceive, express, assimilate, understand, reason, and regulate emotions in themselves and others. The MSCEIT is essentially an ability test capable of measuring one's capacity to reason with emotional content and to use the emotional content to enhance thought.

Building upon the works of Salovey and Mayer (1990), Goleman (1995) popularized the concept that emotions were a valid domain of intelligence. Moreover, Goleman defined EQ as an individual's ability to understand his or her own feelings, as well as the feelings of others, and to use that knowledge to facilitate effective relationships. Goleman's model includes competencies organized into four clusters, (a) self-awareness, (b) relationship management, (c) social awareness, and (d) self-management, each of which a researcher assesses with the multirater Emotional Competence Inventory or Emotional and Social Competence Inventory instruments. Further, this particular model entails a hierarchical relationship where self-awareness lays the foundation for self-management and social awareness, which then provides foundational support for relationship management.

Extending the EQ research by Salovey and Mayer, Goleman (1995) developed an emotional and social dimensions model based on the premise that factors other than innate intelligence play a role in the level of success an individual achieves within the work environment. Goleman's EQ construct is one of the most widely used EQ models in organizational leadership. Moreover, Goleman argued that because conventional intelligence models ignore essential behavioral and character elements, their scope is too narrow to predict success effectively. Goleman contended that individuals with high EQ levels not only possess more effective leadership skills, but are also more successful in life in general, which is a position firmly supported by researchers such as Cherniss (2010), who believed that an individual's success in work and life is not simply a derivative of basic cognitive abilities typically measured by IQ tests, but also depends upon a myriad of personal qualities that involve the perception, understanding, and regulation of emotion.

Goleman's (1995) definition of EQ focused on an individual's ability to understand his or her own feelings and those of others to motivate and manage relationships and generally emphasized four key emotion-related abilities:

- *Self-awareness* is the ability of an individual to understand his or her strengths and weaknesses both as a person and as a leader. This entails not only being able to gauge emotional pulse, but also understanding the impact of emotions on oneself and others.

- *Self-management* is the ability of an individual to refrain from immediate responses. This entails being able to rein in verbal expressions as well as actions, thereby minimizing the chance of compromising personal values.

- *Social awareness* is the ability of an individual to be in touch with the complete demands of the environment and respond in accordance with those conditions.

- *Relationship management* is the ability to resolve conflict, communicate the vision, and create motivation and inspiration throughout the team.

Figure 1 depicts four categories of EQ (self-awareness, self-management, social awareness, and relationship management).

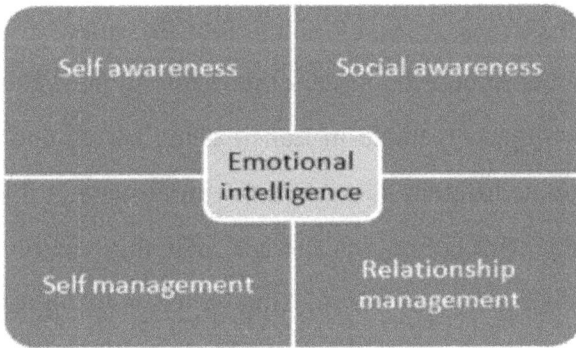

Figure 1: Goleman's (1995) Framework of Emotional Intelligence

Up to this point, emotions have been discussed from the standpoint of individuals being in control of them, but also the link between managing our emotions and effectiveness both in our personal and professional lives. But if it were so easy, why do we sometimes lose it to the point of seemingly not being in charge of our own emotions, much less someone else's? The next section addresses situations where our emotions have seemingly been taken over by outside sources not unlike what occurs during a mutiny. A common definition of mutiny is a refusal to obey the orders of a person in authority. Similarly, we occasionally lose total control of our emotions momentarily to the point of rational thought being nonexistent. Simply being cut off by another vehicle during our normal commute can trigger such an emotional reaction.

Losing Control of Our Emotions

If the word *hijacked* conjures up visible impressions of an aircraft, ship, or vehicle in transit being seized and forced to go to a different destination, your image is likely in alignment with communal thought. For this section, rather than viewing the act of hijacking in terms of objects used for transportation being commandeered, we will instead explore situations where our behavior becomes detrimentally influenced by our thought processes. The focus of this chapter will be on the amygdala, which is an almond shaped mass of nuclei located deep within the temporal lobe of the brain. The amygdala is a limbic system framework that plays a role in many of our emotions and motivations, particularly those analogous to survival. Besides being the emotional center of the human brain capable of regulating fight-or-flight responses essential to survival when a person experiences fear or feels threatened, the amygdala is also instrumental in the processing of emotions such as anger and pleasure.

What about those situations where we appear to not be in total control of our emotions, but once things settle down and we realize that besides being out of character, our behavior was likely a bit over-the-top? If you have ever experienced such an episode and later thought that you must have been out of your mind to act in such a manner, your thinking was not off track. Psychologist and journalist Daniel Goleman, in his 1995 bestseller *Emotional Intelligence*, coined the term amygdala hijack based on the work of neuroscientist Joseph LeDoux that showed how emotional information will occasionally travel directly from the hypothalamus to the amygdala without engaging the higher brain regions, thus causing a strong emotional response that precedes more rational thought (see Figure 2).

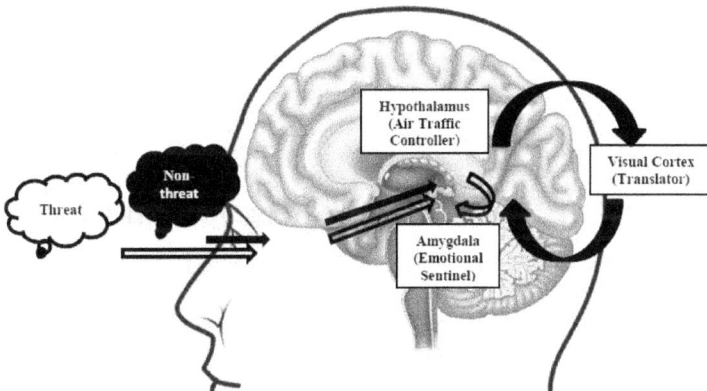

Figure 2: The Amygdala Hijack

Sensory signals received through our eyes are routed through the hypothalamus, which, functioning similar to an air traffic controller, passes that information along to the visual cortex, which is the part of the cerebral cortex that receives and processes sensory nerve impulses experienced through our sight. Once translated through the visual cortex, information is rerouted back through the hypothalamus, on to the amygdala, and finally to the neocortex (thinking brain). There are exceptions where our thinking brain is bypassed altogether and sensory signals are sent straight to the amygdala (emotional brain). See the route depicted by the arrow along the threat path in the above diagram to see what irrational thought might look like.

Under those situations, because our thinking has not gone along the path of being analyzed logically, we experience an immediate, overwhelming emotional reaction disproportionate to the situation at hand, where we may sense feelings of rage long after the incident has subsided. Using the example where one driver was cut off by another while commuting, the ensuing emotions might involve anger that leads to full-blown road rage, where a motorist's uncontrolled anger having been provoked by another motorist's irritating act is expressed in aggressive or violent behavior. But there is a simultaneous physical reaction as well.

Has this has ever happened to you? During a moment of rage, you were thinking and acting against your will. You were unable to read others' emotions accurately. You could not find the right words when attempting to speak. You were unable to focus your thinking or actions. When the fight-or-flight response kicked in, your heart raced while your blood pressure increased. You found yourself sweating profusely and there was an uneasy feeling in your gut.

Also, while you clenched tightly with your jaw, you experienced cold extremities as your brain attempted to rush blood to muscles needed for fighting or fleeing. If this sounds familiar, you likely experienced an emotional hijack. Let us now travel back in time and explore how the amygdala hijack can be our greatest ally when we are faced with fear.

Hundreds of thousands of years ago, such an immediate emotional response served a purpose. Imagine yourself out gathering berries for your family. Along the way, you heard rustling in the bushes and suddenly found yourself face-to-face with a saber-toothed tiger that also happened to be out looking for food.

In this situation, your brain would waste no time in rational thinking, which is a good thing. The typical time it takes the brain to process information through the prefrontal cortex is 100 milliseconds. Thanks to the amygdala hijack, where information is processed in about 15 milliseconds, you would be thrown into a fight-or-flight response with the only two thoughts available to you—do I eat it or does it eat me, after which you would run and hopefully survive to tell someone about your encounter.

Although the chances of coming face-to-face with a saber-toothed tiger today are remote, each of us is prone to facing stressful situations that may trigger an amygdala hijack. For example, similar to the fears faced by our ancestors, police officers routinely encounter situations in their jobs where there is an opportunity for reason being overrun by emotion (triggering an emotional hijack), such as when officers feel they are being disrespected, which are thoughts often expressed by police. Other triggers include being treated unfairly, feeling unappreciated, feeling like you are not being listened to, and being given an unrealistic deadline.

The greatest variance pertains to the decisions an individual might make while in the midst of the fight-or-flight phase of the amygdala hijack, where because of the typical mindset of police officers developed or enhanced through training, running away is not at the top of the list of alternatives. An example of this appears in Chapter 4, which includes an excerpt from an interview between police officer Darren

Wilson, formerly of the Ferguson Police Department and George Stephanopoulos. During the interview, Wilson stated that police officers would be considered less useful if they ran away from threating situations. Officer Wilson does not appear to be alone when it comes to harboring such feelings.

Contemplate the countless number of officer-involved shootings that have resulted in the death of suspects, and sometimes private citizens, who for whatever reason failed to comply with the officer's instructions during a confrontation. The rationale given by involved officers regarding why they believed the encounter escalated to the level of deadly force is something along the line of "I feared for my life," which is an emotion that is hard to disprove and even more difficult to dispute without being in the officer's shoes (or head) during the deadly encounter. Unlike the caveman reacting to fear by running away, police officers are trained to confront danger using whatever force is deemed necessary to eliminate the threat, and it does not matter if the target being engaged happens to be a saber-toothed tiger or a person, because fear feels the same regardless of its genesis. After all, those drawn to the law enforcement profession are likely wired different from individuals who might prefer a job that does not carry with it the daily risks to personal safety often associated with policing.

The million-dollar question still centers on the purported fears on the part of White police officers toward African American men, particularly in the inner city. Why do so many of these types of encounters turn out deadly for African Americans? While some are quick to point to racial differences being the cause, and although race may in fact play a role somewhere in the equation, what cannot be overlooked is the presence of fear that might be linked to something as simple as unfamiliarity. Think about the population of Ferguson, Missouri, and how although census records showed the racial makeup of the city was about 67 percent African American at the time of the Michael Brown shooting, the racial makeup of the police force at the same time was 94 percent White. Regardless of whether the lack of diversity is the result of a general dislike on the part of African Americans for the law enforcement profession, the inability of African Americans to make it through the hiring process, or ineffective hiring practices, a larger issue involves the absence of an emotional connection between law enforcement and the community when police officers have no real involvement with local citizens outside of work, which sets the stage for unfamiliarity.

It is therefore doubtful that the police officers who patrol the streets of Ferguson reside among the general populace, much less socialize with them. Add to this the perception problem likely being created within the minds of White police officers if the only time they spend any significant amount of time around African Americans is during hostile situations and we have the making of a perfect storm, where the dynamics at play might lend some insight into explaining the often explosive nature of engagements between police officers and members of the African American community (see Figure 3).

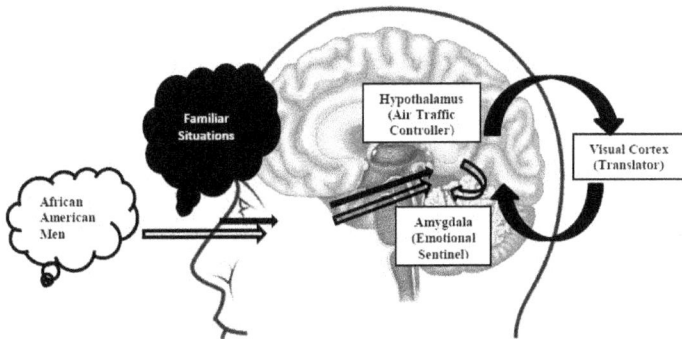

Figure 3: The Amygdala Reacting to Fears Based on Unfamiliarity

Borrowing from our earlier example depicting how the built-in fight-or-flight mechanism in the human brain aided the caveman in terms of being able to differentiate between friend or foe immediately, and then to respond accordingly, Figure 3 shows how the thinking on the part of a police officer would likely follow a similar path when confronted with an unfamiliar situation that triggers a genuine fear within the mind of the officer. Objects along the black arrow might include family members, friends, or other events that are routine to the police officer. However, the fears caused by those things (or people) represented by the white arrow would likely result in the officer elevating the encounter and reacting out of self-preservation, as opposed to retreating and seeking cover, as was the case when the caveman found himself face-to-face with a saber-toothed tiger.

We will now briefly review what occurred in the Tamir Rice case to see what fear might look like, resulting in individuals not being given the benefit of the doubt during encounters between police officers and African Americans. On November 22, 2014, police officers in Cleveland, Ohio, responded to a report of "a male black sitting on a swing and pointing a gun at people" in the park. Upon arrival, the Black male, later identified as 12-year-old Tamir, reportedly reached towards a gun in his waistband, at which time, one of the police officers shot the youth. After the shooting, it was learned that the individual who made the call to law enforcement also indicated to dispatchers that the pistol was "probably fake," and that the individual was "probably a juvenile" (Ellis & Gray, 2015). That piece of information was never relayed to responding officers. Reports and video of the incident appear to show that responding officers opened fire almost immediately upon arriving on scene. Tamir Rice died the following day.

Let's fast forward through the ensuing events surrounding this case, including the protests, the investigation, the non-indictment of involved police officers, and the settlement of $6 million awarded to Tamir's family by the City of Cleveland and address a particular statement that might shed some light on some of the violent encounters between police officers and African American males. A recurring theme within many of the descriptions of Tamir by police officers involved in the investigation was that Tamir looked much older than 12 years old. Officers are reported to have described the child as weighing approximately 200 pounds and appearing to be between 18 and 20 years of age (Lieszkovszky, 2015).

At first, such comments might not strike anyone as being alarming, particularly since young boys often pride themselves in looking older than they really are. However, a research study published online in the *Journal of Personality and Social Psychology* showed that African American boys were viewed to be older than they really were, and consequently, deemed responsible for their actions, while similarly aged Caucasian boys still benefited from the assumption that young children are essentially innocent.

Research participants consisted of 176 mainly Caucasian police officers with an average age of 37 and from large urban areas who were tested to determine their level of two types of bias: (a) prejudice and (b) unconscious dehumanization of African Americans by comparing them to apes (Bump, 2014). Bias was assessed by having the police officers complete widely used psychological questionnaires containing statements such as "It is likely that blacks will bring violence to neighborhoods when they move in" (Bump, 2014). In determining the participants' level of dehumanization of African Americans, police officers were given psychological tests aimed at gauging racial attitudes and subtle associations.

In one such test, participants were primed, by being flashed the names of either apes or great cats, such as lions. The theory was that the less African American boys were thought of as human, the less they were seen as innocent. Additionally, researchers found that in reviewing the personnel records of participants for a history of use-of-force incidents, only those officers where research results indicated the dehumanization of African Americans had a record of documented cases of abuse committed against African American children (Bump, 2014). What is truly concerning about the research is that police officers estimated African American boys on the average to be 4.59 years older than what they really were.

For instance, while adults view children as innocent and in need of protection, similar compassion is typically not expressed toward other adults. This means that if children are viewed as adults (who should know better), they may not be given the benefit of the doubt for lapses in judgment. Assessing this scenario from the standpoint of the threat continuum used by police officers when engaging suspects, there is a high likelihood for African American boys who are as young as 13 years of age to be misperceived as adults, which would undoubtedly impact the thinking of police officers when determining an appropriate use of force when engaging them (Bump, 2014).

Research such as this provides us with the *how* with regard to understanding police officers having a fear of young African American men and how children are at times mistaken for adults. Although fear is a natural part of human nature, processes must be implemented to help law enforcement identify individuals who possess heightened fears of African Americans that might result in police officers acting out of haste rather than being able to navigate through these types of encounters. Numerous studies have been conducted, and research has shown that police officers (similar to many other people within our society) associate African Americans with violence, which may have a bearing on decisions to shoot or not shoot. Combining the former with research showing that during tests using simulations, White participants were more likely to shoot African American suspects than White suspects, and adults were more likely to be shot than children, the concern surrounding African American children being misperceived as being older than they actually are should be quite obvious.

Cultural Impact on EQ

Being able to navigate social and professional environments and possessing the ability to maintain an emotional balance in the midst of adversity are links to greater levels of personal and mental health and distinguish such individuals from those around them as possessing higher levels of EQ. Prior research supports the notion that culture not only has an impact on an individual's EQ level, but that it also affects a person's decision-making process by framing the manner in which individuals initially interpret an event and their subsequent responses. Further, the variance in self-awareness linked to cultural belief systems is likely to have a bearing on the manner in which individuals interact with one another. For example, I can vividly recall the emotions I felt during the arrest of an African American mother and father early one morning in South Los Angeles while a young child stood there crying loudly as his parents were being placed into the rear seat of separate police vehicles.

Part of me wanted to scold the parents for the harm I believed they were causing their son, having committed a crime and thereby creating a situation where Child Protective Services now had to intervene. At the same time, my mind ventured uncontrollably into the future. All I could think of at that moment were the potential misplaced negative perceptions of law enforcement that had now been planted into the child's mind by witnessing police officers taking away his mommy and daddy for reasons well beyond his level of comprehension.

As I reflect on that arrest, one of the thoughts in my head at the time was of the young child growing up fearing or hating police officers or developing such a disregard for law enforcement that he would simply become just another statistic stemming from those early negative perceptions. In addition to those feelings, I also wondered what might have occurred in the parents' lives that they would commit criminal acts with seemingly total disregard for the well-being of their son. Could such behavior be explained through Emile Durkheim's strain theory, which suggests that there are certain goals emphasized by a given society with the presumption that everyone can achieve those goals through education and hard work?

The theory goes on to suggest that not everyone has equal access to the American Dream for a variety of reasons. The unfortunate outcome of such circumstances is that some groups or individuals will resort to illegal means as a course of action toward goal achievement. Another thought is that the parents were exposed to crime as children and rather than breaking a vicious cycle, they continued the trend, which made them the poster children for the profile described by Edwin H. Sutherland's theory of differential association. Sutherland's (1960) theory suggests that the knowledge a criminal possesses is passed along through associations or cliques, whereby the group rationalizes criminal behavior.

Being the type of person who believes that each of us is responsible for our own actions, I find difficulty with individuals who do wrong but blame others for their misdeeds. After observing people being arrested multiple times for the same or similar offenses, I often think that other factors contribute to recidivism. Troubling for me were those times when I would be made aware of the children of people I had arrested early in my law enforcement career who came of age and were subsequently arrested for similar crimes as their parent.

Rather than casting this aside as just another case of the apple not falling far from the tree, I began pouring my time and energy into this dilemma both through conducting research and during conversations with college students enrolled in the criminal justice courses I teach. Bearing in mind that EQ is about broadening our thinking while trying to understand why people do the things they do, I discovered that there are several studies that support connections between one's environment and the likelihood that they will engage in crime. Theories that specifically link poverty and violence include Merton's (1949b) anomie theory, which suggests that because of the inaccessibility of legitimate opportunities to attain culturally defined goals, impoverished youth will experience more frustration and resort to illegitimate means of alleviating poverty. Although not always the case, violence is sometimes a by-product of illegal activity.

The social control theory speaks to the enforcement of conformity by society upon its members, either through law or social pressure. However, impoverished youth have no real attachment or commitment to the local community and, as a result, have fewer barriers between them and delinquent behavior (Hirschi, 1969). Exacerbating the problem is high unemployment rates within the inner city, which essentially makes crime and violence more likely to occur by impeding the formation of critical attachments (Parker & McCall, 1999; Wadsworth, 2000)—a position also supported by Colvin (2000), who agreed that a connection exists between severe poverty, lingering unemployment, and crime.

Although I have retired from the police profession, I continue to seek answers to the precursors to criminal behavior through research and conversations with others. I have always tried to make sense of why some individuals commit crimes while others do not, which might be why I was able to uphold my responsibilities as a federal law enforcement officer and, even after arresting someone, reflect beyond the incident at hand and contemplate potential contributors that may have driven the individual to commit the crime.

Some individuals are just bad, and there is no other way to frame it. However, there are also situations that exist where individuals could find themselves in such a state of hopelessness that they engage in criminal activity for reasons having nothing to do with lawlessness. Dr. Joy DeGruy discussed one such example in her book *Post Traumatic Slave Syndrome: America's Legacy of Enduring Injury and*

Healing (2005), where she linked certain aspects of criminality to posttraumatic slave syndrome, which she described as a set of behaviors, beliefs, and actions associated with, or related to, multigenerational trauma experienced by African Americans. According to DeGruy, this includes centuries of slavery in the United States, followed by systemic and structural racism and oppression, including lynching, Jim Crow laws, unwarranted mass incarceration, and undiagnosed and untreated posttraumatic stress disorder in enslaved Africans and their descendants.

When exploring how culture may have affected EQ associated with the shooting of Michael Brown, consider the results of a national survey conducted by the Pew Research Center that showed 80 percent of African Americans believed that Brown's death raised important racial issues, whereas only 37 percent of Whites polled believed the incident was racially motivated. Consider the manner in which the citizens of Ferguson, Missouri, responded immediately following both the shooting of Michael Brown and the subsequent reading of the grand jury verdict. Such actions on the part of the mainly Black protesters were likely the symptoms of a much larger problem that gives credence to studies showing that there is a real sense among the Ferguson, Missouri, African American community that resources for living a healthy, productive life are unevenly distributed among the races, while as suggested by Coy, Collins, Ingold, and Campbell (2014), many Whites in America convince themselves that the country has become a postracial society.

With there being as many cultures as there are social systems, culture is a social product that affects one's thinking and behavior (Signorini, Wiseman, & Murphy, 2009). In a broad sense, culture may be described as a cultivated behavior that is the totality of one's learned and accumulated experiences that is socially transmitted. Culture can also refer to a collective programming of the mind that distinguishes members of one human group from another, as characterized along Hofstede's (1980) five key elements or dimensions:

- *Power distance*—the degree of tolerance for hierarchical or unequal relationships

- *Uncertainty avoidance*—the degree to which members of a society perceive unknown situations as threatening and attempt to avoid them

- *Individual versus collectivism*—the degree of emphasis placed on personal needs and goals versus the needs and goals of the group, clan, or organization

- *Masculinity versus femininity*—the degree to which a society emphasizes material achievement and assertiveness over consideration for others

- *Long-term orientation*—the degree of stress placed on virtuous living

The above dimensions viewed within the context of one's self-perception mean that an individual's conceptualization of self is not only a product of his or her culture but also dictates the manner in which he or she might interface with others to a large degree. For instance, upon becoming aware of an emotion-eliciting event acting as a filter, an individual's culture facilitates interpretation of the event either positively or negatively, which in turn results in the ensuing behavior in response to the event that initially triggered the emotion (see Figure 4).

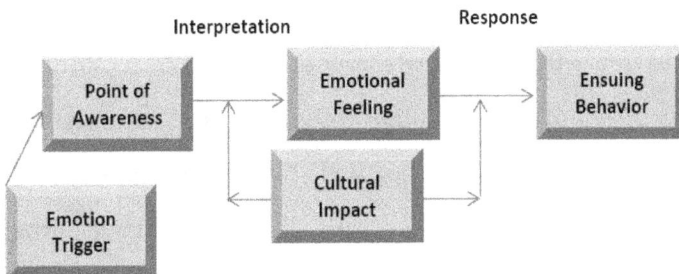

Figure 4: Correlation Between Awareness, Cultural Beliefs, and Actions

The community response immediately following the officer-involved shooting in Ferguson, Missouri, appeared to show alignment along racial lines. While many African Americans across the country gathered in protest of what they perceived to be a wrongful death of an unarmed teenager, there was simultaneous widespread support of the police officer involved in the shooting by Whites, much of which was expressed through the media, fund-raising events, and through a Support Officer Wilson Facebook page that quickly received more than 100,000 likes. Such expressions of support are examples of how emotional stimulation subsequently plays out through individuals' actions in accordance with their respective life experience.

Another example that further illustrates the impact of how one's culture might affect the response to a particular situation was observed in the reactions of individuals to the October 23, 2015, article published in the State University of New York's Plattsburgh campus's student newspaper. In that article, titled "Minority Admission Rates Examined," the cover featured a cartoon portrayal of an African American male in a cap and gown with blackface, a wide smile, and bulging eyes walking through a dilapidated urban neighborhood. The president of the university stated that he found the cartoon "personally offensive," and the editorial staff issued an apology for what they described as a "poor decision." Still, even with what appeared to be widespread social media agreement relative to the insensitive nature of the cartoon, the hurt expressed in many of the comments showed that the emotion trigger connected with the stereotypical image was not experienced the same across the various cultures.

Although no more important than any other skill, self-awareness is critical in the sense that it facilitates learning the remaining EQ competencies because at the core of EQ is self-awareness, where the concept of *self* has different definitions depending upon an individual's culture. For instance, when defining culture within the framework of values, attitudes, and beliefs that affect the behavior of individuals belonging to a particular group, there is a high probability that cultural values will likely vary between groups. Moreover, identified correlations between EQ and culture further strengthen the likelihood that EQ will also contain cross-cultural variations.

Research results conducted using both domestic and international populations showed variances in EQ scores across cultures. For example, in a study conducted by Whitman, Van Rooy, Viswesvaran, and Kraus (2009) on the measurement equivalence of a second-order factor model of EQ across ethnicity, African Americans tended to score higher

81

on EQ tests than Caucasians, whereas in a study assessing racial groups conducted by Gignac and Ekermans (2010), results showed that African Americans and Caucasians scored similarly on measures of EQ. Researchers of other studies that have found African Americans tending to score higher than Caucasians on EQ assessments have attributed research results to the possibility of there being a different EQ construct existing between ethnic minorities and Caucasians. For instance, research has demonstrated that African Americans have a propensity to align with the collectivist society, where the use of emotion is routine when interacting with others, whereas Caucasians in the United States typically learn to be more individualistic and may not be as emotionally attuned as other ethnic groups.

Exploring linkages between EQ and cultural norms, while at the same time differentiating between individualist and collectivist societies, is important when assessing variances in EQ scoring. Hofstede's (1980) work on cultural norms showed that individualist societies are traditionally more self-governing, whereas members of collectivist societies receive encouragement to subordinate their personal needs for the good of the group. Shared collectivist characteristics include identity derived from the system, minimal separation between private and work life, priority on building relationships, and tight social networks. When working with others, these individuals will traditionally either give precedence to or subordinate self-interests, depending on their particular experience. This means that individuals' cultural past affects their quality of interactions with others, as well as their level of self-awareness, as reflected in EQ assessment results.

References

Argyris, C. (1990). *Overcoming organizational defenses.* New York, NY: Prentice-Hall.

Asch, S. E. (1955) Opinions and social pressure. *Scientific American, 193*(5), 31-35. doi:10.1038/scientificamerican1155-31

Bar-On, R. (2006). The Bar-On model of emotional-social intelligence (ESI). *Psicothema, 18,* 13-25. Retrieved from http://www.psicothema.com/english/

Baumeister, R.F., & Leary, M. R. (1995). The need to belong: Desire for interpersonal attachments as a fundamental human motivation. *Psychological Bulletin, 117,* 497-529. doi:10.1037/0033-2909.117.3.497

Bump, P. (2014). *Study: Cops tend to see Black kids as less innocent than White kids.* Retrieved from http://www.theatlantic.com/national/archive/2014/03/cops-tend-to-see-black-kids-as-less-innocent-than-white-kids/383247/

Cherniss, C. (2010). Emotional intelligence: Toward clarification of a concept. *Industrial & Organizational Psychology, 3,* 110-126. doi:10.1111/j.1754-9434.2010.01231.x

Colvin, M. (2000). *Crime and coercion: An integrated theory of chronic criminality*. New York, NY: St. Martin's Press.

Coy, P., Collins, K., Ingold, D., & Campbell, E. (2014). Race, class, and the future of Ferguson. *Bloomberg Businessweek*, (4391), 12-14.

Crawford, H. (2016). *What are Louisiana's gun laws like? Alton Sterling was shot in the state's capital*. Retrieved from http://www.bustle.com/articles/171057-what-are-louisianas-gun-laws-like-alton-sterling-was-shot-in-the-states-capital

DeGruy, J. (2005). Post traumatic slave syndrome: America's legacy of enduring injury and healing. Milwaukie, OR: Uptone Press.

Ellis, T., & Gray, G. (2015*). Tamir Rice report: No proof police officer shouted warning before shooting*. Retrieved from http://www.cnn.com/2015/06/13/us/ tamir-rice-report/

Gardner, H. (1983). *Frames of mind: The theory of multiple intelligences*. New York, NY: Basic Books.

Gignac, G. E., & Ekermans, G. (2010). Group differences in EI within a sample of Black and White South Africans. *Personality and Individual Differences*, *49,* 639-644. doi:10.1016/j.paid.2010.05.039

Goleman, D. (1995). *Emotional intelligence*. New York, NY: Bantam Books.

Hirschi, T. (1969). *Causes of delinquency*. Berkeley: University of California Press.

Hofstede, G. (1980). *Culture's consequences: International difference in work-related values*. Beverly Hills, CA: Sage.

Lieszkovszky, I. (2015). *Tamir Rice investigation released: The big story.* Retrieved from http://www.cleveland.com /metro/index.ssf/2015/06/tamir_rice_investigation_relea.ht ml

Merton, R. K. (1949a). *Discrimination and the American Creed.* In R. M. Maclver (Ed). *Discrimination and national welfare* (pp. 99-126). New York, NY: Harper & Brothers.

Merton, R. K. (1949b). *Social theory and social structure: Towards the codification of theory and research.* New York, NY: Free Press.

Parker, K. F., & McCall, P. L. (1999). Structural conditions and racial homicide patterns: A look at the multiple disadvantages in urban areas. *Criminology, 37,* 447-478.

Salovey, P., & Mayer, J. D. (1990). Emotional intelligence. *Imagination, Cognition, and Personality, 9,* 185-211. doi:10.2190/DUGG-P24E-52WK-6CDG

Senge, P. M. (1990). *The fifth discipline: The art and practice of the learning organization.* New York, NY: Doubleday.

Signorini, P., Wiseman, R., & Murphy, R. (2009). Developing alternative frameworks for exploring intercultural learning: A critique of Hofstede's cultural difference model. *Teaching in Higher Education, 14,* 253-264.

Spearman, C. (1904). "General intelligence," objectively determined and measured. *American Journal of Psychology, 15,* 201-292. doi:10.2307/1412107

Sutherland, E. H. (1960). *Principles of criminology* (6th ed.). Philadelphia, PA: J. B. Lippincott Co.

Thorndike, E. L. (1920). A constant error in psychological ratings. *Journal of Applied Psychology, 4,* 25-29. doi:10.1037/h0071663

Wadsworth, T. (2000). Labor markets, delinquency, and social control theory: An empirical assessment of the mediating process. *Social Forces, 78,* 1041-1066.

Whitman, D., Van Rooy, D., Viswesvaran, C., & Kraus, E. (2009). Testing the second-order factor structure and measurement equivalence of the Wong and Law emotional intelligence scale across gender and ethnicity. *Educational and Psychological Measurement, 69,* 1059-1074. doi:10.1177/0013164409344498

2

An In-Depth Look At Policing

Let me be clear – no one is above the law. Not a politician, not a priest, not a criminal, not a police officer. We are all accountable for our actions

—*Antonio Villaraigosa*

Historical Analysis of American Policing

Turning back the clock on law enforcement and observing how it has transitioned over time in response to public demand will aid in making sense of the current state of American policing and where it is heading. We will begin in the early 17th century, when European settlers in North America saw the use of African slaves as a cheaper, more plentiful labor source than indentured servants, who were mostly poor Europeans, and soon thereafter, a Dutch ship brought 20 Africans ashore at the British colony of Jamestown,

Virginia, which marked the beginning of slavery spreading throughout the American colonies (Beschloss, 2009). Whereas researchers have indicated the mid-1800s and the unification of police departments in several major cities were the starting point in the development of modern policing in the United States, some regard slave patrols as the first formal attempt at policing in America (DuBois, 1904).

In the South, for example, laws were passed that required all plantation owners or their White male employees to be members of the militia and for those armed militia members to make monthly inspections of the quarters of all slaves in the state. The purpose of these sophisticated, government-sponsored slave patrols was to prevent crimes and insurrection by slaves against the Caucasian community. Such actions support the theory that legally sanctioned law enforcement existed in America prior to the Civil War for the express purpose of maintaining ascendancy over the slave population and thereby protecting the economic interests of slave owners (Turner, Giacopassi, & Vandiver, 2006).

The presidential proclamation and executive order issued by President Abraham Lincoln on January 1, 1863, proclaiming the freedom of approximately 3 million of the 4 million slaves in the United States shined a light on not only social issues, but also the measures some in our society would take for the sake of preserving their perception of order. For example, the millions of recently freed African Americans in the South were poor and unemployed, and according to Adamson (1983), "Crime control in the antebellum South was subordinated to race control. With the abolition of slavery, alternative forms of race control had to be found, and race control naturally became a major aim in crime control" (p. 558).

Many social challenges can be traced to the enslavement and subsequent emancipation of millions of individuals, whereby one of the most disgraceful institutions in American history undoubtedly helped in shaping current U.S. society (Silberman 1978; Websdale 2001). Consider the situation where individuals are far more reluctant to trust others if their ancestors were heavily affected by the slave trade. As a result, hundreds of years of insecurity generated by the slave trade has not only created mistrust on the part of African Americans, but has also helped in shaping associated belief systems that continue to pass from parent to child well after the end of the slave trade (Nunn & Wantchekon, 2011). Silberman (1978) provided an example of the manifestation of thoughts of mistrust by alleging that racism has shaped American life for centuries.

The Political Era

The 1800s to the early 1900s represented the political era of policing, whereby politicians hired and retained officers as a means of maintaining their political influence, and, to return the favor for employment, police officers encouraged citizens to vote for specific elected officials, discouraged them from voting for opponents, and, in some instances, assisted with rigging elections (Lombardo, 2013; Marks & Sun, 2007). During this period, police organizations operated in a decentralized fashion that provided loosely supervised officers the flexibility to perform a variety of services, including criminal arrests, social welfare, and routine follow-up on immigrant workers (Schmalleger, 2009). Because politicians were instrumental in the appointment of police chiefs, they wielded enormous influence over decisions that affected employees, as well as organizational decisions whereby the quid pro quo relationship between police leadership and elected officials ultimately led to departmental corruption resulting from political interference.

The Reform Era

The policing reform era in the United States (1900s–1970s) occurred as a result of citizens demanding change in a law enforcement system widely perceived as being brutal and corrupt. Whereas early reform attempts were unsuccessful, progress toward change began to take hold during the latter part of the 20th century. The types of change demanded by citizen groups included improved law enforcement leadership and a set of professional standards employed by police organizations for hiring, retaining, and training officers as opposed to a process whereby politicians appointed police officers for the sole purpose of supporting their political agendas.

Further, while the reform era in American policing provided police administrators with improved processes to include more flexibility for deploying personnel resources based on neighborhood needs, enhanced record-keeping capabilities, improved methods of identifying criminals, and technological advances, because police organizations simultaneously adopted a centralized structure emphasizing professionalism and crime control, law enforcement in general became less engaged with communities (Schmalleger, 2009). Consequently, the relationship between law enforcement and community members deteriorated because leaders of police organizations reprioritized their focus to include less emphasis on service calls (Marks & Sun, 2007; Schmalleger, 2009). Challenges posed by the reform era included the lack of a cooperative effort between the police and citizens that eventually led to the reengagement of law enforcement organizations with the community.

Community Policing Era

Incorporating various aspects from the political and reform periods, community policing was a strategy used by police between the 1980s and 2001 to legitimize the relationship between law enforcement and communities, as well as proactively address conditions believed to precipitate crime. Accompanying community policing initiatives, the slogan, "To Protect and Serve" gained prominence, whereby an objective of community-oriented policing was to forge a collaborative relationship between the community and law enforcement in which citizens became equal partners in public safety (Bullock, 2013; Díaz, 2011; Glaser & Denhardt, 2010; Marks & Sun, 2007; Terpstra, 2011). In essence, community-oriented policing entailed community involvement where citizens partnered with law enforcement in crime-prevention initiatives geared toward reducing crime and creating trust between local communities and police officers who patrolled their neighborhoods. Aside from acknowledging the importance of the citizen in fighting crime, these initiatives cultivated goodwill by providing needed services to local communities. The public welcomed such change, as evidenced in the ongoing popularity of community policing. For example, calendar year 1997 statistics showed there were 21,000 community-policing officers employed at the state and local levels, and by 1999, that number had increased to 113,000 (Hickman & Reaves, 2001).

Adaptation on the part of law enforcement relative to community-oriented policing took the form of police organizational leaders having to abandon outdated operational models and adopt proactive policing philosophies. Under this concept, local police participated on task forces and conducted foot, bike, and horse patrols to enhance community relationships (Marks & Sun, 2007; Schmalleger, 2009). Moreover, within police organizations where operations were intelligence driven based primarily on community input, law enforcement was in a favorable position to respond proactively rather than after the fact, and community satisfaction of the police increased (Lombardo, Olson, & Staton, 2010). The terrorist attacks that occurred on September 11, 2001, changed national conscientiousness related to personal safety and resulted in leaders of police organizations on every level having to reprioritize their organizational strategies to protect American citizens better (Bailey & Cree, 2011; Schmalleger, 2009; Wright, 2011).

American Policing After September 11, 2001

American policing in the 21st century has become increasingly complex as law enforcement executives must not only contend with traditional policing responsibilities in the midst of economic hardship, but must also assume new roles as potential first responders to terrorist incidents and assist federal agencies in developing intelligence on possible terrorist activity. The homeland security era encompasses intelligence-driven terrorism prevention, agency interoperability, and new proactive intervention laws. Moreover, economic realities serve as a constant reminder of the need for law enforcement executives to make efficient use of resources through employing more evidence-based policing, where police organizations incorporate research and analysis into their tactics and strategies (Hoggett & Stott, 2012; McFarlane, 2012; Plecas, McCormick, Levine, Neal, & Cohen, 2011; Scott, 2010) . For instance, although critical factors including politics, resource restraints, and social preferences preclude the likelihood of research ever becoming the sole determinant of law enforcement policy and practice, evidence-based policing where alignments form between law enforcement priorities, scholarly research, and thoughtful and reflective practical experimentation appear to offer leaders of police organizations additional options for adapting to increased demands placed upon police organizations resulting from the homeland security era.

New security initiatives require leaders of police organizations on the local and state level to devise strategies suitable for fulfilling homeland security mandates, which include prioritizing security and enhancing organizational focus on terrorism or the threat of terrorism, while providing traditional law enforcement. Paradigm shifts in law enforcement were most notable through information exchanged between agencies, particularly with the establishment of intelligence-sharing mechanisms such as joint terrorism task forces and regional information sharing networks, which increased collaboration between state and federal law enforcement organizations (Kim & de Guzman, 2012; Marks & Sun, 2007; Schaible & Sheffield, 2012; Schmalleger, 2009). Much of the change experienced by the law enforcement community following the terrorist attacks on September 11, 2001, involved a shift in organizational emphasis from community-oriented policing where police organizations partnered with local communities to address the immediate conditions that give rise to public safety, including crime, social disorder, and fear of crime to an era of ensuring homeland security through threat assessment and information sharing (Lee, 2010; Marks &

Sun, 2007; Morabito, 2010; Randol, 2012; Roberts, Roberts, & Liedka, 2012; Schmalleger, 2009).

Similar to leaders of other businesses, leaders of police organizations continue to face shrinking budgets that affect employee staffing, recruitment, retention, and development. As a result, law enforcement executives are facing a new reality in American policing due to the acceleration of change in operations, politics, and economic (Fischer, 2009; International Association of Chiefs of Police, 2011; Lee, 2010). In addition to the expectation of carrying out their traditional law enforcement duties, agency leaders are being challenged when it comes to devoting resources to community-oriented policing while at the same time realigning operations in a manner that fulfills government mandates associated with homeland security. Still, with crime taking place at all hours of the day and usually out of the immediate observation of police officers, a critical component in crime fighting involves trust and cooperation between law enforcement and individuals who live in the neighborhoods where crime is being committed, which will not occur without a forged partnership between the police and local citizens.

References

Adamson, C. (1983). Punishment after slavery: Southern state penal systems 1865-1890. *Social Problems, 30*, 555-569.

Bailey, A., & Cree, L. (2011). Terrorism preparation by Michigan law enforcement agencies. *American Journal of Criminal Justice, 36,* 434-447. doi:10.1007/s12103-011-9126-2

Bullock, K. (2013). Community, intelligence-led policing and crime control. *Policing & Society, 23,* 125-144. doi:10.1080/10439463.2012.671822

Díaz, J. (2011). Immigration policy, criminalization and the growth of the immigration industrial complex: Restriction, expulsion, and eradication of the undocumented in the U.S. *Western Criminology Review, 12*(2), 35-54. Retrieved from http://wcr.sonoma.edu/

DuBois, W. E. B. (1904). Some notes on negro crime, particularly in Georgia. Atlanta, GA: Atlanta University Press.

Fischer, C. (2009). *Leadership matters: Police chiefs talk about their careers.* Washington, DC: Police Executive Research Forum.

Glaser, M. A., & Denhardt, J. (2010). Community policing and community building: A case study of officer perceptions. *American Review of Public Administration, 40,* 309-325. doi:10.1177/0275074009340050

Hickman, M., & Reaves, B. (2001). *Community policing in local police departments, 1997 and 1999.* Washington, DC: Bureau of Justice Statistics.

Hoggett, J., & Stott, C. (2012). Post G20: The challenge of change, implementing evidence-based public order policing. *Journal of Investigative Psychology & Offender Profiling, 9,* 174-183. doi:10.1002/jip.1360

International Association of Chiefs of Police. (2011). *Policing in the 21st century.* Washington, DC: Author.

Kim, M., & de Guzman, M. C. (2012). Police paradigm shift after the 9/11 terrorist attacks: The empirical evidence from the United States municipal police departments. *Criminal Justice Studies, 25,* 323-342. doi:10.1080/1478601X.2012.707014

Lee, J. (2010). Policing after 9/11: Community policing in an age of homeland security. *Police Quarterly, 13,* 347-366. doi:10.1177/109861111038408

Lombardo, R. M. (2013). Fighting organized crime: A history of law enforcement efforts in Chicago. *Journal of Contemporary Criminal Justice, 29,* 296-316. doi:10.1177/1043986213485635

Lombardo, R. M., Olson, D., & Staton, M. (2010). The Chicago alternative policing strategy: A reassessment of the CAPS program. *Policing, 33,* 586-606. doi:10.1108/13639511011085033

Marks, D. E., & Sun, I. Y. (2007). The impact of 9/11 on organizational development among state and local law enforcement agencies. *Journal of Contemporary Criminal Justice, 23,* 159-173. doi:10.1177/1043986207301364

McFarlane, D. A. (2012). The impact of the global economic recession on the American criminal justice system. *International Journal of Criminal Justice Sciences, 7,* 539-549. Retrieved from http://www.sascv.org/ijcjs/

Morabito, M. S. (2010). Understanding community policing as an innovation: Patterns of adoption. *Crime & Delinquency, 56,* 564-587. Retrieved from http://cad.sagepub.com/

Nunn, N., & Wantchekon, L. (2011). The slave trade and the origins of mistrust in Africa. *American Economic Review, 101,* 3221-3252. doi:10.1257/aer.101.7.3221

Plecas, D., McCormick, A., Levine, J., Neal, P., & Cohen, I. (2011). Evidence-based solution to information sharing between law enforcement agencies. *Policing: An International Journal of Police Strategies & Management, 34,* 120-134. Retrieved from http://www.emeraldinsight.com/journals.htm?issn=1363-951X

Randol, B. K. (2012). The organization correlates of terrorism response preparedness in local police department. *Criminal Justice Policy Review, 23,* 304-326. doi:10.1177/0887403411400729

Roberts, A., Roberts, J., & Liedka, R. V. (2012). Elements of terrorism preparedness in local police agencies, 2003-2007: Impact of vulnerability, organizational characteristics, and contagion in the post-9/11 era. *Crime & Delinquency, 58,* 720-747. doi:10.1177/0011128712452960

Schaible, L. M., & Sheffield, J. (2012). Intelligence-led policing and change in state law enforcement agencies. *Policing, 35,* 761-784. doi:10.1108/13639511211275643

Schmalleger, F. (2009). *Criminal justice: A brief introduction* (8th ed.). Englewood Cliffs, NJ: Prentice Hall.

Scott, M. S. (2010). Policing and police research: Learning to listen, with a Wisconsin case study. *Police Practice & Research: An International Journal, 11*(2), 95-104. doi:10.1080/15614261003590779

Silberman, C. E., (1978). *Criminal violence criminal justice.* New York, NY: Random House.

Terpstra, J. (2011). Governance and accountability in community policing. *Crime, Law & Social Change, 55*(2/3), 87-104. doi:10.1007/s10611-011-9272-y

Turner, K., Giacopassi, D., & Vandiver, M. (2006). Ignoring the past: Coverage of slavery and slave patrols in criminal justice texts. *Journal of Criminal Justice Education, 17,* 181-195. doi:10.1080 /10511250500335627

Websdale, N. (2001). *Policing the poor: From slave plantation to public housing.* Boston, MA: Northeastern University Press.

Wright, M. (2011, Fall). Domestic terrorism, cyber-radicalization, U.S. college students. *Forensic Examiner,* pp. 10-18. Retrieved from http://www.theforensicexaminer.com/

3

Why The Need For Change?

Injustice anywhere is a threat to justice everywhere.

—Martin Luther King, Jr.

A Multicultural Look at the Criminal Justice System

Of the numerous definitions I have come across over the years regarding the meaning of the word multiculturalism, the one that resonates the most with me is that multiculturalism relates to the various cultures being treated equally and respected for their vast differences (Burns, 2008). On the subject of cultural equality as it pertains to the criminal justice system, a widely held belief by some individuals in our society is that crime is overwhelmingly attributable to African Americans, and while statistics are sometimes used to validate that assertion based on population representation and the level at which certain crimes can be associated with African Americans, caution must be exercised when making assertions based solely on statistical profiles, particularly when taking into consideration that research results are sometimes influenced by factors such as bias stemming from ingrained perceptions that link crime with specific races of people.

Before I begin the process of attempting to validate one set of statistics against another, it is important that I introduce the concept of research bias into the conversation at this point. Although prior to beginning my doctoral degree program I was well aware of the possibility of using the same set of data to show opposing views, one of the first things that was drilled into my own head, as well as the heads of my classmates during the initial stages of pursuing our doctoral degrees, was the limitation of arriving at sound research conclusions due to the potential of researcher bias. Researcher bias is a form of response bias that occurs whenever there is a flaw in a survey's research design. This systemic error can be caused by problems with various aspects of a study's research methodology.

Where problems associated with research results might be explained by factors such as inaccurate answers provided by research respondents, other factors that explain why results might not be reliable involve bias on the part of the researcher. Everyone has a bias toward one thing or another, and as a mishap at Google showed, even machinery is prone to exhibiting bias, that is, when manipulated by human input. For instance, a simple Google search for "three Black teenagers" will bring up the mug shots of African American teenagers, as compared to the stock photos of Caucasian men and women smiling and enjoying life displayed when the Google search is for "three White teenagers."

In a June 10, 2016, *Washington Post* article titled "Google Faulted for Racial Bias in Image Search Results for Black Teenagers," algorithms were said to be the cause of the racially insensitive depiction of African Americans. According to a Google spokesperson, image search results are basically the product of the frequency at which images appear and the manner in which they are described online (Chiel, 2016). What I make of all of this is that computers simply spit out what people put in, which gets us to the real question: why do so many people within our society continue to struggle when it comes to cleansing their minds of those negative images of African Americans? When conducting research, it is critically important to set aside those biases to the extent possible and let the data speak for themselves.

To share what the data say, I will use as an example some information provided to me by someone I had engaged in conversation regarding the topic of race and crime, and while I pride myself on being open to learning from those who might hold an opposing view, I am also a bit cautious when someone appears to have an agenda, and the first few words out of their mouth make it obvious that the information being shared with me is merely to prove their point.

One day someone handed me a pamphlet containing an article written by an African American addressing the subject of race and the criminal justice system. The article was well written and had I not been aware of the ability to spin statistics to suit the specific occasion, I would have been convinced that African Americans were 100 percent responsible for the high numbers associated with their incarceration levels without any racial animus. The article addressed crime statistics between 1976 and 2005, and how African Americans committed more than 50 percent of all murders in the United States but constituted only about 13 percent of the population.

Further, the rate of African Americans arrested for crimes such as robbery, aggravated assault, and property crime was about two to three times their population representation. In addressing the argument that jails and prisons are rife with young African American males as a result of racist drug laws, the article rebuked such theories and instead questioned the possibility of such reforms containing any racial undertones, particularly since they received wide support from several African American political leaders who, in the 1980s, also wanted to see harsher penalties handed out to drug dealers. What I found most astounding about the article, even more than the tone, were words to the effect that as long as African Americans continue committing crimes at the rates cited above, they will continue to be viewed suspiciously and tensions will persist between police and individuals who reside in crime-ridden communities. The writer of the previously mentioned article is not alone in his thoughts, for these are the same perceptions held by many people in our society, which as opposed to truly addressing the problem of race and crime, merely serve to perpetuate racial stereotypes.

If you are wondering where I stand on the issue of crime and its purported association with race, I make no excuses for anyone committing crime, regardless of race. That being said, both history and research have shown that it is unwise to simply base one's beliefs on the assertions of others. Along that line, let us turn our attention to an expanded view of crimes broken down along racial lines and explore the manner in which statistics inform us, or not.

According to the FBI Uniform Crime Reports for 2013, 68.9 percent of all individuals arrested were White, 28.3 percent were Black, and 2.9 percent were of other races. Of all juveniles (persons under the age of 18) arrested in 2013, 63.0 percent were White, 34.4 percent were Black, and 2.7 percent were of other races. When assessing the adult arrest percentages for 2013, 69.6 percent were White, 27.6 percent were Black, and 2.9 percent were of other races (U.S. Department of Justice, Federal Bureau of Investigation [FBI], 2013).

White individuals were arrested more often for violent crimes than individuals of any other race and accounted for 58.4 percent of those arrests. Of adults arrested for murder, 52.1 percent were Black, and 45.5 percent were White. Black juveniles comprised 53.3 percent of all juveniles arrested for violent crimes, while White juveniles accounted for 59.7 percent of all juveniles arrested for property crimes. Of juveniles arrested for drug abuse violations, 73.0 percent were White, while White juveniles comprised 54.4 percent of juveniles arrested for aggravated assaults. And as concise as these numbers from the FBI might appear, they have limitations. The lack of consistency in reporting by police departments relative to reporting methodologies or whether or not crime statistics are even reported to the FBI must not be overlooked. At first glance, the data appear to show that African Americans, who comprise approximately 13 percent of the population, represent 38 percent of the inmates in state and federal prisons (U.S. Department of Justice, FBI, 2013). This means that African Americans are locked up at a rate of three times their population representation, and while such data are often used to support agendas wishing to make correlations between race and crime, the data contains many flaws that are difficult to overcome.

As mentioned before, because there is not a requirement relative to crime reporting, not every police department reports its numbers to the FBI. Because a large number of incarcerations involve nonviolent offences such as marijuana possession, the statistics best reflect those who have been apprehended and locked up, as opposed to those responsible for the majority of criminal acts. For example, Miller (1996) suggested that whereas drug use among racial minorities, including African Americans, is proportionate to their population percentage, they comprise 35 percent of all drug arrests, 55 percent of all drug convictions, and 75 percent of all prison admissions for drug offenses. But what really stands out is that African Americans are approximately 18 times more likely to be arrested for a drug offense than Whites, thereby adding to their incarceration numbers, which further skews criminal statistics along racial lines.

Adding to the potential flaws in research data due to researcher bias is the slant put on the data by whoever is using the research to make a point. Just like other well-intentioned ideas or concepts that have been used for means other than their original purpose, users of statistics occasionally rely on this information simply to back up their preconceived ideas. What usually comes to mind when discussing this issue with others is how the media use a set of identical statistics depending on their political leanings. To test this theory for yourselves, the next time a significant event is broadcast over the news channels, try turning back and forth between the various networks and notice the differences in how the same event is being covered, particularly if it involves controversial issues. The point is that statistics at best merely point us in a particular direction, but they are far from an exact science.

Remember the article I referenced earlier that suggested that between 1976 and 2005, African Americans constituted about 13 percent of the population but were responsible for committing more than 50 percent of all murders in the United States? A cursory review of FBI crime statistics might appear to lend credibility to such assertions; however, an important statistic the article failed to mention was that for the reporting year 2005, Whites were charged at a higher rate than African Americans with murder and nonnegligent manslaughter offenses in the United States at a rate of 49.1 to 48.6 percent, respectively (U.S. Department of Justice, FBI, 2005).

Why are some individuals quick to point to criminal statistics where African Americans are the worst offenders and hold them up to seemingly indict an entire race of people? Is this somehow linked to societal thought, where individuals truly believe that crime can be factually linked to a particular racial group, or do statistics simply confirm or support what some individuals choose to believe? Think about the disparity in how the early South engaged Black and White criminals. During those days, police practices routinely treated African Americans more harshly, while Whites who committed crimes were typically given undue leniency (DuBois, 1903). In the section titled Is Racial Profiling a Myth? we will further explore some of the dangers behind the misuse of crime statistics, but for now, I offer an alternative position to the article presented earlier that asserted African Americans, absent the impact of societal injustice, were responsible for their higher than average incarceration numbers.

Since the 1980s, policies aimed at curbing crime and drugs in the United States have resulted in an exorbitant number of young African American males being taken off the streets and placed behind bars. Although the high incarceration levels can partly be blamed on the misdeeds of individuals who commit crimes, there is no denying the negative impact caused to impoverished neighborhoods by the implementation of harsher penalties that although designed to enhance public safety, unquestionably lowered the threshold needed to lock up African Americans. As noted by Tonry (1995), the emphasis on low-level drug dealers in the war on drugs had virtually no lasting effect on the drug trade, but instead resulted in increased numbers of young African American males from the inner city being incarcerated. For example, the prison population tripled during the 1980s and in the 1990s, where a quarter of all young African American males were either behind bars, on probation, or on parole. Before jumping to the conclusion that such high incarceration levels are simply attributable to wrongdoing on the part of African American men, let us first consider the possibility of the criminal justice system itself playing a role in the make-up of jail occupancy.

The criminal justice system is a set of agencies and processes established by governments to control crime and impose penalties on those who violate laws and essentially accomplished through investigating, apprehending, prosecuting, defending, sentencing, and punishing those suspected or convicted of criminal offenses. Once a law is violated, becoming a part of the system follows a course of action that encompasses the following basic steps:

- Law enforcement officers receive the crime report from victims, witnesses, or other parties or witness the crime themselves and make a report.

- The crime is investigated, and the officers try to identify a suspect and find enough evidence to arrest the individual they believe is responsible.

- If a suspect is identified and there is sufficient evidence, officers may arrest the suspect or issue a citation for the individual to appear in court at a specific time.

This sounds simple enough, but the large disparities between the numbers relative to African American versus White inmates should at least pique one's interest to look behind the numbers to determine whether there is more to the story.

One place to begin such an inquiry is the war on drugs, which immediately comes to mind when contemplating problems associated with drug enforcement and sentencing practices that have led to both prison overcrowding and a downstream impact on local communities. For example, even as recent as 2013 when we saw an increased emphasis on drug treatment and prevention programs, our government budgeted more than $25 billion in federal spending on the drug war, with approximately $15 billion earmarked for law enforcement, drug interdictions, and international efforts to combat drug trafficking. Today, approximately 2 million Americans are in prison or jail, many of them African American, and despite more relaxed attitudes among the public toward nonviolent offenses like marijuana use, according to U.S. Department of Justice reports, the number of people in federal prison for drug offenses spiked from 74,276 in 2000 to 97,472 in 2010 (U.S. Department of Justice, FBI, 2000, 2010). But what was the war on drugs about in the first place?

The term *war on drugs* was a media creation that gained popularity following a press conference given by President Nixon on June 18, 1971, related to his declaration of drug abuse as "public enemy number one" (Vulliamy, 2011). Therefore, a viable war strategy was to cut off the head of the snake, which in battle usually means to remove the most dangerous opponent or the leader first, so that the other enemies will be easier to deal with. Along those lines, one would naturally assume that an effective strategy would entail focused attention on those presumably at the top, such as drug czars and others responsible for supplying drugs to neighborhoods. Instead, what has occurred is that

each succeeding U.S. president has at least in part continued a similar war on drugs strategy that was particularly
problematic during from 1980 to 1997, when the number of
people behind bars for nonviolent drug law offenses increased from 50,000 to over 400,000 (Human Rights
Watch, 2016).

Not discounting the efforts of President Jimmy Carter, who
was inaugurated on a campaign platform that included marijuana decriminalization; President Bill Clinton, who initially advocated for treatment instead of incarceration during his presidential campaign before reverting to many of
the same war on drug strategies of his Republican prede-
cessors; or even President Barack Obama, who supported
state medical marijuana laws, shrinking the gap in disparity
relative to the number of incarcerated African American
men behind bars does not appear to have been the top
agenda item, regardless of which administration has been in
office.

Before abandoning the discussion on the laws that might
have contributed to prison overcrowding, a consideration of
the judicial system that laypersons rarely if ever consider
involves the unenviable position federal judges often found
themselves in by having to abide by sentencing laws that
contained mandatory minimum penalties driven more by

quantities of drugs than the defendant's role in the crime. The impact of such guidelines meant that for a crime involving 50 grams of methamphetamine, for example, individuals were subjected to spending 40 years behind bars, regardless of whether they were a kingpin or a low-level drug runner.

For as long as I can remember, countless people, particularly individuals living within or having connections to impoverished neighborhoods, have alleged a government conspiracy is behind the high incarceration levels of African American men. At the same time, such claims have been brushed off as either mere speculation or blatant excuses for wrongdoing. Being able to articulate the drug problem within African American communities from a holistic standpoint has been a monumental task. That is, until the release of *The New Jim Crow: Mass Incarceration in the Age of Colorblindness* by Michelle Alexander (2010), which addresses the dynamics of this situation that makes it difficult to continue turning a blind eye to a glaring wrong within our society without making a conscientious effort to do so.

Alexander discussed how mass incarceration practices of the 21st century are actually no different from pre-Civil War slavery and the post-Civil War Jim Crow laws in terms of intent, which she asserts was primarily to maintain a racial caste system. Whereas the definition of the word *caste* in the Merriam-Webster dictionary speaks to a system of rigid social stratification characterized by hereditary status, endogamy, and social barriers sanctioned by custom, law, or religion, Alexander framed the term *racial caste* as a racial group locked into an inferior position by law and custom. Within that context, she suggests that the criminal justice system is merely a mechanism designed for racial control through targeting African American men made simple by the passage of initiatives such as the war on drugs.

An example Alexander used in supporting her assertion detailed how the Anti-Drug Abuse Act of 1986 carried much harsher penalties for distributors of crack, which was mainly associated with African Americans, as compared with the punishment for distributors of powder, which was the substance mainly associated with White drug offenders. In addition to the skewed penalties levied against African Americans, civil penalties associated with drug offenses created eligibility problems for offenders, many of whom were later denied access to public housing and student loans.

Then, as if an explosion had just gone off, it happened. *It was an article by journalist Dan Baum titled "Legalize It*

All—How to Win the War on Drugs" published in the April 2016 issue of *Harper's Magazine* that caught nearly everyone off-guard and gave further credence to widely held beliefs within the African American community relative to the disparities surrounding drug sentencing (Baum, 2016). Baum recounted an interview he once had with John Ehrlichman when Baum was writing a book on the politics of drug prohibition, when Ehrlichman, who served as President Richard Nixon's domestic policy chief, surprised him by asking, "You want to know what this was really all about?" According to Baum, Ehrlichman then said,

> The Nixon campaign in 1968, and the Nixon White House after that, had two enemies: the antiwar left and black people. You understand what I'm saying? We knew we couldn't make it illegal to be either against the war or black [*sic*], but by getting the public to associate the hippies with marijuana and blacks with heroin, and then criminalizing both heavily, we could disrupt those communities. We could arrest their leaders, raid their homes, break up their meetings, and vilify them night after night on the evening news. Did we know we were lying about the drugs? Of course we did.

Talk about creating, and in some cases cementing, perceptions about the criminal justice system. In the conversations surrounding this issue that I have been a part of over the years, a great majority of people, particularly those connected in some way to the inner city, typically believed that the war on drugs carried with it racial undertones. The problem with those types of allegations has been the absence of proof to substantiate such claims. And while the strategies of the Nixon years as recounted in the Baum article may not be actual proof that a program aimed at locking up African Americans ever existed, the information contained within the article will nonetheless harden the already negative perceptions of those mostly affected by U.S. drug enforcement policies.

Regardless of your personal beliefs regarding where fault should be placed when contemplating the reasons behind our criminal justice system being overrun with African American men, the fact remains that such a dynamic does have an impact on societal thought. Think about it from the perspective of felons being unable to acquire meaningful work due to questions raised on employment applications requiring applicants to divulge whether they have been convicted of a felonious crime. While seemingly a fair question in terms of the selection process employers go through in filling vacancies, what about the innocent individuals who become entangled in police narcotics investigations along with hardened criminals and become haunted by blemished records? But only criminals commit crimes, right? As unconventional as that statement might sound to some, some individuals suggest that people finding themselves on the wrong side of the law for whatever reason must have had, at the very least, a propensity to commit a crime in the first place, which makes them no better than others who break the law. Such a sentiment will unquestionably play into who in our society is considered a criminal.

In terms of the label *criminal* being affixed to a person, Dr. J. W. Wiley, in his book *The Nigger in You: Challenging Dysfunctional Language, Engaging Leadership Moments* (2013), addressed a possible connection between criminality and race that appears to have developed immediately after slavery. Using the same transitive law found in mathematics and logic, that is, if $a = b$ and $b = c$, then $a = c$, Wiley constructed the equation $P = C = N$, which uses variables in a manner that renders a complex outcome. In one of his examples, the variables paired together involved a sudden uptick in crime and the change in federal legal status of more than 3 million enslaved persons from slave to free following the signing of the emancipation proclamation in 1863.

Next, depending on the intent and timing of the conversation, the letter P in the equation reflects individuals considered *property* prior to the emancipation and a *problem* for society afterwards. Here is where we get down and dirty, but in keeping things in proper context, there is really no getting around it. The letter N in the equation represents the word *nigger*. I will pause here for a moment to allow you to regain your composure.

Yes, I am keenly aware of the derogatory nature of *that* word and am not a fan of its usage in any context; however, I would like to emphasize that the usage of the word in this instance is merely to coincide with common references made during those times, which was well before any thought of political correctness. We now have our first equivalence, $P = N$, which reflects the problem asserted by Wiley and was associated with the newly emancipated. To understand further the problem being referenced here, it must also be taken into account that many of those who were newly emancipated became part of the homeless, lacked economic spending power, and were competing with poor Whites for the same type jobs in an economy recently devastated by war. The next equivalence in the equation, $C = N$, represents the mental model that occupied the minds of many within our society, where the newly emancipated people, left without resources, were framed as *criminals*, as denoted by C.

The backdrop of such labeling relates to the reality faced by many of the disenfranchised, who, upon finding that no real infrastructure existed to allow assimilation into mainstream society, began committing criminal acts as a means of survival. With our correlation complete and using the same transitive law in the earlier equation, we now have $P = C = N$, which symbolizes Problem = Criminal = Nigger (Wiley, 2013). The burning question relates to whether these types of correlations are being made today, and if so, how are they impacting the fair treatment of individuals who, for whatever reason, become caught up in the criminal justice system?

Continuing our convicted felon scenario with those who are now labeled and are for the most part unemployable, attempts at reintroducing convicted persons to society through prisoner reentry programs often result in many of the same individuals returning to similar and occasionally new crimes out of either habit or perceived necessity. According to U.S. Department of Justice records, more than 650,000 people, many of them with untreated mental illness and substance abuse disorders, are released from state and federal prisons every year, and approximately two thirds of them become recidivists where they are either rearrested or returned to prison within 3 years of being released.

The perpetual commission of crime by a segment of our society further ingrains our perceptions, often without delving into the actual origin of the problem. Because of our ability to access archived legislation, we can take a close look at how the Violent Crime Control and Law Enforcement Act of 1994, and support for such an initiative without consideration for the ensuing downstream impact, resulted in the need for countless apologies decades later. Remember the media reports of the incident that occurred on February 24, 2016, during a fund-raiser at a private South Carolina residence when in the middle of a speech, hopeful presidential candidate Hillary Clinton was suddenly interrupted by an activist holding a sign that read, "We have to bring them to heel – Hillary Clinton"?

On the video of the incident, the young lady can be heard asking Ms. Clinton if she was going to "apologize to Black people for mass incarceration," adding, "I'm not a super-predator." Being unfamiliar with what was meant by that statement, I actually had to conduct a little research to get up to speed on what the activist was attempting to convey in her message. What I learned was that Ms. Clinton, in support of President Bill Clinton's crime bill, the Violent

Crime Control and Law Enforcement Act of 1994, had given a speech at Keene State College where she defended the bill's legislation.

Among other things in her speech, Ms. Clinton is both observed and heard on the video stating the words,

> They are not just gangs of kids anymore. They are often the kinds of kids that are called 'superpredators.' No conscience, no empathy. We can talk about why they ended up that way, but first we have to bring them to heel.

With copies of the video being circulated during the time when Ms. Clinton was seeking the Democratic presidential nomination, her words from the past have come back to bite—hard.

Let's review an example of just how quickly things can get out of control when society becomes desensitized to hearing words such as *predator* in describing our youth and such indifference leads to the abuse of children. I am referring to the countless numbers of youth victimized by the Scranton, Pennsylvania, court system between 2003 to 2008, which is a classic example of prioritizing profits over people. As reported in a February 23, 2014, *New York Post* article, a former Luzerne County judge was ordered to spend 28 years in prison for his part in a bribery scandal that ultimately resulted in the state's high court having to overturn about 4,000 juvenile convictions. According to the article, the judge was convicted of taking more than $1 million from the builder of two juvenile detention centers in what the media dubbed as "kids for cash," where in blatant violation of constitutional rights, children as young as 10 years old (many of them first time offenders and without legal representation) were placed in for-profit detention centers in exchange for kickbacks (Getlen, 2014).

So, outside of simplifying the ability of those with the intention of camouflaging the type of mistreatment of individuals as with what occurred in Scranton, Pennsylvania, what exactly did the 1994 crime bill accomplish? While parts of the bill were designed for the express protection of crime victims, including women, the elderly, and children, through various support programs, other parts of the bill such as the amendments contained within Title II that allowed for juveniles within the criminal justice system to be treated as if they were adults effectively subjected the young to many of the same, if not worse, dangers that the bill was said to be designed to mitigate. For example, studies have shown that juveniles confined to prisons for extended periods of time face serious threats to their well-being, particularly when forced to share the same facilities as adults, where they face the risk of being both physically and sexually assaulted from not only other inmates, but from prison guards as well. But we are just getting started, and the scenario gets much worse.

There were provisions allowing for the development, modification, expansion, and operation of state prisons, and while some might rationalize such funding through a statement along the lines of, "We have to put prisoners somewhere," the idiom "The devil is in the details" has probably never been a more appropriate statement, particularly when considering how sections of the crime bill took away the federal court's power to hold prison or jail crowding unconstitutional under the Eighth Amendment.

This portion of the legislation effectively made it permissible to disregard rules governing cruel and unusual punishment. The amendment lifted the ceiling on inmate population to the point where overcrowding was only deemed a problem in cases where harm was sustained by a specific prisoner. Then, because of the manner in which the bill was written, the onus was placed on the inmate (plaintiff) to prove that prison overcrowding was the actual cause of the condition that resulted in undue suffering, pain, or humiliation.

This is where we lock them up and throw away the key—that is, it is time to address provisions within the crime bill that mandated life sentences for persons convicted of certain felonies. If someone was convicted of two or more serious violent felonies or of one or more serious violent felonies and one or more serious drug offenses on separate (and unassociated) prior occasions in a federal or state court, that person would be sentenced as prescribed under the mandatory life imprisonment guidelines the next time he or she was convicted in a U.S. court of a serious violent felony. If the bill contained allowances where judges had the discretion to reserve the harshest penalties for individuals who committed the worst types of crimes, the bill would likely not be picked apart for its faults in the manner it is today. The three-strikes law resulted in record numbers of prisoners being locked up for nonviolent and second-tier felonies.

Looking back on the progressively worsening condition of crime in local neighborhoods during the early 1990s might give insight into some of the thinking behind an initiative such as the 1994 crime bill. With inner-city violence seemingly out of control at that time, support for what was being proposed under the crime bill was received from many African American politicians and from African American church leaders who although wary of the potential impact of such legislation on the African American community, found themselves in a no-win scenario of having to choose between doing something or maintaining the status quo while inner-city communities were being ruined by gang violence (Fortner, 2015). Although over 20 years have passed since my days in the academy and receiving my first assignment working the streets of Long Beach and Compton, California, I can still remember the dated training film showing suspects having the upper hand on federal agents during a gunfight, where pinned-down agents attempted to return fire using six-shooters, while the bad guys fired continuously at them with semiautomatic weapons.

I bring that up because the type of images depicted in that training film very likely contributed to some of the safety concerns of police officers working in the inner city at that time, for the well-being of local residents and themselves. Being new to the law enforcement profession and having a fairly good idea about the types of weapons I would likely encounter in the neighborhoods where I would be working (having grown up there), when given the opportunity shortly after leaving the academy to swap out my standard- issued, six-shot Ruger for a Glock semiautomatic handgun, I jumped at the opportunity. And while amendments within the crime bill may have had the intention of enhancing the overall effectiveness of police departments through hiring, training, and equipping officers with the tools needed to enforce the new legislation, even with mass agreement that individuals should be held accountable for their actions, there must still be a sense of fairness when administering justice.

Trying to make sense of certain lengthy prison sentences handed out under the tough-on-crime bill is difficult at best. For example, a homeless man in Los Angeles, California, was sentenced in 1995 under the law to a term of 25 years for the theft of four cookies from a restaurant, and a man was sentenced in 1994 to a term of 25 years behind bars under the three-strikes law for stealing a slice of pizza from children. In both of those cases and several others like them, the 1994 crime bill legislation was just as, if not more, egregious than the offenses that led to individuals sentenced to unspeakable lengths of time behind bars in proportion to their crime.

Also within the theme of fairness, consider the following almost identical cases and determine for yourself the level of equality within the criminal justice system. The first case involved a 16-year-old African American high school football linebacker who in 2002 was accused of a rape that was later found to be a false allegation. Being charged as an adult and facing the prospect of spending the remainder of his life behind bars, coupled with being convinced by his attorney that the all-White jury would certainly find a big Black teenager guilty, the young man accepted a plea deal that resulted in him spending more than 5 years in prison and several more on parole.

The second case involved a 20-year old Caucasian swimmer at Stanford University who was convicted of three felony counts for a crime he committed in 2015, including assault with the intent to commit rape of an unconscious person, sexual penetration of an unconscious person, and sexual penetration of an intoxicated person. Although facing a maximum sentence of 14 years behind bars, the defendant received a reduced sentence of only 6 months in county jail and 3 years of probation, where in line with California's felony sentencing guidelines, he will likely only have to serve half of that sentence. In an attempt at justifying the lenient sentence, the judge pointed to the presumed severe impact a prison sentence would have on the defendant.

But what about the severe impact caused to the African American student? After all, neither student was on record as having a criminal past. Here we are once again, seeking balance for the scales of justice and questioning whether Lady Justice can actually see through her blindfold, which, the story tells us, is there to denote her impartiality in matters of justice and law. It is an almost sure bet that perceptions have been formed in response to the obvious disparities in sentencing, making it difficult for many people, particularly those within the African American community, to view the criminal justice system as a process that is fair for all, as opposed to an institution where the fate of those who come before it largely depends on social status.

Moving to another critical component of the crime bill, some of the most thought-provoking debates I have ever witnessed have been between criminal justice students in the classes I have taught, where although total agreement was not always reached, there was usually consensus surrounding the indoctrination of new inmates into the prison system. The prevailing belief was that individuals actually hone their craft during their time behind bars, resulting in them becoming even better criminals when (and if) they are released. Such a position was supported by Wood (2012), who noted that because juveniles lack access to services critical to their learning, they become vulnerable to criminal socialization. That brings us to another extreme that was among the many amendments of the tough on crime legislation, namely, Section 20411, which prohibits individuals serving time in either a federal or state penal institution from receiving Pell Grants.

There are some critical points under Section 20411. From inception, Pell Grants were established to provide grants to college students based on their financial need, and while prisoners were initially allowed to take advantage of the program, amendments contained within the 1994 crime bill revised eligibility criteria surrounding the receipt of those grants. In evaluating the costs of funding the program, according to the U.S. Department of Education Office of Postsecondary Education, for the 1994-1995 school year, the average grant was $1,502, with a maximum allowance of $2,300. Of all Pell Grants awarded in the early 1990s, only between .82 percent and 1.2 percent went to prisoners (Wright, 2001).

As there was clearly not much of a financial savings associated with the elimination of education for prisoners, this brings up not only the question of intent, but also the thinking behind disallowing prisoners to improve their education. In a discussion with my son about problems associated with not educating prisoners, he shared a quote by Horace Mann: "Education then, beyond all other devices of human origin, is the great equalizer of the conditions of men, the balance-wheel of the social machinery." After affixing my own meaning to that quote and determining that it speaks to equality derived through educating people, I couldn't help but wonder about the benefit of the government focusing more effort on housing prisoners than on educating them, which as it turned out, was exactly what occurred with the tough on crime legislation.

So let's discuss some of the real costs associated with prioritizing incarceration over education. According to a 2012 report by the Vera Institute of Justice, among the 40 states surveyed, the average cost of keeping an inmate behind bars was approximately $32,000 per year, with New York topping the list with an average cost of $60,000 per inmate. Regardless of your thoughts regarding whether the costs of keeping someone behind bars is worth the financial burden, many of those currently incarcerated will return to local neighborhoods at some point.

We cannot lose sight of the fact that, without learned skills and an infrastructure that facilitates change on the part of incarcerated individuals, all that would have been accomplished through putting countless numbers of people behind bars to simply get them off the streets, is continued recidivism, more impacted perceptions, and an even greater divide among people within our society. Although minuscule when compared to the overall costs to society resulting from recidivism, educating prisoners does require funding. The benefits to the inmate and to society, however, are difficult to argue against.

According to a study by the Graduate Center of the City University of New York, inmates who take college classes while in prison are four times less likely to be rearrested and convicted after they are released. Furthermore, less than 8 percent of those who took college courses returned to prison, compared to 29.9 percent of those who did not (Garmon, 2002). It really comes down to the objective of putting people behind bars and whether the goal is to rehabilitate or punish offenders.

There are individuals who remain behind bars who should not be there, not because they are innocent, but because of the criminalization of behavior related to nonviolent offenses coupled with a warped set of guidelines surrounding sentencing. I am not trying to mitigate crimes committed by hardened criminals; rather, it is my intent to launch an honest dialogue to discuss the reasons behind the high number of incarcerated African American men, which is a vitally important phenomenon when considering how criminality commonly has a bearing on the regard society holds for others. Increased concern is being expressed for the manner in which individuals were unfairly sentenced, and it appears President Obama is hearing the message. Eggleston (2016) noted the 348 individuals released from prison through June 2016 under President Obama's clemency program that targets individuals who received severe mandatory life sentences for nonviolent offenses surpassed the total number of commuted sentences by the past seven presidents combined.

Lessons From the Michael Brown and Eric Garner Incidents

The many safety initiatives implemented following the September 11, 2001, World Trade Center attacks are a clear indication of the priority the law enforcement community places on protecting American citizens from terrorists. Anyone who has traveled aboard a commercial airline knows the precautions taken by the Transportation Safety Administration to ensure passengers' safety, but numerous other safety precautions are not as apparent, such as those put in place to protect our national monuments or other high-profile potential terrorist targets. Law enforcement has also shifted organizational priorities to guard against attacks on city streets to the extent possible. Still, as the saying goes, where it might take years to establish goodwill, all can be lost in a split second, which is what occurs anytime private citizens perceive wrongdoing on the part of the law enforcement community. Consider the following two examples, where confrontations between police officers and community members negatively affected the public perception of police.

August 9, 2014, Ferguson, Missouri—Michael Brown, an unarmed 18-year-old Black man was fatally shot by police. A private autopsy conducted for the Brown family showed that Brown had been shot at least six times, including twice in the head. Protests and civil disorder began the day after the fatal shooting and lasted for over 2 weeks. Along with peaceful protests, there was looting and violent unrest near the site of the original shooting that prompted local law enforcement to establish curfews and deploy riot squads. Media coverage of the events of the shooting showed police officers wore camouflage uniforms similar to those worn by military personnel, carried military-grade weapons, and drove around local neighborhoods in the same type of armored vehicles used for patrol missions by the military in Afghanistan. The police response to this incident heightened public unrest and created a further divide between law enforcement and the community that resulted from public perceptions of police militarization.

December 3, 2014, Staten Island, New York—A grand jury failed to indict the officer involved in the July 17, 2014, death of Eric Garner, which stirred public protests and rallies in the face of perceived police brutality in several cities across the United States. Garner died after a police officer put him in an apparent chokehold for about 19 seconds. Officers initially approached Garner on suspicion of selling

134

single cigarettes, or loosies as they are commonly called. After Garner told the police that he was tired of being harassed and that he was not selling cigarettes, one of the officers moved in to effect Garner's arrest by placing his arms around the much taller Garner's neck, applying an apparent chokehold that was captured in a video recording of the event showing Garner lying face down on the sidewalk surrounded by four officers, where he was heard repeating the words, "I can't breathe." Garner was pronounced dead approximately 1 hour later at the hospital. Although city medical examiners concluded that Garner was killed by neck compressions from the apparent chokehold, along with "the compression of his chest and prone positioning during physical restraint by police," other contributing factors included bronchial asthma, heart disease, obesity, and hypertensive cardiovascular disease.

While the public outrage following the deaths of both Brown and Garner focused national attention on the work of police officers, it is important to keep things in perspective and not take for granted the many sacrifices made by law enforcement personnel to protect our freedom. Unfortunately, many will focus solely on the perceived unjust behavior of select law enforcement officers. After all, aren't police trained to deal with confrontations and unruly citizens?

Accepting that proposition, the following questions then come into play: Why do so many unarmed private citizens lose their lives during confrontations with police officers? Why are a disproportionate number of African American men behind bars? These are just a couple of the questions consistently voiced by everyday people that ultimately lead to the distrust of the law enforcement community, which detracts from the ability of police officers and local citizens to engage in the type of dialogue needed to address social issues.

As you have probably surmised, and if we are going to take a holistic approach to viewing these incidents, the other side of the coin is a slightly different story where many of the perceived wrongdoings by the involved police officers are justified through either case law or policy. For instance, in the case of both Michael Brown and Eric Garner, regardless of what you might think regarding the involved officers following agency protocols, there was nothing to indicate that either individual complied with the demands of police officers, which also played a role in each untimely death. This is a good time to discuss the source of police officers' arrest authority.

The authority given to police officers will typically vary slightly depending upon jurisdiction. For example, the credentials that accompanied the badge I carried during my time in federal law enforcement were as follows:

To Whom It May Concern:

By my direction the individual whose signature and photograph appear hereon is a duty accredited Postal Inspector and as such is authorized to investigate Postal offenses and civil matters relating to the Postal Service; to carry firearms; serve warrants and subpoenas and make arrests (18 U.S.C. 3061); administer oaths (39 U.S.C. 1010); and perform other official duties as may be established by the Chief Postal Inspector.

Likewise, officers at the state and local level are granted constitutional authority that gives them certain enforcement powers to carry out their law enforcement duties, which include making arrests and gaining control of situations in accordance with their respective organization's use-of-force policy, which are the standards governing the amount of force police officers may use against someone in gaining compliance in a given situation. The levels, or continuum, of force police officers use begins at officer presence, where the appearance of police officers in many instances is sufficient in gaining compliance. As the threat progresses, so does the responding action by the law enforcement officer, which transitions to verbal commands and, if needed, physical restraint if officers must place their hands on subjects to gain compliance.

Even higher on the continuum is less-than-lethal force, for example, batons, rubber pellets, and bean bags, while at the very highest end is lethal force for encounters that rise to such a level. Part of the training received by police officers is designed to reinforce the use of only the amount of force necessary to control an incident, effect an arrest, or protect themselves or others from harm or death. While those are the facts, perception as viewed by most is tantamount to reality, and because a vacuum exists between the work performed by police officers and how that work is assessed in terms of effectiveness by local communities, there is much work to do in bridging that gap.

Law Enforcement and Organizational Change

Environmental factors associated with each new era of policing have dramatically influenced the prevailing leadership practices within police organizations and the interface between police leaders and stakeholders both within and outside their organizations. Malfeasance prevalent among the police profession in the early 20th century resulted in police reforms designed to curb police corruption. Misuse of police powers posed potential threats to the functioning of a free society; consequently, police leaders adopted a paramilitary structure as a means of bringing order to their departments, a more rigid bureaucracy, and enhanced accountability, while simultaneously closing ranks against corrupt political influences (Biggs & Naimi, 2012; Wuestewald & Steinheider, 2012).

The leadership that accompanied this model entailed autocratic forms of oversight that allowed police leaders to better gauge the actions of their subordinates. Police organizations experienced additional changes in response to the ensuing disconnect that developed between law enforcement and local communities resulting from the implementation of rigid police structures that while allowing for better accountability of police actions, had the unintended consequences of law enforcement objectives and community needs being in conflict with one another. In addressing such concerns, police organizations transitioned to a community policing philosophy with the intention of solving problems through a decentralized approach, which challenged the authoritarian management paradigms practiced within police organizations (Biggs & Naimi, 2012). For instance, the type of leadership most appropriate for supporting community-oriented policing required police organizations to make allowances for some aspects of decision making relative to subordinates working within communities and facing situations requiring them to make time-sensitive decisions without first consulting superiors.

The homeland security era served as the impetus for continued organizational change for the police profession, as law enforcement executives struggled with managing tighter budgets while adhering to government mandates requiring police organizations to take on larger security roles, in addition to performing their traditional law enforcement responsibilities. The need to strengthen communication between the various layers of law enforcement was also readily apparent following the terror attacks of September 11, 2001. Organizational change accompanying this latest shift in priorities involved police leaders having to taper operational expenses previously earmarked for community policing while managing personnel resources in a manner that allowed police organizations to maintain alliances with local communities due to the realization that law enforcement cannot tackle crime or solve problems without community involvement (Neyroud, 2011).

Leadership can function at any level of the organization, and through their constant encounters with citizens, subordinate law enforcement personnel working within communities routinely demonstrate the ability to make critical leadership decisions. Further, police organizations that shift their leadership paradigm from quasi-militaristic to one with employee participative mechanisms are exponentially more conducive to meeting the challenges posed by 21st-century law enforcement. For instance, studies have shown that organizations where leaders openly communicate the need for change to employees and include the entire work-force in the change process drastically reduce resistance to change and garner wider support for change initiatives (Biggs & Naimi, 2012; Burke, 2011; Rafferty & Jim-mieson, 2010; Smet, Lavoie, & Hioe, 2012; Vito & Hig-gins, 2010; Wuestewald & Steinheider, 2012).

Moreover, although employee participation does not imply that employees have decision-making authority on the same level as organizational leaders, leadership styles that make allowances for employees to have input in workplace deci-sions typically provide employees with a sense of agency control that translates into higher organizational outcomes, which is a factor that looms large, particularly since non-supervisory personnel are in most cases the first to engage the public and therefore play a key role in the perception external stakeholders hold of the organization. Law en-forcement leadership that has fostered employee engage-ment during the homeland security era has involved chal-lenges. For instance, on June 6, 2013, British newspaper

The Guardian exposed a secret U.S. National Security Agency program to collect domestic telecommunications metadata that at the very least presented opposing views involving Fourth Amendment rights against unreasonable searches and seizures versus the government's perceived right to collect data in support of initiatives designed to protect American citizens (Landau, 2013).

Although increased leadership oversight may have forestalled such leaks from occurring, disallowing employees sufficient latitude when making certain decisions relative to their work is also counterproductive. In light of the prominence of information gathering and exchange during the homeland security era, it is critical that law enforcement leaders achieve parity between employee empowerment and work process that makes possible the unauthorized disclosure of information that potentially detracts from diplomatic relations. Because of the complexities involved with organizational change, law enforcement executives must possess the skills necessary to modify work strategies in accordance with the many law enforcement challenges faced by police organizations.

Revamping Law Enforcement Leadership

Because of the changing dynamics of the work environment resulting from globalization, leading in the 21st century requires individuals who possess strategic vision, are aware of their internal and external surroundings, and are capable of adapting to the many uncertainties confronting organizations. Moreover, changes in the expectations of employees relative to their desires for increased involvement in workplace decisions further emphasize the need for individuals placed in positions of leading organizations to possess leadership competencies suitable for not only garnering the support of followers, but also enabling them to influence those they lead toward achieving organizational objectives. Whereas mechanistic work environments of the past may have realized certain aspects of success in terms of goal attainment under a command-and-control form of leadership, the intricacies of contemporary organizations require leaders to have the ability to inspire others through facilitating work environments conducive to followers feeling valued for their contributions and consequently accepting larger roles in ensuring organizational success.

Although leaders are capable of using the perceived power in their positions to ensure employees perform at minimum standards, inspiring organizational commitment requires a form of leadership that connects with employee emotions to the point where employees willingly support the strategic vision of organizational leaders. Transformational leaders use emotional support in motivating followers by sharing their own emotion and through their understanding of other's emotion. Moreover, through their presentation of nonverbal cues, transformational leaders are effective and charismatic and consequently benefit from the emotional commitment of followers. Leaders must possess four basic levels of emotional abilities to be effective: the ability to recognize and interpret facial expressions of others, the ability to weigh conflicting emotion against each other and determine the best course of action, the ability to understand the relationships associated with shifts in one's emotions, and the ability to regulate emotion in oneself and others.

Emotions are bodily impulses that are generated unconsciously in response to a sudden physiological change. Emotions may be triggered by anger, fear, surprise, disgust, joy, or sadness. The ability to self-direct impulsive behavior enhances overall leadership effectiveness by channeling unexpected impulses in a manner that benefits both the individual and the organization. Emotional intelligence relates to individuals being able to manage not only their own emotions, but also the emotions of others with whom they interact. Further, EQ relates to one's ability to identify, understand, and manage emotions in positive ways to relieve stress, communicate effectively, empathize with others, and diffuse challenges.

Policing traditionally involved an individualist approach to leadership, where decisions emanated through a top-down organizational hierarchy. Bureaucracy, while often questioned in terms of its usefulness in contemporary work environments, continues to have a place in law enforcement, particularly in situations where employee safety is at risk. However, because of the uncertainties faced by organizations in an ever-changing environment, an organization's effectiveness is dependent upon its leaders' ability to shrink the power distance between position levels and implement creative strategies through the innovative talents of its people. The current state of law enforcement shows that it has become increasingly more complex in response to globalization, technological advances, and increased demands placed upon police organizations in general, which indicates a need for a full range of leadership and EQ traits to address the operational, social, and economic challenges of the 21st century. For example, over 85 percent of agency representatives who responded to a 2011 survey conducted through the International Association of Chiefs of Police reported that they had to reduce their expenditures and anticipated having to make further budgetary reductions over the next several years due to continued financial constraints, while at the same time they had to implement mechanisms designed to mitigate the onslaught of crimes brought on by globalization, technological advances, and terrorism.

Community-oriented policing has received an abundance of credit for minimizing incidences of street crime, particularly when coupled with modern advances in crime fighting such as psychological profiling and high-technology surveillance. A by-product of the same technological advances that allow law enforcement to monitor criminal activity from afar is the ability of criminals to commit insidious types of offenses that include terrorism and Internet-based crimes while remaining distant from the location of the crime. A new reality in American policing is that law enforcement executives must devise innovative approaches to combat 21st-century crimes made possible by technology, but must carry out their responsibilities while simultaneously managing significant change that includes reduced budgets, higher societal expectations of law enforcement, and the changing mind-set of employees who comprise the workforce in contemporary police organizations.

As mentioned earlier, budget cuts have been detrimental to law enforcement, as reflected in leaders having to furlough staff, reduce expenditures for equipment replacement and technological upgrades, and face the inability to respond adequately to emergency calls from citizens. Another factor that appears to be standing in the way of efficiency within police organizations involves the inability to lead and motivate employees effectively. It also appears that the failure to develop employees to become effective leaders is largely to blame for the lack of leadership in police organizations, where the outcome of poor leadership often emerges in unmotivated, highly stressed employees who often demonstrate their dissatisfaction with leadership practices through poor productivity, absenteeism, and attrition (Schafer, 2009).

Law enforcement personnel have expressed a preference for a more supportive and participatory approach to leadership, and whereas some leaders have demonstrated a willingness to employ a range of leadership styles beyond autocratic, bringing about change in this profession is challenging in part due to the nature of law enforcement, where police organization protocols are generally quasi-military and predicated on command-and-obey relations between leaders and followers. Transformational leaders are able to motivate followers through their emotional senses to where employees willingly delay immediate personal gratification for the greater good of the organization. Further, while followers view leaders who possess traits that align with the values of their followers favorably, emotions in the field of law enforcement are generally a less desired trait when compared to a leader's ability to make rational decisions.

Research has shown that transformational leaders are more adept at leading followers through uncertain times due to the soft skills these leaders possess that enable them to communicate with employees effectively. Reasons cited for this is that effective leadership is seen as people-centered, where organizational leaders prioritize the needs, values, and goals of followers, as opposed to focusing solely on productivity measures. Praxis on the part of leaders to value people over organizational performance is one of the basic pillars of EQ.

Developing a more effective leadership style has become increasingly important in the public sector, particularly in law enforcement agencies, where a universal characteristic distinguishing police organizations from other public institutions is the paramilitary structure and climate that encourage an authoritarian approach to leadership that in essence conflicts with any movement toward a more participative leadership model. Although early attempts at leadership research centered on understanding trait behaviors whereby labels for successful leaders included being intelligent, imaginative, and possessing the capacity to make good decisions, the researchers of modern studies have not only questioned the effectiveness of highly directive leadership, but have increased research on problems of motivation, participation, and human relations.

Leadership stretches well beyond the ability to make decisions and direct employees. Moreover, in addition to intellect, effective leadership entails the ability to execute a vision through motivating, guiding, listening, and persuading in a manner that evokes trust and willingness on the part of others to follow. Work environments should have leaders who possess EQ competencies, which refer to the ability to manage one's own emotions and the emotions of others, and while pushing individuals' emotions toward the range of enthusiasm might result in performance beyond expectations, employees may perform at less than optimal levels when they are exposed to leadership styles that facilitate anxiety within a work environment.

The repeated questionable shootings that have generated nationwide public debate surrounding law enforcement's use-of-force policies lead to categorizing the conduct of some police officers as less than optimal, which begs the question, were the actions of the officers involved in questionable police shootings simply a derivative of the leadership paradigms that exist within the organizations that employed those officers? Before attempting to answer that question, consider that we have already established that, for various reasons and as is the case with the military, police organizations are not the most participative work environments, which means communication is typically one way and flows from the upper echelons of the organization, with little if any room for questioning decisions much less orders. Moving forward with our example, if we imagine a scenario on a city street where a police officer is engaging someone who has the audacity to question the officer's commands or, rather than immediately comply, pulls out a cellphone and begins recording the incident, we can all reasonably predict how an officer might respond to such defiance, particularly if their organizational culture has conditioned them to simply follow orders without questioning authority.

Deconstructing the communication process will enable us to have a better understanding of the critical role communication plays during engagements between police officers and private citizens. For example, once a message is created in the sender's mind and targets (receivers) are identified, the encoded message is then transmitted to the selected receiver via the selected channel. Upon receipt of the message, the receiver decodes the message for meaning and then generates an appropriate response to send back to the sender in accordance with how the message was interpreted (see Figure 5).

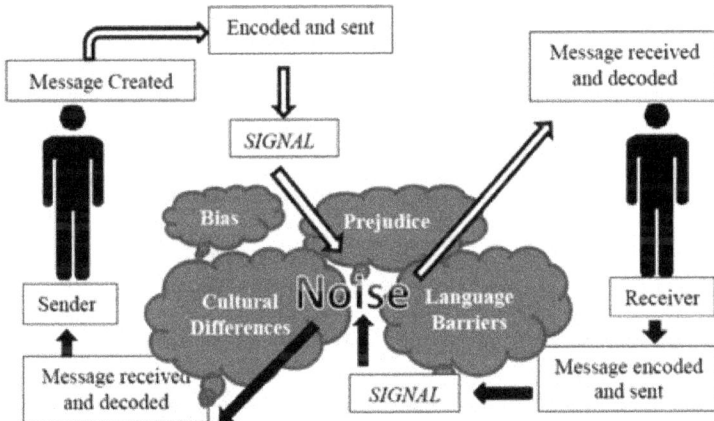

Figure 5: The Communication Process

The reference to noise in the above figure is reflective of the detractors to effective communication that may include outside distractions, language barriers, cultural differences, or negative perceptions, all of which could generate a series of verbal and nonverbal reactions, including a return message, smile, frown, or physical response.

Although communication is often considered an integral component of community policing, a complaint often expressed by private citizens relates to rudeness on the part of police officers, where in some instances, officers have been described as being both condescending and arrogant. As a result, ineffective communication can potentially result in police officers transmitting a message that is not what was intended. While poor communication feeds into trust problems related to police officers, and reluctance on the part of local communities to provide police officers with information critical to combating crime, studies have shown that police officers can also gain public trust through something as simple as a kind word.

Communication however, is not only what we hear, but also what we observe. For example, as a matter of safety, basic police training conditions officers to remain on-guard when interacting with the public. During my initial days in the academy, I can recall learning the importance of vocal tone, body language, and the proper distance police officers should maintain between themselves and suspects being questioned. Such distances allow for conducting street interviews without the officer becoming vulnerable to physical attack. That said, unless police officers employ flexibility in their communication styles, so not everyone is treated as if they were a suspect, some of the communication styles routinely used by police officers may be rendered ineffective under certain circumstances, particularly when communicating with law-abiding citizens.

As simple as it might sound, something that might help to improve communication between police officers and local communities is if law enforcement would begin to rethink their role in such a way that police culture was transformed from being a culture of crime fighting to one of social service. The effectiveness of policing in the 21st century will depend upon police leaders finding ways to break the norms of traditional law enforcement bureaucracies by devising strategies that are effective at both inspiring workers to perform beyond expectations while simultaneously maintaining an appropriate level of structure conducive to minimizing the risks law enforcement personnel are subjected to daily in the performance of their job. Along that line of thinking, it is paramount that police executives reevaluate current strategies and begin to explore alternate methods of leading contemporary law enforcement work environments. The need for leadership change within the law enforcement profession looms as a critical component of organizational effectiveness. Leaders perceived to be open and honest with their subordinates tend to generate greater organizational commitment from the workforce (Schafer, 2010), although a uniqueness prevalent among the law enforcement profession relates to the desire for the symbolism represented by structure and authority (Wuestewald & Steinheider, 2012).

Effective law enforcement leadership will require leaders who are not only visionaries skilled in strategic direction and performance achievement, but also aptly capable of breaking down prevailing bureaucratic cultures of police organizations in a way that inspires higher degrees of employee commitment, particularly related to social justice. Leadership styles significantly affect organizational outcomes, including job satisfaction, morale, and employee organizational commitment. And what was abundantly clear from the studies conducted on police personnel is that although the law enforcement profession is by nature resistive to change, organizational efficiency in 21st-century policing will require police executives to adopt leadership orientations that both achieve their goals and inspire workforce commitment. The expectation of contemporary workers requires leaders to be knowledgeable, trustworthy, and respectful of the workforce and to empower employees through a form of shared leadership, each of which is a critical component of organizational performance. Keeping in mind that organizational performance as it pertains to the law enforcement community must also account for the interactions between officers and private citizens, it is important that leaders of police organizations devise strategies that ensure officers who have the most contact with the public are exposed to methodologies that will allow for the necessary arrest of private citizens, while at the same time maintaining a level of civility. Several of these methodologies are contained within the EQ competencies.

Whereas it is a tribute to the law enforcement community that research showed that police leaders tested high in EQ regardless of race, the encounters between law enforcement and private citizens that have generated debate about perceived injustices traditionally do not involve law enforcement executives but involve officers on the front line who were hired using assessments that likely did not contain EQ competencies. This means that leaders of police organizations are going to have to come up with a process of transferring the high level of EQ possessed by police leaders to the rank and file, thereby raising the overall EQ level of the entire organization. Being in tune with the environment both within and outside the organization would enable police leaders to adapt to the immense change affecting police organizations, thereby enhancing individual and operational efficiency. Later chapters include examples of various encounters between police officers and the public that allow for a closer examination of how working within such a rigid work environment might impact the manner in which police on the front line engage the public during stressful situations when police leaders are not on the scene to monitor their behavior. While some of these incidents will clearly show EQ at work, others typify the rapid pace at which these types of encounters can escalate when emotions are not properly controlled.

When Situations Warrant the Use of Deadly Force

Because police officers often encounter situations where split-second decisions must be made regarding the use of deadly force, part of the training that officers go through includes the Firearms Training Simulator, which is a virtual training simulator used during police officer training to reinforce marksmanship skills, judgmental training objectives, and situations where less than lethal force is appropriate. Although resembling an oversized video game, officers going through the training experience anxieties similar to those present during an actual shooting situation. I can recall occasions when our range officer would come forward with information regarding some of our employees being a bit quick on the trigger, where someone might experience difficulty distinguishing between "good guys" and suspects in scenarios resulting in unjustified shootings. Although employees lacking in this area received additional training, firearms proficiency was probably the part of my job that kept me up the most at night. My primary concern was that once outside of a controlled environment where an instructor could manipulate the outcome of scenarios by pressing a few buttons on a console, the decisions made by police officers on the street often spell the difference between life and death.

When officer-involved shootings resulting in unarmed suspects being killed, the involved officer is disciplined in less than 8% of the allegations of excessive force . The first question that usually arises anytime the judicial system allows an officer to walk away from the incident unscathed is something along the lines of, "How can police just shoot unarmed people and get away with it?" Such confusion might only be capable of being explained through a thorough understanding of the allowances afforded police officers relative to the use of deadly force by the U.S. Supreme Court, where officers are given latitude in shooting situations as long as they can articulate that they feared for their life. This does not always sit well with those outside the law enforcement community, especially when I explain that in some instances, officers are also allowed to shoot individuals in the back while suspects are running away if they are perceived to be a threat to society. There are countless media accounts claiming a widespread use of excessive force by police officers in America, and although the unjustified loss of a single life is one too many, what is often portrayed by the media relative to police brutality does not tell the story in its entirety. This is not an attempt to bash the media or rationalize police shootings. The loss of life inflicts pain upon all concerned.

Studies show that a significant number of police officers have encountered situations in which they could have easily justified the use of deadly force, but resolved the incident without serious harm to either party. For example, I vividly recall a specific incident that occurred several years ago when some officers and I were effecting an arrest of a suspect in a hotel who was lying in the bed at the time we gained access to the room. After announcing ourselves as police and giving the order "Show me your hands," rather than comply with orders given, the individual we were attempting to arrest unexpectedly shoved his hands under the cover. Not knowing whether the individual had a weapon under the covers, my immediate reaction was to close the gap between him and myself, at which point I positioned my firearm only inches from his head and yelled at the top of my lungs to the suspect "Don't move!"

Were it not for the quick thinking of the accompanying local police officers who moved in and pulled back the covers so that I could see that the individual was lying in bed naked and was merely trying to put his pants on, that incident could have easily been added to the list of unarmed men being fatally shot by law enforcement officers. I tell that story to my son and my friends anytime the issue of officer-involved shootings comes up to make two critical points. The first relates to the immediacy in which police officers must make a determination about whether the situation they are encountering rises to the level of deadly force. Second, these types of encounters are rarely, if ever, as they first appear, and there are often mitigating factors that might better explain what actually prompted the unfortunate shooting of an unarmed individual by a police officer.

The results of a study conducted by Pinizzotto, Davis, Bohrer, and Infanti (2012) showed that 80 percent of police officers reported being assaulted during their careers, where the average number of assaults experienced by police officers was approximately seven times in the line of duty. Because some officers consider assaults as part of the job, unless the officer sustained injuries requiring medical attention, many such incidents experienced by police officers go unreported. The study also showed that approximately 70 percent of police officers in the study had been in situations where they could have fired their weapons during confrontations with private citizens, but chose not to.

A significant finding in the study showed that although officers were involved in 1,189 situations in which, in accordance with organizational policy, they could have legally and ethically fired their weapon, officers only did so during 87 of these incidents. There were not 87 incidents where someone was killed, but an officer fired a weapon during the confrontation, which is a critical point for any discussion on excessive use of force by police officers. It is equally important to note that the focus of the study was on organizational factors such as departmental policy that might have an impact on the use of force by police officers and was not intended to assess the perceptions, beliefs, and thought processes experienced by police officers in the midst of deadly force situations. Again, although studies such as this will never legitimize the unwarranted taking of one's life, they do show significant restraint on the part of police officers when dealing with hostile situations, even when their own safety is at stake. So we are left with the following questions: If police officers risk personal safety by using restraint in legitimate deadly force situations, why isn't there more focus on instances where police officers elected not to fire their weapons during violent confrontations although they would have been justified in accordance with departmental policy to do so? Why do the vast majority of incidents involving police shootings seemingly start from the perception of police brutality and work backward? What steps can the law enforcement community take in curbing public perception that often results in local communities immediately thinking the worst about officer-involved shootings? Such questions provoke extensive conversations surrounding the tactics used by police organizations and will likely propagate debate well into the future.

Is Racial Profiling a Myth?

One school of thought is that racially and ethnically underrepresented people are more likely than White Americans to be arrested, stopped, questioned, searched, victimized by excessive physical force, and shot and killed by the police (Walker, Spohn, & DeLone, 2011). Such a statement has leanings of racial profiling, and if racial profiling does exist, some writers have theorized that this national problem has persisted in cities and towns across the country. They further suggest that people of color are targeted, detained, interrogated, and searched, based solely on their race without any evidence of criminal activity. Rather than draw any conclusions, let's place judgment in abeyance while we take some time to ponder both sides of this highly explosive subject.

There has been a lot of debate about whether police officers indiscriminately harass and arrest African Americans. While some individuals believe such acts are racially motivated, others point to statistics depicting African Americans committing offenses commensurate with incarceration levels as a means of dispelling such accusations, suggesting that racial profiling is no more than a reliance upon statistical evidence reflective of racial differences in crime rates in an attempt to increase the likelihood of both identifying and apprehending offenders. Although certainly not representative of every police organization, the U.S. Department of Justice report detailing the treatment of African Americans by the Ferguson, Missouri, Police Department reinforces views held by many people. What follows is a recap of highlights of the U.S. Department of Justice report based on observations of engagement between the Ferguson Police Department and local citizens:

1. The city's practices are shaped by revenue rather than by public safety needs.

2. The 67% of African Americans in Ferguson account for 93% of arrests made between 2012 and 2014.

3. The disproportionate number of arrests and tickets and the disproportionate amount of force used stems from unlawful bias rather than African Americans committing more crime.

4. A single missed, late, or partial payment of a fine could mean jail time.

5. Arrest warrants are almost exclusively used as threats to push for payments. And, if time is served, no credit for jail time is received and the length of time isn't recorded by the court.

6. Officers used a dog to attack an unarmed 14-year-old African American male and then struck him while he was lying on the ground, all while he was waiting for his friends in an abandoned house. The report concluded that in every dog bite incident reported, the person bitten was African American.

7. After an officer assaulted a man, he demanded the man not pass out because the officer did not want to carry the man to his patrol car.

8. From October 2012 to October 2014, every time a person was arrested because he or she was resisting arrest, that person was African American.

Anyone unable to escape the barrage of information floating throughout the information superhighway learned that, shortly after the report went viral, several public officials either resigned or were fired from their positions, including the city manager, the police chief, a police captain, a sergeant, and the municipal court judge. The city's top court clerk was also fired in connection with sending racist e-mails. Although the allegations in Ferguson, Missouri, represent an extreme case of misconduct, literature on the topic of racial profiling has uncovered a lack of confidence on the part of African Americans toward law enforcement, particularly when seemingly routine encounters between citizens and police unnecessarily escalate.

The cause of such escalations appears to be a combination of both perception and actual accounts of unfairness, and while statistics continually show that police officers stop African American males at a higher proportion than any other group, logic tells us that race cannot be the motive behind every stop police officers make involving African American motorists. Perceptions can also affect the decisions made by police officers during vehicle stops involving African American motorists. One example is when a police officer decides to conduct a vehicle search based in large part on the demeanor of the person stopped. What is often overlooked during these encounters is the symbiotic relationship between a motorist's prior experience with police officers and how the motorist might respond when being pulled over.

If you recall from my earlier points about how in accordance with the ladder of inference each of us responds in accordance with our respective experiences, if African American motorists believe they are the target of frequent harassment and discourteous treatment by police officers during traffic stops, the most plausible outcome of such encounters will be distrust and possibly dislike of police officers, both of which are routinely displayed in the attitude of African American motorists toward officers. You probably know where this is headed, but it is important to complete the cycle by addressing the subsequent actions on the part of the police officer initiating the traffic stop (see Figure 6).

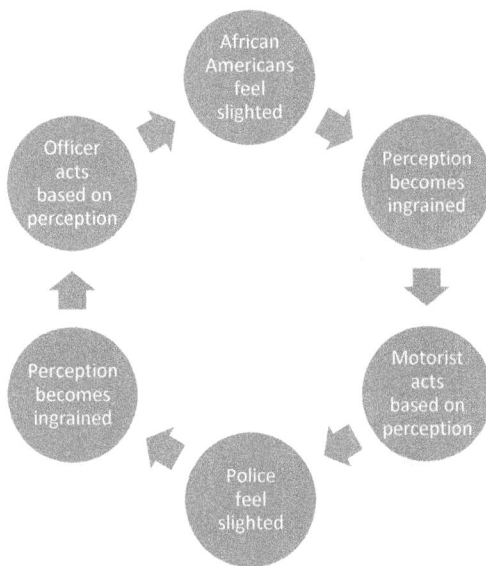

Figure 6: How Perceptions Become Ingrained Through Experiences

Countless studies have shown that the demeanor of African Americans during traffic stops is a determining factor on the likelihood of them being not only searched but also arrested, resulting from police officers perceiving such actions as disrespectful or antagonistic (Lundman, 1974; Smith & Klein, 1983; Sykes & Clark, 1975; Worden, 1989). It has also been suggested that police officers are four times more likely to form nonbehavioral suspicions of African Americans, where the actions of police officers were based purely on an individual's appearance (Alpert, Macdonald, & Dunham, 2005). Statistics show that African Americans do not violate traffic laws with greater frequency than White motorists; therefore, stopping them more frequently results in the appearance of injustice. A problem with the routineness of such events is that regardless of which action is selected as the initiator, there is an unremitting negative string of responses that will continue to unfold unless a substantial change in perception takes place among all the actors in these types of encounters.

While we continue to set aside judgment on whether racial profiling actually exists, consider the comments made by New York's Mayor de Blasio regarding he and his African American wife's attempts to ensure their biracial son remained safe by conducting himself appropriately if ever stopped by police officers. The mayor said that he and his wife had to train their son on how to act during police engagements, telling him that if he were ever pulled over by a police officer that he was to do everything the officer told him and that he was not to make any sudden moves, including reaching for his cell phone, out of fear that such an action might be misinterpreted by the officer simply because he was a young man of color. This is without question the type of important dialogue that has been missing from discussions on race, not because people outside of the African American community are unaware that problems exist, but instead because there is really no way of fully understanding the impact of mistreatment on the grounds of racial differences without actually being there.

An episode of *Black-ish* aired on ABC on the evening of February 24, 2016, addressing this very difficult subject. In the episode, African American parents faced a dilemma of having to decide between protecting the innocence of their young children by shielding them from the state of race relations in America or educating them on the harsh realities associated with life in the inner city that would effectively rob them of their childhood. While the decision to expose their children to cases involving conflicts between police officers and citizens did not come easy, weighing heavily on the decision to engage in such difficult conversation was the inherent risks associated with allowing their children's first encounter with race relations to be learned through outside sources as opposed to lessons passed along from their parents.

As I contemplate what Mayor de Blasio must have experienced when addressing the subject of race and social justice with his son, I can't help but think that the racial make-up of his family and the need to understand African American survival skills has given him a glimpse of how life exists through the eyes of African Americans, which is about as close as one can come without actually being Black. Further, I am confident that what he has discovered from his unique vantage point not only changed his worldview, but also continues to influence the conversations he feels compelled to have with those close to him. Still, the mayor's comments were met with a backlash from the head of the police union in New York, who suggested the mayor "threw cops under the bus."

The mayor found himself torn between standing up for police officers and protecting the well-being of his son. The mayor's support of his police officers is indisputable, but for decades, parents of African American children have spent dinner time discussing life issues that include how they should conduct themselves if ever stopped by police officers, and just as the mayor said during an interview with George Stephanopoulos on this subject, "It's different for a White child. That's just the reality in this country." The exclamation point behind this reality came in the form of statements made by Democratic presidential candidate Hillary Clinton during the South Carolina town hall meeting on February 23, 2016, when she said, "White people should be honest and recognize that our experiences may not equip us to understand what a lot of our African American fellow citizens go through every single day."

Immediately following the shooting of Trayvon Martin in Florida, I told my son that I would appreciate it if he no longer wore his hoodie, out of fear of the potential harm that might come to him should he somehow be mistaken for a hoodlum. Before I could explain that I know that some individuals are law-abiding citizens, like he was, and only wear hoodies to keep warm, my son stated that this was America and he should be able to wear whatever he wanted. Although in theory my son was correct, I directed his attention to one word he used in his response. The word "should" made all the difference in how his version of reality might differ from how a great number of people viewed young men wearing hoodies.

I went on to explain that many individuals within our society have somehow made the connection between specific items of clothing and criminality. I also suggested that although he *should* be able to wear whatever he wanted, the risks far outweighed the rights he believed were on his side in accordance with the freedoms granted to American citizens. Again, this is just an example of conversations taking place within African American circles to lessen the chances of harm coming to our children that while appearing not to be a big deal on the surface, actually occupies a significant amount of space within the minds of African Americans when examining issues surrounding equality.

We will pause for a brief perception check to see if you find one position more credible than the other with regard to determining whether racial profiling is real. Whether you were swayed in one direction or another, or remain encased within the confines of your original beliefs on racial profiling, is irrelevant. The point was to show the powerful impact negative encounters between African Americans and police officers have on perceptions surrounding racial profiling, particularly among African Americans. We will now explore how the types of blatant wrongdoing the U.S. Department of Justice alleged have been committed by the Ferguson Police Department could be allowed to persist in an effort to understand the explosive relationship between law enforcement and the local community.

Spending a number of years in leadership roles both in organizations and within law enforcement, I have always believed (and acted) from the perspective of the argument that what you fail to confront, you validate, so when I consider the disparate treatment of African Americans reported to have taken place within Ferguson, Missouri, at the hands of the local police between 2012 and 2014, much of this has to fall on management's shoulders. Further, if the allegations asserted in the report are to be taken at face value, it is highly unlikely that rank and file police officers acted on their own volition without management having knowledge or at least some idea of their conduct. My assessment as to why some police officers might act in such a manner is not that they are bad people. Instead, I propose that such instances of poor judgment by the officers had to do with a perceived lack of negative consequences that reinforced negative behavior.

B. F. Skinner's operant conditioning theory will help to create an understanding around how such behavior on the part of police officers might occur. According to the theory, human free will is an illusion, and any human action is the result of the consequences of the same action (Skinner, 1935). Think about a teenage student smoking in school and the only consequence of being caught was that he was now thought to be cool and was accepted into the crowd he always wanted to run around with. The result of those actions would be a reward, and as such, the student's behavior, smoking in this instance, would likely be repeated. On the other hand, if the student was caught by school administration and subsequently punished through suspensions and parental involvement, the student would be less inclined to smoke going forward. This means that if the consequences are bad, there is a high likelihood that the action will not be repeated; however, if the consequences are good, the actions that led to it will become more probable. Because management within the Ferguson Police Department failed to confront the actions of their rank and file officers, they in essence validated their actions, which resulted in the officers believing that what they were doing was not only acceptable in the eyes of management, but encouraged, thus reinforcing the types of abusive behaviors alleged in the report.

Before leaving this discussion, I would like to reference the movie *Crash*, a 2004 film where writer-director Paul Haggis interweaves several connected stories about race, class, family and gender in Los Angeles in the aftermath of 9/11. More specifically, there is a scene in the film where Cameron, a well-to-do African American television producer played by Terrence Howard, and his beautiful wife Christine, played by Thandie Newton, were pulled over by Los

Angeles Police Department (LAPD) officers while returning home from a party. During the officer-initiated traffic stop, one of the police officers subjects the couple to a humiliating interrogation and the wife to an inappropriate search while the husband helplessly watches, believing his inaction is the best way to survive the encounter.

Later in the film, there is a scene where Cameron is again stopped by LAPD officers; however, because of the ill-feelings he harbors for police officers resulting from the previous engagement, he escalates the situation with police officers. Cameron then comes close to being shot, which would have easily been judged a justified police shooting when considering his aggression toward police officers during the traffic stop. Were this an actual confrontation between police officers and a private citizen, it is not likely that the driver would be allowed to leave the scene and go home.

Although the media accounts of the shooting would have reported something along the lines of an African American man being shot and killed during a traffic stop after he failed to comply with commands to yield and continued his charge toward officers in an aggressive manner, those hearing of the officer-involved shooting through the media likely would not have been aware that the reason for the driver's aggression toward police officers was at least partially due to the pent-up frustration he harbored resulting from how police officers had mistreated him and his wife during a prior stop or that the conduct of the officers during the prior stop had damaged not only his marriage but both his and his wife's self-esteem.

I have a real-life story involving my family and law enforcement that, similar to the events that unfolded in the film *Crash*, could have easily escalated out of control. Over the course of 365 days, everyone in my immediate family experienced encounters with police officers, beginning with my son being stopped by officers while transporting a television from an apartment to his car. The police officers were unaware that my son had just been given the television by his friend who lived in the apartment complex he was observed coming out of. According to my son, he was forced to sit on the curb for an extended period while police officers checked out his story, after which he was allowed to continue along his way.

Needless to say, he was extremely upset at the embarrassment of having passersby in the neighborhood witnessing him being detained on the curbside by officers for what he perceived as profiling; however, the two of us discussed the situation and concluded that because the officers were courteous and ultimately let him leave the area, there was no *real* harm done. A few months later, my daughter was driving my wife back to our home after spending the day together when they were pulled over by police officers about a block from our home. My wife told me that both she and my daughter saw the police vehicle on the side of them and that they looked in the direction of the officers. The next thing they noticed was the police vehicle had pulled behind them with the emergency lights flashing for them to pull over.

When the officers approached their vehicle, my wife asked the one standing at the passenger side window what had they done wrong and was told that she would have to ask the officer standing at the driver-side window. My wife then informed the officers that she and my daughter did not want any trouble and only wanted to know what they had done wrong. She also let the policers officers know that her husband was a retired federal law enforcement officer and that she and my daughter had every intention of cooperating.

The officers retreated to their vehicle momentarily before returning to tell my wife that they were pulled over because my daughter had "driven her vehicle into the bike lane too early before making a right-hand turn." To this day, my wife and daughter both insist that was not the case and they did not break any traffic laws, but since they were allowed to leave the scene with merely a warning and no (there we go again with that word) *real* harm was done, they have decided not to spend their time reliving the incident. As you might have imagined, by now I am growing a bit tired of having members of my family detained by police officers, and with a backdrop strikingly similar to the rage that began to form within Cameron in *Crash*, I continued to return to my law enforcement background in maintaining my optimism that these were merely isolated incidents and nothing more.

Around 7:30 one morning, my wife accidentally set off our home burglar alarm by opening our bedroom window, thinking that because I was already up, I had turned off our alarm system as I usually do. According to routine security protocol, we received our follow-up call from the alarm monitoring center to ensure everything was all right, and they asked me for our password. After I provided the information, the dispatcher simply said, "Thank you. Have a nice day." However, I did not realize that I had provided the incorrect password and the dispatcher, unbeknownst to me, had alerted local law enforcement to roll out to our home to ensure we were not under duress.

To better frame this incident, the neighborhood where we resided is predominantly White, with only a few African American residents. Making matters worse, during this same period, there had been a rash of home burglaries where residential surveillance cameras showed the suspects were African American. I believe it is worth mentioning that, coincidentally, a crime alert for our neighborhood was disseminated by local law enforcement, which read in part,

> A homeowner called to report that at approximately 1 pm today there was an attempted break-in at their home. Two residents had left the house and one resident remained inside. When someone knocked on the door, he did not answer the door. After more knocking, the individual broke the glass in the door. (Everyone in the home is safe.) It was reported that the individual was a male, black, wearing a button down shirt, slacks, dress shoes and a baseball cap. A grey SUV was also seen....

Continuing to build the story, with Governor Jerry Brown declaring a drought state of emergency in January 2015, we were in the process of having our lawn removed and replaced with artificial turf. As such, during the demolition phase of the project, we were expecting the contractors to arrive at our home on the same morning my wife accidentally set off our alarm. At around 8:00 a.m., I heard loud knocking on my front door and my first instinct was to open the garage door to allow the contractors to retrieve their tools they had left the day before so that they could begin their work for the day. Fortunately, for whatever reason, I instead went to the front door and to my surprise, there were two officers from the Orange County Sherriff's Department standing there. I was told by the officers that they were there to follow-up on an alarm report and after I produced identification validating that I was in fact the owner of the property, they jotted down my name, thanked me and left.

Now, let's play the what-if game, because that is exactly what I did when contemplating the potential outcome of my encounter with police officers that morning had I simply followed through on my initial plan and exited my home through the garage thinking the contractors were the ones knocking on my front door. Although I would have immediately observed the police car in front of my home once I opened my garage door, what if the officers were somehow startled by me coming through the garage when they had knocked on the front door? Remember, there had been several home break-ins during this period, and profiling or not, I resembled the individuals believed to be responsible for crimes being committed in my neighborhood, at least in terms of race.

As we continue with the what-if game, being startled and not knowing whether I was the homeowner or a suspect attempting to flee the scene, what if the officers pointed their weapons at me and ordered me to the ground so that they could sort things out. What if the sight of other home-owners standing on their front porches with full view of what was taking place, out of embarrassment of being ordered to lay on the pavement in front of my neighbors, not to mention on the very grounds where my wife and I pay the monthly mortgage, I disobeyed the officer's command and refused to lay down, thereby exacerbating the situation. What if things spiraled so much out of control that unlike the situation in *Crash*, where one of the officers recognized Cameron from a prior encounter and persuaded his fellow officers to lower their weapons, I sustained injury or worse during the police encounter as a result of my defiance?

What if the news headlines read, African American man was injured or fatally shot by police officers in front of his home after officers responded to what turned out to be a false alarm? Although initial news reports of such an incident would have undoubtedly resulted in law enforcement once again defending the actions of the responding officers, should the blame for this scenario spiraling out of control fall on the shoulders of law enforcement? Enough of the what-if game. Now it is time to play Monday morning quarterback, where we assess the police officer's conduct, and because this was merely a scenario, we can assess things within what constitutes a sterile environment. Do you believe the officers acted appropriately? Who was at fault for the outcome presented in the scenario? Had this actually occurred, do you see anything that I (the homeowner) might have done that contributed to the situation rising to a level where police officers felt justified in resorting to an increased level of force to contain the situation?

Just like the actions of the police officers who actually responded to my home on that morning, my assessment of the officers in the what-if scenario is that they too acted appropriately based on the circumstances they faced in that situation. After all, I raised the stakes that resulted in the officers responding in accordance with their threat continuum by meeting my advances with the force deemed appropriate in containing the situation. The truth is that the outcome of the scenario is unfortunately a situation that plays out from time to time during confrontations between police officers and private citizens, many of whom happen to be African American.

This is a good time to revisit the racial profiling issue introduced a while back in terms of its prevalence. It is an indisputable fact that a select number of individuals within the ranks of policing have abused, and are going to abuse, the latitude afforded their position. There are also going to be situations where police officers detain African Americans for no other purpose than the legitimate performance of their jobs, and although the word *compliance* sometimes carries with it negative connotations synonymous with submissiveness, the name of the game is to survive to fight another day. Dispatching police officers to my residence after I had accidentally provided the incorrect password was the proper thing to do, and both the alarm monitoring center and Orange County Sherriff's Department did their jobs exceptionally.

Just like other consumers who pay their hard-earned money for home security, I would have not expected anything less than the response I received on that day. The what-if scenario evolved out of the subsequent thoughts running through my mind following the police response, where all I imagined for a while was how badly this situation could have turned out had I followed my initial plan of exiting though my garage. Such a decision would have undoubtedly surprised the officers standing at my front door, and while the element of surprise is at times exhilarating, it can also be extremely dangerous.

The good thing is that the what-if scenario was only in my mind, and the actual response to my residential alarm going off that morning was exemplary, as both the alarm monitoring company and the officers dispatched to my residence did just as they should have under the circumstances. I was the one who had inadvertently given the incorrect password when asked for it by the operator, and the officers were simply there to make sure the alarm going off was not an indication of my family being restrained against our will. So the question remains, is there such a thing as racial profiling? Although logic informs us that not every officer-initiated engagement with an African American is intertwined with racial undertones, personal realties as to the realness of racial profiling is something for us to decide for ourselves based on our experiences, whether they are actual or indirect.

When Citizens No Longer Trust the Police

There have been countless times when someone has asked me, "How can police officers get away with things that I would be arrested for?" What people are really saying is that although police officers are human beings like the rest of us, individuals belonging to this profession are held to a higher degree when it comes to exercising decorum. Police officers are both similar and dissimilar to the clergy, in that, analogous to the openness one might share with church leaders, when police officers respond to the calls of the local community, they too engage individuals when they are the most vulnerable. The greatest difference between the two relates to the ability to hold individuals against their will, where outside of the spoken word, the clergy have no real power to impede the movement of others, while police officers possess the power to detain and arrest people and to use whatever amount of restraint is deemed appropriate for gaining compliance, up to and including deadly force, in the performance of their duties.

Police officers hold positions of public trust, and as such, the actions of members of this highly visible profession affect society's perception of justice. If someone were tasked with constructing a list detailing what a police officer might do that would diminish the confidence the public holds of the law enforcement community, failure to act in an ethical manner would likely rank among the top of that list. For the purpose of this discussion, ethics will be defined as one's beliefs in relation to distinguishing between right and wrong, where an individual's value system is to a large degree shaped by his or her own perceptions, as well as external influences stemming from interactions with parents, friends, and the surrounding community.

One area where policing differs from other professions that emphasize adherence to ethical guidelines as part of employee training involves police socialization, where the application of ethics is best described as situational and might actually conflict with the ethical values brought into the police environment by new recruits. For example, the pressure to fit in with their fellow officers might require recruits to prove that they are both trustworthy and part of the team by engaging in behavior that runs counter to departmental policy. While the public's assessment of police ethics is based on the interactions between officers and private citizens, the conduct displayed by officers is largely the product of environmental influences both within and outside the police department.

In the book, *Breaking Rank: A Top Cop's Exposé of the Dark Side of American Policing*, there is a chapter titled "Why White Cops Kill Black Men," where former police chief Norm Stamper addressed the fears of African American men on the part of White police officers and how those fears were as much a part of police training for new officers as indoctrinating recruits to the laws governing arrests. Even more disturbing, according to Stamper, new officers, including himself, were groomed by their superiors to believe that "Black men and White cops don't mix" (p. 93) and that African American men posed the greatest threat to their personal safety and survival among any race of people White officers would encounter on the streets. Such conditioning led to officers developing an utter disrespect for minorities that was eventually displayed in officer conduct both during arrest situations and in the language White police officers used toward describing African Americans.

Stamper further discussed how his fellow officers falsely accused minorities for crimes they did not commit and how it was not until he ascended to the leadership ranks and was in a position to conduct an inner-office assessment of employee conduct that he truly realized the magnitude of racism among the police ranks. In a subsequent chapter titled "Racism in the Ranks," Stamper told of how during inquires with his officers, where they were given immunity for being forthcoming, he learned that White police officers routinely referred to African Americans using such disgraceful terms as niggers, buckwheats, sambos, and jigaboos (Stamper, 2005). Although the inquiry focused attention on the actions of officers assigned to one police department, and while such blatant racism might not be as prevalent as the example described above, the likelihood that such feelings can be isolated to a single police department is remote based on the persistence of reported incidents of police misconduct with which we have become familiar.

For example, a short time after his discharge from the armed services, my younger brother, Don, set his sights on becoming a law enforcement officer, which was something he had wanted to become since donning his first uniform as a high school cadet. I watched as my brother attended classes at night in preparation of fulfilling his dream of securing a job in policing, only to quit the force within a year of being hired. Knowing the effort he expended and personal sacrifices he made to put himself in a positon for a career he longed for, although admittedly clueless as to why he left the force and returned to active military duty, I felt it was best at the time not to delve too much into his personal affairs. One day I asked him what occurred during his time on the force and without going into detail, he just said it did not work out.

While writing this portion of my book, I decided to revisit the subject with my brother by asking him to tell me again why he left the police force so abruptly. I also asked for his views on some of the things cited in the book *Breaking Rank* relative to inappropriate police conduct, as he worked within the same city where Chief Stamper had described blatant police abuses. I was caught totally off guard when my brother told me that he could relate to the chief's assertions and actually experienced similar inappropriate conduct by his fellow officers during his probationary period, which was the reason he decided that perhaps a career in policing was not for him. I asked for specifics and was told that as a rookie, he was assigned to work in the jail, where aside from witnessing police officers "beat the hell out of an inmate until the man defecated on himself," he began to sense that he was "on the outskirts" and not trusted among his fellow officers due to his expressions of disapproval of such treatment. It was now abundantly clear why he left a job he had worked so hard to acquire after such a brief period of time.

Let us now explore the elements used by private citizens to form their perceptions of police officers. How is trust on the part of officers earned by the public? According to Tyler (2001), following interactions with police officers, individuals usually ask themselves two questions when assessing their experience. The first relates to the extent they believe they were treated with respect, and the other relates to a sense of fairness. While positive experiences usually enhance the level of trust the public holds for law enforcement officers, when private citizens do not believe they were treated fairly by officers, they hold the police profession in lower regard. Moreover, personal experience with police officers are without question the most direct way of evaluating police trustworthiness, but it is not the only way the public gauges police conduct. Indirect knowledge of police actions, referred to as vicarious experiences, where individuals form their opinions of officers based on the information received from their family, friends, and the media following interactions with officers, also contribute to the perceptions of police officers held by the public (Brunson, 2007; Weitzer & Tuch, 2005).

From time to time, I am approached by individuals who know about my connection to the law enforcement profession who have recounted the experiences they have had with police officers, and while not all of the encounters were negative, similar to the manner in which goodwill is associated with particular businesses based on positive customer interactions, negative experiences typically receive the most attention when individuals convey their interactions with police to others. The most difficult conversations for me are those where I am dragged into situations where I seemingly have to defend the actions of officers while not sounding as if I am merely attempting to cover up police misconduct. While I am generally able to move the conversation along by resorting to my patent statement, "Let's wait until the investigation has been completed before jumping to conclusions," there are situations where even I am at a loss for words when it comes to attempting to explain why specific actions were taken by police officers during interactions with the public.

One that immediately comes to mind is the October 20, 2014, shooting of Laquan McDonald, where former Chicago police officer Jason Van Dyke shot the 17-year-old 16 times. Although authorities have said McDonald was in possession of a 3-inch knife, video of the incident that was first released to the public approximately 13 months after the shooting appeared to show McDonald walking away from the officers during the time Officer Van Dyke exited his vehicle and began firing his weapon almost immediately upon arriving on the scene. Police accounts of the shooting indicated that McDonald was found to have PCP in his system, exhibited erratic behavior, and refused commands to drop the knife, and as expected, the attorney for Officer Van Dyke said the officer feared for his life and acted lawfully in his actions. Still, the difficulty in defending the officer's actions relates first to the actual threat posed to the officers at the time of the shooting, as well as police protocol as it pertains to the use of deadly force when the threat no longer exists. Officer Van Dyke continued to discharge his firearm, striking the body of McDonald several times while he lay still on the ground several feet from where the officers had taken position and certainly unable to pose any threat, which were actions that undoubtedly were considered in the first-degree murder charges subsequently filed against the officer.

Another police shooting that grabbed the headlines was the April 8, 2015, incident when a witness with a cellphone captured the unjustified shooting death of a private citizen, where the video shows former North Charleston police officer Michael Slager discharging his firearm eight times as Walter Scott ran from a traffic stop that began over a broken taillight. Without question, this incident served to diminish public trust of law enforcement further, and fed into the growing public perception that police are out of control. How do I know that? Because those are the actual words I have heard not just from social settings, but from everyday citizens who only need access to the news media to remain current on the most recent deadly encounter between police officers and private citizens. A picture is worth a thousand words, but even the most vivid portrait is not always capable of portraying the story in its entirety.

Without getting into a debate or even into case law that might justify incidents where police officers can shoot fleeing suspects in the back, from the onset, the North Charleston incident did not appear to rise to such a level. Still, there are likely to be those who due to variables that have nothing to do with use-of-force policies will find no fault on the part of the officer. Based on public reaction to the incident, I am fairly confident that a significant number of individuals within and around the law enforcement community share in the disgust held by the public relative to the actions of Officer Slager, if for no other reason than the harm such incidents cause to relations between police and local communities. Although the efforts of public officials in North Charleston to get out in front of the media by addressing the unprovoked shooting in the hours immediately following the incident were commendable, not even such valiant efforts appear capable of thwarting the dwindling relationship between police officers and local communities. The untimely death of Freddie Gray in Baltimore, Maryland, further underscores that point.

On April 12, 2015, Freddie Gray, a 25-year-old African American man, was taken into custody by the Baltimore Police Department for allegedly possessing a switchblade. While being transported in a police van, Gray fell into a coma and was taken to a trauma center, where he died 7 days later as a result of injuries to his spinal cord alleged to have occurred during transport following his arrest. Within weeks of the riots first erupting in Baltimore, criminal charges were filed against the six police officers believed to have caused Gray's death when prosecutors received the medical examiner's report that ruled Gray's death a homicide. Baltimore prosecutors failed to reach a conviction on the first three officers brought to trial, which led to acquittals. In July 2016, charges were dropped on the remaining three officers in connection with Gray's death.

The public unrest that occurred in Baltimore resulting in the arrest of protestors as well as police officers sustaining injury during the riots, while strikingly similar to the protests and damage caused to local businesses witnessed in Ferguson following the shooting death of Michael Brown, the Baltimore incident was also different on many levels. Take, for example, the delay in police response time after the eruption of the first indications that protests had eclipsed the point of peaceful demonstrations. Although law enforcement officers were out in force in response to a reported call to *purge* (a reference to a 2013 film depicting a 12-hour period when all crimes were legalized) circulated on social media among Baltimore students on the morning of the riots, unlike the clashes between law enforcement and the public in the early stages of the protests, the Baltimore police department were told to stand down, presumably on the orders of the mayor.

Some accounts of the police presence still place the blame on the shoulders of law enforcement alleging that had students been allowed to leave the area, they would not have been in the area in the first place. The ensuing riots that turned violent and resulted in a reported 34 arrests and injuries to approximately 15 police officers were somewhat predictable. Assessments of this incident will forever focus on the orders given to police officers during the initial stages of the riots, presumably by the mayor, to hold their positions. The point must be made that the civil unrest that occurred in Baltimore was no more in response to the death of Freddie Gray than the burning and looting of local businesses in Ferguson can be associated exclusively to the shooting death of Michael Brown. A better explanation would be that those types of incidents are part of a much larger societal issue where both have served to underscore the public relations nightmare faced by law enforcement organizations across the nation as a result of the diminished level of trust local communities have of police officers.

Whether it is the result of perceived injustice or other issues that occasionally detract from the credibility of police officers, anytime interactions between law enforcement and the public turn violent, even before the ink on the initial report dries, much less the finalization of the after-incident investigation, one of the first thoughts that cross the minds of many is that the police were somehow in the wrong. While in some instances members of the public who hold such beliefs are correct in their assumptions, the truth is that there are significantly more good cops out there doing an exceptional job day in and day out, in spite of the select number of officers who bring shame on the profession when they are shown in the media displaying a seeming disregard for the ethics portion of the oaths they took when signing onto the force.

Earlier I addressed differentiators between police officers and the public. More than any other quality, having ethics tops the list in level of importance due to the level of trust police officers hold within our society. Before ending this section, I want to address an argument held seemingly in defense of police officers who sometimes display unethical behavior. Some individuals I have spoken to, while forth-right in their acknowledgment that the positon of police officer carries with it an expectation of ethics, they also compare the actions of police officers to those of the public by suggesting that it would be a difficult task to identify anyone who has not at one time or another acted in an un-ethical manner, and as such, why should police officers be held to what may be an unrealistic standard when they are human too?

While initially this might appear to be a legitimate question, I do not believe debating the fairness surrounding the expectation of police officers adhering to a higher ethical standard than the public warrants an excessive amount of time and attention, but I will at least provide my thoughts on the matter. Without attempting to sway anyone else's opinion in one direction or another, my feeling is that answering such a question merely requires the acknowledgment that police officers are sworn to protect and to serve the communities under their jurisdiction. If we can agree to start with such a premise, answering that question should be exponentially simplified for both the public and the law enforcement community. Yes, police officers are human, but the similarities cease when you consider that members of the public are not held in the same regard as police officers, nor do they possess the powers to detain others against their will. Consequently, police officers must adhere to a higher ethical standard if they are going to be trusted by local citizens while at the same time work toward rebuilding severely damaged police relations with the communities they serve.

Restoring trust between police officers and local communities is challenging. Just like any other organization with a goal of improving its image, if the police community is to engender trust, it must place attention on becoming more transparent with both its internal and its external stakeholders. When you think about how each person appreciates transparent qualities within other people, it makes sense that people would also be drawn to businesses that are transparent. That means to be viewed as trustworthy, as opposed to keeping police matters close to the vest as if under a cloak of secrecy, the law enforcement community will have to develop strategies that not only guard against premature release of investigative evidence, but at the same time, facilitate a culture of being more forthcoming with regard to disseminating information involving engagements between police officers and the public.

At the forefront of convincing police organizations of the need to transition to a culture of sharing, and perhaps the one thing that has influenced such a change beyond anything else, is social media, where encounters between the police and the public are routinely displayed over the Internet, particularly if the engagement has any possibility of spurring controversy. This is where we begin our conversation on police body cameras and the potential impact such footage might have on the number of grievances levied against police officers by the public. Throughout this book, I have contended there are far more good cops than the exceptional few who, through their own actions, demonstrate that they do not possess the type of personality suitable for functioning well in the role of police officer. Doesn't this mean that the majority of police officers have nothing to hide and would not object to being required to wear a body cam while on duty?

While the current trend appears to show that police organizations have somewhat warmed to the idea of equipping officers with body cameras, not everyone in law enforcement favors the idea, citing reasons that include the potential infringement on a police officer's private conversations. However, such arguments do not hold water, particularly when accounting for the fact that other organizations, industry-wide, have been using various forms of monitoring to track the work habits of their employees for years. Besides, since 9/11, there are very few public places anyone can go, where there isn't a strategically placed surveillance camera cataloging every move.

The potential benefits of outfitting police officers with body cameras appear to outweigh not doing so. For example, body cameras offer an advantage over the type of stationary cameras mounted on police vehicles by capturing a much clearer picture of what the police officer is seeing at the time of the incident, thereby eliminating much of the uncertainty when attempting to reconstruct encounters between police officers and the public. Further, similar to what occurs with the use of surveillance cameras to monitor the actions of employees within work environments, body cameras would likely result in not only police officers but also private citizens being mindful of their behavior, knowing that the encounter is being recorded.

For example, a 12-month study conducted by researchers at the University of South Florida showed where randomly selected officers wearing police body cameras during the research period experienced a 53 percent reduction in reported use-of-force incidents and a 65 percent decline in civilian complaints against the officers. In a similar study conducted within the Rialto, California, Police Department, results showed complaints against police officers wearing the body cameras were reduced by 87.5 percent, while use of force reduced by 59 percent over the course of 1 year (Wing, 2015). Regardless of whether the positive nature of the monitored engagements between the law enforcement community and civilians is the result of behavioral changes on the part of police officers taking part in the study or the public, the early results of studies on the use of police body cameras certainly appear to show promise. Still, we must all be mindful that regardless of whether video footage is captured via police body cameras or a cellphone that a witness might have pointing in the direction of the incident, there is no getting around the impact of perceptions, and as we have learned from past incidents, while it is true on some level that video does not lie, much of what each of us considers reality is in conjunction with our perspective.

References

Alexander, M. (2010). *The New Jim Crow: Mass incarceration in the age of colorblindness*. New York, NY: The New Press.

Alpert, G., Macdonald, J. & Dunham, R. (2005). Police suspicion and discretionary decision making during citizen stops. *Criminology*, 43, 407-434.

Baum, D. (2016, April). Legalize it all—How to win the war on drugs. *Harper's Magazine*. Retrieved from https://harpers.org/archive/2016/04/legalize-it-all/

Biggs, B. A., & Naimi, L. L. (2012). Ethics in traditional policing: Reflecting on a paramilitary paradigm. *Franklin Business & Law Journal, 2012*(4), 19-39. Retrieved from http://www.franklinpublishing.net/businesslaw.html

Brunson, R. (2007). Police don't like Black people: African-American young men's accumulated police experiences. *Criminology & Public Policy, 6*, 71-101. doi:10.1111/j.1745-9133.2007.00423.x

Burke, W. (2011). Who is the client? A different perspective. *OD Practitioner, 43*(3), 44-49. Retrieved from http://www.odnetwork.org/?OutstandingODPract

Burns, R. (2008). What does diversity mean for employees? *Black Enterprise, 39*(5), 69.

Chiel, E. (2016). Black teenagers' vs. white teenagers: Why Google's algorithm displays racist results. Retrieved from http://fusion.net/story/312527/google-image-search-algorithm-three-black-teenagers-vs-three-white-teenagers/

DuBois, W. E. B. (1903). *The souls of black folk.* Chicago, IL: A. C. McClurg and Co.

Eggleston, N. (2016). *President Obama has now commuted the sentences of 348 individuals.* Retrieved from https://www.whitehouse.gov/blog/2016/03/30/president-obama-has-now-commuted-sentences-348-individuals

Fortner, M. (2015). The Clintons aren't the only ones to blame for the crime bill. Retrieved from https://www.themarshallproject.org/2015/10/07/the-clintons-aren-t-the-only-ones-to-blame-for-the-crime-bill#.iHZWWI8EU

Garmon, J. (2002). Higher education for prisoners will lower rates for taxpayers. *Community College Week, 14*(11), 4.

Getlen, L. (2014, February 23). Corrupt 'Kids for Cash' judge ruined more than 2,000 lives. *New York Post.* Retrieved from http://nypost.com/

Human Rights Watch. (2016). *The impact of the war on drugs on U.S. incarceration.* Retrieved from https://www.hrw.org/reports/2000/usa/Rcedrg00-03.htm

Landau, S. (2013). Making sense from Snowden: What's significant in the NSA surveillance revelations. *IEEE Security & Privacy Magazine, 11*(4), 54-63. doi:10.1109/MSP.2013.90

Lundman, R. J. (1974). Routine police arrest practices; a commonwealth perspective. *Social Problems, 22,* 127-141.

Miller, J. G. (1996). *Search and destroy: African-American males in the criminal justice system*. New York, NY: Cambridge University Press.

Neyroud, P. (2011). Leading policing in the 21st century: Leadership, democracy, deficits and the new professionalism. *Public Money & Management, 31*, 347-354. doi:10.1080/09540962.2011.598346

Pinizzotto, A., Davis, E., Bohrer, S., & Infanti, B. (2012). Restraint in the use of deadly force: A preliminary study. *FBI Law Enforcement Bulletin, 81*(6), 1-11.

Rafferty, A., & Jimmieson, N. (2010). Team change climate: A group-level analysis of the relationships among change information and change participation, role stressors, and well-being. *European Journal of Work and Organizational Psychology, 19*, 551-586. doi:10.1080/13594320903007869

Schafer, J. (2009). Developing effective leadership in policing: perils, pitfalls, and paths forward. *Policing: An International Journal of Police Strategies & Management, 32*, 238-260. doi:10.1108%2F13639510910958163

Schafer, J. A. (2010). The ineffective police leader: Acts of commission and omission. *Journal of Criminal Justice, 38*, 737-746. doi:10.1016/j.jcrimjus.2010.04.048

Skinner, B. F. (1935). The generic nature of the concepts of stimulus and response. *Journal of General Psychology, 12*, 40-65.

Smet, A., Lavoie, J., & Hioe, E. (2012, April). Developing better change leaders. *McKinsey Quarterly, (2)*, 98-104. Retrieved from http://www.mckinsey.com/

Smith, D. A., & Klein, J. R. (1983). Police agency characteristics and arrest decisions. In G. P Whitaker & C.

D. Phillips (Eds.), Evaluating performance of criminal justice agencies (pp. 63-97). Beverly Hills, CA: Sage.

Solis, S. (2016). Protests break out after Baton Rouge police fatally shoot man. Retrieved from http://www.usatoday.com/story/news/nation/2016/07/05/baton-rouge-alton-sterling-police-shooting/86738368/

Stamper, N. (2005). *Breaking rank: A top cop's exposé of the dark side of American policing*. New York, NY: Nation Books.

Sykes, R. E., & Clark, J. P (1975). A theory of deference exchange in police—Civilian encounters. *American Journal of Sociology, 81,* 584-600.

Tonry, M. (1995). *Malign neglect.* New York: Oxford University Press.

Tyler, T. (2001). Public trust and confidence in legal authorities: What do majority and minority group members want from the law and legal institutions?. *Behavioral Sciences and the Law, 19,* 215-235. doi:10.1002/bsl.438

U.S. Department of Education Office of Postsecondary Education. (2004). 1994-95 Federal Pell Grant Program end-of-year report. Retrieved from http://www2.ed.gov/finaid/prof/resources/data/pell-end-of-year-94-95.html

U.S. Department of Justice, Federal Bureau of Investigation. (2000). *Crime in the United States 2000.* Retrieved from https://www.fbi.gov/about-us/cjis/ucr/crime-in-the-u.s/2000

U.S. Department of Justice, Federal Bureau of Investigation. (2005). *Crime in the United States 2005.* Retrieved from https://www2.fbi.gov/ucr/05cius/

U.S. Department of Justice, Federal Bureau of Investigation. (2010). *Crime in the United States 2010.* Retrieved from https://www.fbi.gov/about-us/cjis/ucr/crime-in-the-u.s/2010/crime-in-the-u.s.-2010

U.S. Department of Justice, Federal Bureau of Investigation. (2013*). Crime in the United States 2013.* Retrieved from https://www.fbi.gov/about-us/cjis/ucr/crime-in-the-u.s/2013/crime-in-the-u.s.-2013

VERA Institute of Justice. (2012). The price of prisons: What incarceration costs taxpayers. Retrieved from http://www.vera.org/news/new-vera-report-price-prisons-what-incarceration-costs-taxpayers

Vito, G. F., & Higgins, G. E. (2010). Examining the validity of the leadership challenge inventory: The case for law enforcement. *International Journal of Police Science & Management, 12,* 305-319. doi:10.1350/ijps.2010.12.3.169

Vulliamy, E. (2011, July 24). Nixon's 'war on drugs' began 40 years ago, and the battle is still raging. *The Guardian.* Retrieved from http://www.theguardian.com

Walker, S., Spohn, C., & DeLone, M. (2011). *The color of justice: race, ethnicity, and crime in America.* Independence, KY: Cengage Learning.

Weitzer, R., & Tuch. S. (2005). Racially biased policing: Determinants of citizen perceptions. *Social Forces, 83,* 1009-1030.

Wiley, J. (2013). *The nigger in you: Challenging dysfunctional language, engaging leadership moments.* Sterling, VA: Stylus Publishing.

Wing, N. (2015). *Study shows less violence, fewer complaints when cops wear body cameras.* Retrieved from http://www.huffingtonpost.com/entry/police-body-camera-study_us_561d2ea1e4b028dd7ea53a56

Wood, A. (2012). Cruel and unusual punishment: Confining juveniles with adults after Graham and Miller. *Emory Law Journal, 61,* 1445-1491.

Worden, R. E. (1989). Situational and attitudinal explanations of police behavior: A theoretical reappraisal and empirical assessment. *Law and Society Review, 23,* 667-711.

Wright, M. C. (2001). Pell Grants, politics and the penitentiary: Connections between the development of U.S. higher education and prisoner post-secondary programs. *Journal of Correctional Education 52,* 11-16.

Wuestewald, T., & Steinheider, B. (2012). Police managerial perceptions of organizational democracy: A matter of style and substance. *Police Practice & Research, 13,* 44-58. doi:10.1080/15614263.2011.589568

4

EQ And American Policing

Our dehumanization of the Negro then is indivisible from our dehumanization of ourselves; the loss of our own identity is the price we pay for our annulment of his

—*James A. Baldwin*

Dehumanization and the Ferguson Incident

In further exploring how emotions affect our actions, let us revisit the shooting death of Michael Brown in Ferguson, Missouri, not by engaging in a dialogue centered on the sometimes-asserted racist actions of police officers, but instead, by striving to grasp an understanding of the actions of police officers and community members through the lens of the EQ construct. The grand jury testimony of police officer Darren Wilson provides insight into his thinking during the fatal shooting of Brown and demonstrates the impact of fear on rational thought. The following are excerpts taken from Officer Wilson's grand jury testimony:

- "He was just staring at me, almost like to intimidate me or to overpower me."

- "When I grabbed him, the only way I can describe it is I felt like a five-year-old holding onto Hulk Hogan."

- "And then after he did that, he looked up at me and had the most intense aggressive face. The only way I can describe it, he looked like a demon, that's how angry he looked."

- "It looked like he was almost bulking up to run through the shots, like it was making him mad that I'm shooting at him. And the face he had was looking straight through me, like I wasn't even there, I wasn't even anything in his way."

- "And then when it went into him, the demeanor on his face went blank, the aggression was gone, it was gone, I mean, I knew he stopped, the threat was stopped."

While some might view Officer Wilson's testimony as a hodgepodge of excuses, my initial instincts was that his statements were without question the mere tip of the iceberg in terms of his subsurface beliefs. From there, I questioned the various processes that occur within an individual's psyche that might cause that person to view others as objects as opposed to humans, and while there is a plethora of worthy psychological explanations, during my research on the topic, I came across the word *dehumanization*, which was something I had not previously considered. Dehumanization broadly refers to perceiving a person or group of people as lacking humanness. African Americans have historically been dehumanized, from constitutional denial of full legal personhood to enslavement as chattel. Today, a subtler form of dehumanization persists chiefly through public endorsement of police brutality against African Americans stemming from negative perceptions that operate beneath conscious awareness (Goff, Eberhardt, Williams, & Jackson, 2008).

Take, for example, a study conducted by Northwestern University titled "A Superhumanization Bias in Whites' Perceptions of Blacks," which suggested that the historical dehumanization of Blacks through slavery coupled with societal prejudices has resulted in some Whites believing that Blacks possess abnormal strengths or abilities. Differentiating between physical abilities based on race is nothing new and has crept into the world of sports for many years when describing athletes. I recall the time during an NFL pregame commentary in 1988 when Brent Musburger, speaking on behalf of CBS Sports, told fans that "Jimmy the Greek" Snyder's remarks were not representative of his former colleagues and that he had been fired by the network for his comments alleging that African Americans by nature were better athletes because of the size of their thigh muscles, something he attributed to selective breeding by slave owners in the antebellum South. Some perceived the comments as racist, whereas others saw them as either inappropriate, spoken out of ignorance, or simply taken out of context. Still, when we move beyond reckless debates surrounding racial superiority in terms of athleticism, the outcome of the Northwestern University study is both scary and dangerous, particularly if there is a subconscious belief on the part of Whites that African Americans possess super strengths or are somehow immune to pain.

Think about this within the context of confrontations between police officers and African American males. More specifically, consider the application of a use-of-force threat continuum where officers are authorized to counteract a suspect's aggression with the level of force believed to be appropriate in controlling the situation. When revisiting the grand jury testimony of police officer Darren Wilson and analyzing his words carefully, can you now see correlations between the officer's description of his encounter with Michael Brown and the potential that subconsciously he may have truly believed that African Americans somehow possess super strengths and are therefore incapable of being restrained in the same manner as other human beings? Do you see the potential correlations between the officer's perceptions and his subsequent actions? Again, this is not meant to support or justify an officer-involved shooting, but instead to show that what occurred in Ferguson, Missouri, was considerably more than simply a case of a White police officer shooting an African American male. It is also meant to illuminate a significant problem if African Americans are viewed by some police officers in the context of being other than human, and the potential dangers associated with officers harboring such beliefs.

Applying EQ to Real Life Situations

Rather than admitting the obvious, that is, that a problem does exist in the manner in which some police officers engage the African American community, think for a moment about how many of the so-called experts were paraded before the public to provide news commentary following the Michael Brown and Eric Garner grand jury decisions and how the focus of their dialogue centered on the protests, burning buildings, and looting. Some of those so-called experts presumably thought it would enlighten the public to hear that there are more Blacks killed by other Blacks within their own communities than at the hands of White police officers, and although a case might be able to be made for such a statement statistically speaking, it makes about as much sense as suggesting that it is socially acceptable to cause harm to another person as long as there is documentation showing that the person being injured is on record as being a victim of abuse. When did we as a society begin comparing the actions of sworn police officers to the conduct of common criminals? More than anyone else, police officers must uphold the law, and there is no logical way of explaining away unjustified police shootings of African Americans simply by using the actions of street criminals as a barometer.

Statistics do not always tell the entire story. For example, while statistics taken from U.S. Department of Justice crime reports from 1980 to 2008 showed that 93 percent of African American victims were murdered by an African American, what often goes unsaid is that according to the same crime statistics, 84 percent of Whites were killed by another White person (Cooper & Smith, 2011). What it comes down to is that, although it is well documented that homicides typically involve individuals who know one another, statistics will likely continue to be manipulated for the sole purpose of validating perceptions of correlations between race and crime, and it is incumbent upon each of us to perform our due diligence before blindly accepting statistics as facts.

From the Mouths of Police Officers

If you were under the impression that police officers always speak with one voice, think again. Similar to how we interpret our surroundings in accordance with our respective belief system, the manner in which police officers think and process information will sometime vary based on things that include the officer's race, upbringing, and life experiences. To show divergent thought between officers from dissimilar backgrounds, I asked two former colleagues of mine who are federal agents to respond to identical questions related to a few of the high-profile encounters between police officers and the public to see how such a scenario might play out. Below are the questions asked of each officer with the officer's respective responses:

1. **What is your impression of race relations in the United States?**

African American officer's response: "I believe that race relations have worsened with the creation of political groups such as the Tea Party. I think with the in-

211

crease of minorities obtaining college educations, better paying jobs, stable government jobs, and with the loss of jobs normally held by White Americans such as steel mills, auto industry and union workers (out sourcing) has only fueled the *Blacks and minorities are taking our jobs mindset* which has added to the resentment."

White officer's response: "Overall I believe they are quite good, although there is always room to improve. I believe one way the improvement can be seen is the rise of minorities to the highest levels in politics, entertainment and business. No longer is race a barrier to achievement if someone is dedicated and focused and persists with hard work."

2. **Do you believe there is disparity in the manner in which citizens are treated by law enforcement officers based on race. Why or why not?**

African American officer's response: "Yes! A good example of this was when my former partner who is White was interviewing a CFO [chief financial officer] of a major corporation who was a suspect in the investigation along with a White AUSA [assistant United States attorney] and another White agent. My former partner began to ask the CFO some very pointed questions about the fraud and was stopped by the AUSA.

The AUSA said, Hey—, he is just like you and me! My former partner turned to the AUSA and said, "No he is not like me because he is a crook and to me he is no different than any dope dealer."

White officer's response: "I believe there is disparity in the manner in which citizens are treated by law enforcement but race is only a part of it, much of it is based on such things as appearance, age, dress and demeanor. Other factors include the time of day and vehicle driven. All these factors will contribute to how an officer may react to someone which may seem unfair to the subject but actually has basis for the officer as they approach and interact with citizens."

3. **Do you believe racial profiling is real or a myth? Have any of your close friends ever told you that they were mistreated by police officers? If so, please describe the incident. DO NOT USE ANY NAMES.**

African American officer's response: "About two months ago, I was driving on a popular interstate at about 65 mph in a 70 mph zone in my unmarked law enforcement vehicle. A State Police Officer pulled up beside my vehicle then pulled behind me and turned on his lights. The police officer told me he stopped me because I had two ear buds in my ears (one in each ear). I explained to him that I was talking to my office on my cell phone and wanted to be hands free. After seeing that I was a federal law enforcement officer, he said it was against state law to have two ear buds in your ears and let me go. You be the judge."

White officer's response: "I know someone who feels he has been mistreated by the police, however when I tried to tell him why he may be stopped frequently in certain neighborhoods he did not want to be open to my way of explaining it. I partially blame the officers who have stopped him because they have done a poor job of telling him why they have stopped him after clearing him of any wrong doing. Note: He is White but drives an old vehicle that appears in poor condition and his unkempt looking long hair and colored dark glasses are key factors. He does handyman type work and has been stopped midday in certain areas around parks that have been known for drug activity."

4. **During the incidents where police officers have killed suspects, the officer routinely stated that they "feared for their life." Along those lines, during the time you worked in the inner-city, did you ever have a "fear" of approaching African**

214

American suspects? Why or why not? Also, as it pertains to arresting suspects, was your level of apprehension any different depending on whether your suspect was White or Black? Explain in detail.

African American officer's response: "Depending on the person's criminal history and whether there was a previous weapons charge, I would take extra precautions. I never feared approaching African American suspects because I tried to respect them and still do what I was tasked to do. As it pertains to any apprehension on my part, if it was a drug case I approached each suspect the same way. I knew if it involved meth (usually used by Whites suspects) that this person might be "tweaking" and/or paranoid which may result in the residence being booby-trapped. I also knew if the case involved crack and/or cocaine in predominantly African American neighborhoods, the suspect was more than likely going to be armed."

White officer's response: "Because of where I worked, I did not have any recollection specifically about dealing with many Black suspects, most of my experiences were involving White or Asian (Philippine nationals). Those Black suspects I did have contact with

I don't believe I had any higher level of concern just based on race. In answering the second part of the question and based on my response to the above, I mainly felt "apprehension" in making arrests or approaching suspects based on type of crime involved, as opposed to the race of the individual since, unlike uniform officers, we usually didn't approach or have contact with individuals in a random manner. However, to add to this thought, I feel more apprehension if walking in certain areas and someone is coming in my direction, the race of the individual, along with the age, demeanor, dress and overall appearance, may make me feel more caution as the person approaches, which may mean crossing the street or walking closer to the outside."

5. **Please provide your thoughts on the following officer-involved incidents. Do you feel the amount of force used in each of these incidents was justified? Please explain in detail:**

The Michael Brown shooting in Ferguson, Missouri

African American officer's response: "Understanding the full scope of what transpired I believe this was justified. I am taking in account from the strong armed robbery to the incident at the police officer's vehicle as well as the size of the officer and suspect. I also believe that if Brown and his friend had been walking on one of the sidewalks on either side of the street instead of in the street, this would have never occurred."

White officer's response: "I believe this was a justified shooting based on the evidence presented—Brown was a suspect in a felony and attacked the officer once, broke away and in pursuit of him further Brown came back towards the officer at which time he believed his life was being threatened and he fired, killing Brown."

The Eric Garner death at the hands of police officers in Staten Island, New York

African American officer's response: "I believe that this was excessive force. Keep in mind, this all happened over him selling individual cigarettes."

White officer's response: "This was unfortunate as Garner was approached for a relatively minor offense but when officers tried to take him into custody he resisted and a struggle resulted leading to Garner's death, which may have been enhanced by him being in poor health. Could he have just been issued a citation? However, Garner's resistance was primary in leading to the situation escalating."

The Ezell Ford shooting in Los Angeles, California

African American officer's response: "With regards to Ezell Ford I believe that the officer did not follow the force continuum. I also believe that a struggle ensued which led to the shooting. The officer was predisposed because of his past treatment of Black people and suspect although has a history of mental illness was predisposed with several arrests for gang activity, drug and weapons possessions."

White officer's response: "With Ford if he had mental health issues then his reaction may have been due to this problem and again he escalated the situation by offering resistance. He was approached at first only for questioning but the situation changed quickly with the resistance. Most police departments are still not adequately trained in handling subjects with mental health issues and the results can be seen in cases such as this."

6. **Do you feel it is the responsibility of the law enforcement community to bridge the gap between police officers and local communities, or the other way around? Why?**

African American officer's response: "I think that both parties should work together to bridge the gap. Everyone has a responsibility to bridge the gap."

White officer's response: "I feel both sides are responsible for improving relations, the police by being open and available and the community by having an understanding of the crime trends in their area and what's involved in the police doing their day to day job of protecting and enforcing."

7. **What ideas do you have for improving the level of trust between police officers and those they are sworn to protect and to serve?**

African American officer's response: "We, as citizens can no longer harbor individuals or withhold information regarding individuals who terrorize our communities. Law enforcement officers should not have a preconceived notion about every person they meet who does not look like them. Also, hiring and promoting diversity within the local police departments will go a long way towards breaking stereotypes."

White officer's response: "Community policing is a tried and true method but needs to be taken seriously by both sides. Attending community meetings and reviewing police websites for current data is very helpful. Officers getting out of their cars and walking the beat also has a proven positive impact."

The questionnaire was not meant to replicate a scientific study. Instead, the intent was to show that while police officers might share similar beliefs when it comes to assessing innocence or guilt, there is no way of getting around the impact of one's life experience on how they might perceive the world around them. As observed in the above responses, these officers provided similar answers to the question relating to the responsible party when it comes to bridging the gap between police officers and local communities, which suggests that both play an integral role in this endeavor. In responding to the question related to enhancing the level of trust the public holds of police officers, both officers suggested the need for community involvement and better dialogue between police officers and stakeholders. Although their answers were not identical, both officers gave very similar answers to the questions about appropriate use of force related to the deaths of Michael Brown, Eric Garner, and Ezell Ford.

A few questions required introspection on the part of both officers, where the responses they provided not only reflected their law enforcement roles, but were also a product of factors associated with life experiences outside of work, and as expected, the answers provided by these officers did just that. For example, if you peel back the layers of the onion on the answers provided by the officers when addressing race relations in American, racial disparity, and racial profiling, you will immediately sense that the answers are more personal. Those answers were not framed in accordance with police protocol, which is typically easy for law enforcement officers to address simply by assessing what occurred and then applying it to routine police procedures. The point is to reiterate the fact that all humans have experiences, and not even donning a uniform or wearing a badge will enable an individual to escape from the feelings, beliefs, or perceptions that reside within each of us.

Capturing EQ Teaching Moments

As we continue to expand our discussion on EQ, we will now look at it from within the social environment to get a better feel of how EQ can be applied to encounters between police officers and the communities they serve. For this illustration, social environment implies the immediate physical and social setting in which people reside or in which an event takes place or evolves. It includes the culture that the individual was educated or lives in, as well as the people and institutions with whom they interact. We will also further explore Goleman's EQ model, which as previously described in Figure 1, includes competencies organized into four clusters: (a) self-awareness, (b) self-management, (c) social awareness, and (d) relationship management.

Competencies describe the specific characteristics necessary to perform a job well. Further, they differentiate level of performance in a job, role, organization, or culture. The following attributes enable a person to exhibit competency behaviors:

- Skills—things a person knows how to do well

- Knowledge—what a person knows about a particular substantive area

- Values—what behaviors a person sees as important or not important

- Self-image—the way a person sees him or herself internally

- Traits—relatively enduring characteristics of a person's behavior

- Motives—unconsciously focus individuals on behaviors they find intrinsically satisfying

To assist with identifying the various competencies on the pages that follow, I have highlighted each of them where they show up within the scenarios to illustrate not only how the EQ competencies are being used, but also where EQ might have enhanced the outcome of some of the engagements.

The next section will be used to link several of the competencies associated with Goleman's EQ model to some of the most highly publicized confrontations involving police officers and private citizens. Throughout this section is the phrase *"Where's The EQ?"* accompanied by a magnifying glass. At each of these locations, we will take a closer look at various engagements between police officers and the public from the perspective of EQ, with an overarching goal of better understanding how EQ might look within policing by showing situations that demonstrate high levels of EQ or where EQ may have been lacking. Beginning with the Michael Brown shooting, the information found in both the self-awareness and the self-management clusters will be useful in assessing the actions of Officer Wilson.

Self-awareness is foundational to EQ and starts with an individual's level of self-confidence. It also relates to how aware someone is of his or her thoughts and mood. Individuals high in this competency have a good sense of self and are attuned with their emotions, which allows them to understand the emotions of others and opens the door for empathy. Consequently, they are able to process and use that information to guide their behavior to where they routinely give themselves ample time to consider the potential downstream impact before they act.

To evaluate the level at which Officer Wilson may or may not have been completely aware of his emotions at the time of the shooting, we will revisit the interview between he and George Stephanopoulos. Through that information exchange, we have the ability to gain at least some perspective of Officer Wilson's thinking. The first part of the interview we will focus on involves Officer Wilson responding to the statement where he was told that some witnesses to the incident reported that he was out of control and that he had snapped, to which he responded that he was never angry. Wilson also stated that the only emotion he felt was fear, and after that, his training took over and he went into survival mode.

Where's The EQ?

Having experience with people assuming that I was angry when I was not, I can relate to others having the impression that Officer Wilson was angry, in light of the circumstances, when he might not have been. All things being equal, an individual is usually the best judge of what he or she is feeling internally, so I give Officer Wilson the benefit of doubt that he was *self-aware* of what he was experiencing at the time. Besides, from personal experience, I know that when you are in the middle of situations where there is even a remote possibility of having to resort to the use of deadly force, so much of your energy is devoted toward ensuring you survive the encounter that there is little if any time left for anger. After things settle down, it is quite normal to experience any number of emotions, but with police officers having the ability to compartmentalize emotions, I believe Officer Wilson when he said that anger was not one of the emotions he felt during the encounter with Michael Brown.

I found it even more compelling during the interview when Officer Wilson said, "My training took over and I went into survival mode." Wilson made it sound as if he was on automatic pilot rather than giving any critical thought to his actions during his encounter with Brown when things began to deteriorate. That is exactly what police field training officers want to occur in those situations, where split-second decisions can make the difference between life and death, and the only thing police officers have at their disposal at that moment is their training. The next part of the interview warrants more scrutiny.

Throughout the interview, Officer Wilson was inexpressive and responded to questions in what appeared to be a rehearsed, or at least calculated, manner, where he repeatedly tied his actions to his training. That is, until he was asked why he did not get behind his car when Brown was advancing toward him, where Officer Wilson's response was quite telling both in his vocal and facial expressions. With a slight smirk on his face, Wilson appeared to momentarily lose a bit of his composure when he replied, "Run away? That is not what we are there for."

After a brief pause, he then said, "If we ran away every time something scared us, we would not be very good at our job. We are taught and trained to deal with the threat at hand, and that is what I did." When I heard this exchange during the interview, my initial thought was that Officer Wilson was potentially reliving the incident in his mind as he spoke, and if this was the case, this was likely the very point when he made the decision that the opportunity for negotiation was over and that it was time for him to gain control of the situation regardless of the outcome.

Another part of the interview that stood out to me was Officer Wilson's assertions that nothing in his police training gave him the option of retreating and taking cover, specifically, his statement that running away from scary situations was outside of the police officer role. During that exchange, Wilson emphasized that officers were trained to deal with threats, and if they ran away every time they were afraid, they would not be very good at their job. Although such feelings might be more of an indication that Officer Wilson himself (as opposed to his training) ruled out the option of backing off and reassessing things once the situation "went south," it remains difficult at best and possibly unfair to question Officer Wilson's tactics without being there and experiencing exactly what he encountered at that critical moment.

As I continued through the interview, listening to Officer Wilson's every word and hearing nothing that made me question his tactics, I began to think this was simply another interview where the interviewee was provided the questions beforehand so that he could prepare his responses. Then I heard the type of open-ended question I had been waiting for throughout the interview. A question that would finally provide insight into Officer Wilson's thinking on the day he encountered Michael Brown and would require more than a yes or no answer or an answer that could be easily placed under the umbrella of police training.

George Stephanopoulos said to Officer Wilson, "You have worked in African American communities for a long time. You have described the neighborhood where you encountered Michael Brown as anti-law enforcement. What does that mean?" Officer Wilson responded saying, "There is a lot of criminal activity. There is drugs, guns, burglaries, assaults, violence, that is one of our high crime areas for the city."

The very next follow-up question presented to Officer Wilson was absolutely brilliant in that it appeared to be at the crux of many of the problems the entire world saw unfold in Ferguson, Missouri, following the reading of the grand jury verdict. George Stephanopoulos said to Officer Wilson, "What was the relations like every day as you were working? You talked about a criminal element where you talked about drugs and crime. Did you feel any racial tensions?" Hearing that question, I thought to myself that this is going to be interesting. After all, during the same time the interview was taking place, the presence of handheld signs and posters addressing perceived racial injustice were still in plain view, not only in Ferguson, but across the country.

Where's The EQ?

To my surprise, Officer Wilson's response to the question of racial tension was "No. Ferguson loves Ferguson. That community loves its community. When people say it's a diverse community, it is a diverse community."

Again, Stephanopoulos followed up with a question that forced Officer Wilson to share a bit more of his thinking when he said, "But the police force is overwhelmingly White and the community is predominantly Black. That didn't create tension, that didn't create problems?" to which Officer Wilson simply said, "Not with me."

As a person who is rarely surprised, I was not only taken aback by Officer Wilson's response, but for the first time during the interview, I thought to myself that this is a person who is truly out of touch with the events taking place directly in front of him. Are we not talking about the same Ferguson, Missouri, that was the recipient of a U.S. Department of Justice investigative report disclosing disparate treatment of African Americans at the hands of the very police department he worked for? Officer Wilson's assessment of race relations in Ferguson, provides an excellent example of social awareness or lack thereof.

Research shows that socially aware individuals are not only attuned to what others need, but they act on that knowledge. Social awareness involves first carefully considering what others want and then communicating with them in such a way that their need is met. Social awareness more or less refers to individuals who are cognizant of the social constructs and culture around them.

Along those lines, social awareness, for our purpose, is defined as one understanding that there exists different cultures and opinions outside of their own. In applying that to the responses of Officer Wilson relative to race relations in Ferguson, Missouri, as presented during the interview, at best he typifies an individual who "can't see the forest for the trees." It appears that Officer Wilson was so wrapped up in the specifics of law enforcement, such as crime rates associated with the community where he was assigned, that he either missed, or had chosen to overlook, the larger problem involving race relations taking place in Ferguson, Missouri.

The question remains, how could Officer Wilson not see that anything was out of the ordinary in Ferguson, Missouri? The answer is twofold, with the first part having plenty to do with organizational leadership, including the court system, city administration, and the Ferguson Police Department, who by their very silence in response to reports of wrongdoing sent a clear message to police officers that disparate treatment of African Americans was condoned. The second part is a bit more complex; still, with the likelihood of race relations between the Ferguson Police Department and the local community being the subject of water-cooler talk, the chances of members of the police force not being aware of what was taking place in the community are remote. While Officer Wilson's interview with George Stephanopoulos might be indicative of someone being in sync with his emotional self, his assessment of race relations in Ferguson, Missouri, at the time of the Michael Brown shooting, without question, exemplifies someone devoid of social awareness.

Turning our attention to how the Ferguson Police Department responded immediately following the shooting death of Michael Brown gives us some insight into how those actions might have contributed to the ensuing public unrest. For this discussion, we will focus on self-management and relationship management, both of which assess the degree to which individuals are capable of regulating their actions. Self-management measures one's ability to adapt in response to factors that might dictate a need for change while maintaining composure in the midst of potentially disruptive circumstances. Individuals high in this competency are innovative, adaptable, restrained, responsible, and guided by a strong sense of trustworthiness, where they hold themselves accountable for acting in ways commensurate with such feelings.

With the protests and riots following the reading of the grand jury verdict in Ferguson, Missouri, well behind us, although certainly not forgotten, what are your thoughts now relative to how the Ferguson, Missouri, Police Department might measure up against the EQ self-management component? The tactics officers used in attempting to quash the riots will provide a treasure trove of information to make our assessment. If you recall, officers responded by donning their riot gear, driving armored vehicles down city streets, and firing tear gas into the crowds of people, and while some individuals were without question there only to wreak havoc, there were plenty of peaceful protestors gathered in the streets wrongfully treated by police officers. So how did things go so wrong?

When I engage others in conversation about the day riots broke out in Ferguson, Missouri, although stated in a multitude of ways, what usually surfaces are perceptions that American policing has become overly militaristic. Several individuals I spoke with stated that when they first saw the military vehicles deployed on city streets in Ferguson, Missouri, they had to remind themselves that these were police officers and not our military soldiers engaging enemy forces in the Middle East. Some felt that American policing had lost its way and rather than subscribing to a mission to *protect and to serve*, the mind-set of some police officers appeared to be more akin to *seek and destroy*, again resembling conduct more appropriate for the battlefield than city streets where American citizens are protected by the Bill of Rights.

Where's The EQ?

The problem is that the police profession continues to struggle with image, and when the media capture officers at their very worse, as was the case when officers were observed cursing, pushing, and pointing loaded firearms at peaceful protestors in Ferguson, Missouri, such actions only serve to accentuate negatively held perceptions. Maintaining a sense of calm in the midst of chaos is foundational to the **self-control** competency, and although police officers in Ferguson had their work cut out for them in their attempt to restore order to local neighborhoods after the riots broke out, the conduct of many officers epitomized inordinate disdain. Several individuals I have spoken with regarding the tactics of the Ferguson Police Department in response to the riots find difficulty erasing from their memory the images of what they described as out-of-control police officers further agitating the crowds by shoving citizens, handcuffing members of the press, and, according to some, leaving them with uneasy feelings about American policing, with one individual relating the state of policing to the Eldridge Cleaver quote, "You either have to be part of the solution, or you're going to be part of the problem," adding that in the eyes of many, because police officers consistently appear to show little restraint relative to the use of force when faced with citizens exhibiting defiance, their conduct unfortunately is more in line with the latter.

Although giving the appearance of being either overlooked or disregarded, the problems between the Ferguson Police Department and local communities did not begin with the death of Michael Brown. In fact, we now know that numerous complaints were lodged by the residents of Ferguson, Missouri, alleging that police officers were mistreating African Americans. And if the allegations were not sufficient in rising to the level of an inquiry, the racial disparity of offenders documented within police reports should have at least raised a red flag warranting an internal investigation, although this does not appear to have been done according to what was learned from the U.S. Department of Justice report on the Ferguson Police Department.

Where's The EQ?

Whether the complaints were thought to be baseless, or were purposely ignored by police leadership, a volatile situation ensued within the community whereby local citizens developed both a distrust and a dislike for police officers, which is not exactly a recipe for effective relationship management. The first competency the police department showed that they were lacking was **trustworthiness**, which relates to maintaining standards of honesty and integrity. Individuals possessing this competency are able to build trusting relationships with those they engage by acting ethically and above reproach. Failure to establish trust with the local community created a situation whereby the Ferguson Police Department remained under public scrutiny and, without a trusting relationship, any misstep by the police department was viewed by local citizens as validation of perceived corruption within the ranks of the police department.

There are a slew of other EQ competencies that if used when engaging the public, the Ferguson Police Department likely would not have found itself in such an unenviable position. For example, **building bonds** involves nurturing relationships where individuals possessing this competency build rapport with others through making connections that are mutually beneficial. Another critical area where the department appears to struggle relates to the **leveraging diversity** competency. Aside from respecting people from varied backgrounds, individuals possessing this competency create an environment where diverse people can thrive, which sounds nothing like the state of Ferguson, Missouri, during the time of the Michael Brown shooting and the aftermath. The last competency that will be associated with this section relates to **empathy**, where individuals possessing this competency take an active interest in the concerns expressed by others. Circling back to the previously mentioned scenario where local community members reportedly made allegations of police misconduct only to have their complaints seemingly fall on deaf ears, not only did the Ferguson Police Department fail in terms of showing sensitivity to the perspectives of those they were sworn to protect and to serve, but it appears they also missed vital emotional cues that in all probability were right there for the finding.

New Mexico Van Shooting Incident

You may recall the incident where a New Mexico state police officer fired shots at a minivan with a female driver and five children as the vehicle fled away from the scene after being pulled over for reportedly driving 71 mph in a 55 mph zone. The vehicle stop escalated into a heated argument whereby the driver's 14-year old son became so enraged at the argument that had ensued between the officer and his mother that he exited the vehicle and confronted the police officer just prior to the mother getting her children back into the vehicle and speeding away. Although the driver's refusal to comply with the officer indisputably placed her children in harm's way, the decision of one of the responding officers to discharge his firearm at the passenger vehicle as it sped away is contrary to fundamental firearms safety, which instructs officers to always know their target, backstop, and what is beyond.

Officers are taught that to the extent possible, whenever a firearm is discharged, the officer must know what is beyond their intended target on the chance bullets miss or go through the target. An obvious observation involving this situation is that, being unaware that there were five children inside the minivan when he discharged his weapon, the officer's actions unnecessarily placed the lives of innocent people at risk. Like most situations, there are opposing views when it comes to placing blame, with some suggesting that the speed of the fleeing vehicle placed the children as well as other citizens in as much danger as the officer who fired the shots; however, even with the video showing the officer presumably aiming at the minivan's tires, it remains difficult to defend the discharging of the firearm on the basis of imminent danger, particularly since the vehicle was leaving the scene. Regardless of what you might have been led to believe through television shows, with officers having to account for each round fired from their weapons, there is no such thing as a warning shot.

Where's The EQ?

Applying EQ to this situation, rather than acting to save lives, the officer's decision to shoot at the fleeing vehicle was likely the result of a loss of composure in the heat of the moment, not unlike what many of us experience from time to time. The difference being, unlike someone outside of the law enforcement profession losing control and flinging an object when things don't go according to plan, with agency-issued firearms being one of the primary tools police officers carry, demonstrating high levels of EQ by being able to manage one's behavior under stressful situations is vitally important. Individuals who possess the **self-control** competency are able to remain composed and manage their impulses when they find themselves in the type of situations these officers encountered with a fleeing suspect. Up to this point, the discussion has been on the officer firing the shots at the fleeing minivan, who was not the first police officer on the scene. But what about the officer who made the initial stop?

In assessing the actions of the officer who initially pulled over the minivan, it is difficult to argue that he acted professionally as he attempted to explain the reason for the traffic stop as well as options for the driver, which were to either pay a fine or contest the citation in court, which meant she would have to be taken before a magistrate on the spot. The video clearly shows that the officer's intent was to issue the citation and the driver would have been free to go. It was not until the driver increased the intensity of the situation by driving away the first time that the officer began to show a loss of composure, which would have likely been difficult for many people to maintain under the circumstances. When the officer switched from explaining the reason for the traffic stop to attempting to extract the driver from the minivan, his intent was no longer to simply issue a citation, as he was really left with no choice based on the actions of the driver.

Outside of the one area where the initial officer appeared to lose his composure at the end by first attempting to pull the driver out of the van and then attempting to break out the rear side window of the minivan with his baton, he actually receives high marks in several EQ competencies. For example, the officer showed **empathy** when, although he knew the driver had crossed the line and was going to be arrested, he is heard patiently telling her that she needed to come to the back of the van so that her children did not have to witness what was going to occur, which I think meant placing her in handcuffs. Knowing children were in the van, the officer showed sensitivity.

When assessing the officer's **communication** capabilities, again it is difficult to find fault. Although the officer was faced with a difficult situation when the driver refused to decide whether she wanted to sign for the warrant or go before the magistrate, he listened intently and ensured the lines of communication remained open throughout. This was a bad situation, and there is no excusing the actions of the officer who subsequently responded to the scene and thought it was a good idea to attempt to shoot out the tires of the fleeing minivan. Remember that pendulums swing both directions, and although when it points toward the actions taken by the police officers things certainly looked bad for law enforcement, swinging in the other direction exposed the actions of the driver (failing to comply) as possibly the main culprit in this dangerous officer-initiated traffic stop that could have ended worse than it did.

McKinney, Texas, Pool Party Incident

A pool party in McKinney, Texas, generated a lot of media attention when a video showed a police officer who had responded to the location due to a reported disturbance throwing a 15-year-old girl wearing a bikini to the ground and then placing his knee in her back while she cried out in pain. The officer is then heard on the audio portion of the video cursing loudly at bystanders, and at one point, he is observed pointing his agency-issued firearm at the crowd of onlookers who verbally protested what they believed to be unjust treatment by the officer. Although it does not take a significant amount of convincing to conclude that the officer's actions were over the top, this situation allows us to explore a number of the competencies associated with EQ.

Where's The EQ?

At the core of exercising control over oneself is the ability to gauge our personal limitations, which immediately brings into question why the officer remained on his shift as opposed to being removed for debriefing after reportedly responding to an attempted suicide and another situation where someone actually took their own life earlier in the day. The officer's **emotional awareness** is being questioned in this case due to his attorney suggesting that being exposed to such trauma likely impaired the officer's judgment. Similarly to athletes who convince their coach that they are okay to return to the playing field after sustaining an injury, police officers also experience difficulty admitting that help is needed or that they are somehow incapable of responding to a call. It is important that each of us has the capacity to assess our own emotions and understand when we are functioning on all cylinders, and when we are ill-prepared mentally to deal with a particular situation.

Although it is difficult to tell what was in the mind of the officer at the time of the incident, we can make an educated guess that the officer failed to recognize how his feelings would affect his performance. We do know the officer lost his composure during the time he engaged the bystanders who had encircled him while he pinned the young girl on the ground, indicating a loss in **self-control**. Was this excessive force or simply a case where the officer was trying to restore order to an unruly crowd and things got out of hand?

If we are to believe the words of the McKinney, Texas, police chief whom the officer reported to prior to his resignation, the officer's actions were clearly against departmental policy. Still, with such statements often being viewed as pure politics and nothing more than the law enforcement community caving to public uproar over racial injustice, I will attempt to assess this incident using only the EQ competencies regarding what actually occurred, absent of race. Starting with the **communication** competency, it appears the officer missed an opportunity to get to the bottom of what was actually taking place. Individuals who are good communicators listen well, seek mutual understanding of what is actually taking place, and are able to deal with difficult situations while using emotional cues in tailoring their message.

Another area where individuals possessing high levels of EQ excel is in the area of **conflict management**, where they are able to engage difficult people and tense situations with diplomacy and tact. Not only are these individuals good at spotting conflict, but they are also adept at deescalating tense situations. The final competency discussed within the context of this scenario is a part of social competence and involves **empathy**, where individuals possessing this competency act on the premise of understanding other people's needs and feelings. Something that I find somewhat amusing when I am engaged in conversation with people about the McKinney incident, particularly when someone tries to defend the police officer's actions, is when I simply ask, "How would you feel if that was your 15-year-old daughter being thrown around by a police officer?" What I notice is that perspectives immediately begin to shift. It is interesting how the way an individual might feel about a situation has a tendency to change when the scenario hits close to home. Similar to the courtroom scenario in the 1996 film *A Time to Kill*, where jurors in a court in the South seemingly had a difficult time administering fair justice in a case involving an African American man, played by actor Samuel L. Jackson, on trial for a revenge death where he was being tried for killing two White men who had physically abused his young daughter. In getting the jurors to overlook their racial biases, the defense attorney, played by actor Matthew McConaughey, asked the jurors to close their eyes while he methodically walked them through the facts of the case. Once he was done with describing what had taken place and while the jurors still had their eyes closed, he asked the jurors to imagine the little girl was White instead of African American, and, for the first time, the jurors were able to assess what had occurred based on the incident as opposed to the players. Using the film example as a backdrop, ask yourselves if when evaluating the McKinney, Texas, incident from the perspective of what has been reported as taking place as opposed to within the context of a Black or White issue, how do you rate the police officer's actions? Does the officer's conduct pass scrutiny when judged solely against the EQ competencies?

Hempstead, Texas, Officer-Initiated Traffic Stop

Staying in Texas for our next example, we turn our attention to an officer-initiated traffic stop that occurred in Hempstead, involving the death of 28-year-old Sandra Bland, an African American woman who was found hanging in her jail cell only days after being taken into custody. On the heels of the rallies against police violence that began immediately following the announcement of her death, reports were released indicating that Bland suffered from depression and likely took her own life while in police custody. As things have turned out, results of an autopsy on Bland supported the medical examiner's initial ruling of suicide according to the county prosecutor. Closed case, right? I mean, based on what we know about the events of that situation, Bland caused her own death. After all, the problem stems from Bland failing to cooperate with the officer during the initial stop, and had she simply followed orders, she probably would still be alive.

That is how some would choose to assess this situation, but it is much more complex, and there appears to be plenty of fault to go around. A case can always be made that bad things usually occur when private citizens fail to yield to the orders of police officers, but truly assessing these types of situations typically requires looking well below surface information to get to the real cause of things going badly. Let us look at this situation from an emotionally intelligent point of view to see if an alternate approach might have resulted in a different outcome.

Where's The EQ?

Let's begin with the traffic stop. The officer was well within his rights to pull over Bland if he perceived her as violating the law. The video of the incident showed the officer approaching the passenger side of Bland's vehicle, and he can be heard rather calmly advising her that the reason for the stop was because she had failed to signal a lane change. After requesting her driver's license and registration information, the officer is observed returning to his vehicle momentarily before returning to Bland's vehicle on the driver's side with a clipboard in his hand presumably to have her sign for the citation he was about to issue her for the violation. But that is when things took a sudden turn for the worse.

The officer asked Bland if she was all right, telling her that she seemed a bit agitated, and she immediately began expressing her dissatisfaction regarding being pulled over in the first place, and her demeanor unquestionably added to things spiraling out of control between her and the police officer. Was she disrespectful in the manner in which she responded to the officer? Absolutely. Now agitated himself, the officer is heard asking Bland to put out her cigarette, and when she objected, his demeanor changed drastically, which was the first sign that the situation had truly transitioned to an elevated state and was no longer simply about a traffic violation. **Communication** between the two deteriorated, and now the engagement became a situation where the police officer's primary intention was that Bland obey his orders, and that was the crucial point of where EQ would have helped the officer deescalate the situation. Instead, the officer's composure continued to worsen and in addition to his repeated demands for her to get out of the vehicle, at one point the officer is heard telling Bland that he will "light her up."

The law is very clear that the officer did have the legal authority to order Bland out of the car. The only question seemingly left unanswered relates to whether it was necessary to do so under the circumstances, particularly since it appears his intent was to have her sign for the citation and only changed his mind after she refused his demands to extinguish her cigarette. If we somehow had the ability to rewind this situation and equip the police officer with high levels of EQ, the **self-control** competency would have likely kicked in whereby rather than reacting impulsively to Bland's defiance, the officer would have expressed an outward calmness, even though he may well have experienced feelings of irritation on the inside. The self-control competency describes individuals capable of remaining composed and unflappable in the middle of intense situations, which if used in this instance, likely would have resulted in Bland calming down or at least ceasing her tirade long enough for the officer to issue her a citation and thereby bringing to a conclusion the initial intent of the traffic stop. Again, the officer was within his rights to order Bland out of the car. Now set police protocols aside for a moment and ask yourself if you truly believe this officer-initiated traffic stop was carried out in an emotionally intelligent manner, particularly the actions of the officer when he ordered Bland to extinguish her cigarette while she sat in her own car waiting to receive a citation. For anyone attempting to uncover the specific action that really set this engagement on a negative track, the controversy surrounding the cigarette is probably a good point at which to begin your inquiry.

Councilman Tased by Police in Texas

Jonathan Miller, a 26-year-old city council member, was tased and arrested by police officers in Prairie View, Texas, after failing to comply with the demands of responding officers to back away from the scene where they were interviewing three of his friends in front of the councilman's residence. While Councilman Miller was attempting to obtain information from the first responding officer regarding why his friends were being questioned, a second officer is observed arriving and ordering Miller to back away from the scene. The video of the incident showed the officers ordering Miller to back away, but also showed his continued resistance to those orders, at which time both officers turned their focus away from questioning his friends and initiated arrest procedures on Miller due to his failure to comply with orders to back away from the scene. The video then showed Miller on his knees with his back toward the officers where he is given orders to place his hands behind his back, which he again refused to comply with, even though the officers are heard on the audio portion of the video telling Miller that he will be tased if he does not comply with their orders.

In summing up this scenario, the officers were well within their rights to order Councilman Miller to step away from the scene while they conducted their investigation, and his refusal to do so was in clear violation of the law, meaning he placed himself in jeopardy of being arrested and taken to jail by refusing lawful orders of police officers. Now let's assess what transpired through an emotionally intelligent lens to determine if things were truly handled in the most appropriate way possible or if there might have been a better approach to this type of situation.

Where's The EQ?

Plenty of people viewed this scenario as an open and shut case. After all, the officers gave a private citizen clear and concise orders, which included the consequences of not complying. When those orders were not obeyed, the officers simply followed routine police procedures and did exactly what they said they would do. But as the saying goes, "You can be right and still be wrong."

We will dive into the EQ competencies and attempt to match emotionally intelligent behavior against what actually occurred in this situation. If we take into account the components that make up the **communication** competency and lay them side by side with the verbal responses of the female officer who was the first to arrive on the scene, more than a few occasions will surface depicting where she lacked in this competency. For example, individuals possessing this competency are effective both in reaching compromise and in registering emotional cues when attuning their message. These individuals are also adept at resolving difficult issues and fostering open lines of communication, and are good listeners. Now take a close look at the video from this incident and it immediately becomes obvious that the officer was not in the mood to listen to anything the councilman had to offer and was intent on him backing off and moving away from the scene. We can also apply the **adaptability** competency as well. Individuals possessing this competency are able to smoothly handle multiple demands, easily adapt their responses and tactics to fit fluid situations, and be flexible in how they perceive events.

Although we are not able to peer inside the officer's mind to know what she felt at that particular moment, the video shows that as soon as the councilman approached the scene and altered the dynamics of the situation, her demeanor changed and her priority also appears to have changed. The officer's focus became to force the councilman to back away from the scene, irrespective of the fact that she knew he was a public servant who was inquiring why his friends were being questioned outside of his residence. Let's now switch gears and assess the actions of the second officer who responded to the scene and who actually tased the councilman. As soon as the officer arrived, rather than demonstrating behavior of someone understanding the connectedness between what they felt, thought, said, and did, the officer's initial comments indicated that he was lacking in the areas of **emotional awareness** and **leveraging diversity**.

Individuals possessing the above-mentioned competencies have both an understanding of how their feelings affect their performance, as well as the ability to respect and relate well to people from varied backgrounds. They also understand diverse worldviews and are sensitive to group differences. Where are we going with this? Listen to the officer's words on the video of the incident, where shortly after he arrives, he tells the councilman, "Go back there to the end, man. You always starting problems, so go back over there."

Were there prior interactions between the two that led to the officer telling the councilman that he always started problems? The officer then says, "We are not going to keep playing these games, brother," to which the councilman retorted, "You are not my brother first of all." Whether the officer's words were simply a figure of speech and not meant as a slight, it was abundantly clear from the video that the councilman did not like being addressed in such a manner, although his feelings apparently failed to register with the officer.

On two other occasions, the officer is again heard referring to the councilman as "brother," once when he is walking Miller to the police vehicle and while the two are talking, the officer said to Miller, "Two feet wasn't enough, brother" in reference to an appropriate distance the councilman was expected to back up when ordered. The next occurrence is when the officer said to the councilman, "Have a seat, brother," while Miller was placed in the vehicle. Why is this such a big deal when we all know that there are plenty of words one might be called that are significantly worse than *brother*? The answer is because our discussion is about EQ competencies with a purpose of assessing how our behavior either adds to or detracts from positive engagements between people.

Take, for example, the **empathy** competency, which is all about sensing another person's feelings and perspective. Even if the initial instance where the officer referred to Miller as "brother" was not meant in a negative manner, the councilman's response made it clear that continuing down such a track would not make for a positive engagement. But as was observed in the video, the officer disregarded those cues and repeatedly used those words, either out of defiance on his part or simply because he was not attuned to the situation unfolding before him.

Before we wrap up this section, we need to address the tasing of the councilman. Although the initial account of the incident by the responding officers was that Miller was tased because he was fighting, the video showed Miller on his knees with both hands at his side at the time he was tased by the officer. He clearly did not comply with the officer's orders to move his hands around to his back, but he was on his knees and did not appear to be offering any physical resistance at the moment he was tased. Let's again turn to our list of EQ competencies and see if things were handled in the most emotionally intelligent manner based on the circumstances.

From a safety standpoint and based on personal experience, it is routine for police officers to order an individual to position their hands behind their back when effecting an arrest, particularly when it is unclear whether an individual is in possession of a weapon. There is no way of gauging from the video the mind-set of the officers relative to whether they had concerns about Miller possessing weapons during the time he was on his knees. But for the sake of argument, let's say they did, thus supporting their rationale for ordering him to position his hands at his back so that his hands were in plain view.

Now here is where discretion comes into play. In showing the rapid pace at which police officers might alter their tactics, I will be referencing portions of a typical use-of-force policy published by the National Institute of Justice and used by police officers to gain control of a situation. You will then have an opportunity to judge for yourself where this situation might have fallen along that continuum.

The first level refers to the officer's presence, where visual presence of authority is typically enough for individuals to comply with an officer's lawful demands. Verbal commands are next, where in response to a police officer's legal demands, which in some instances contain consequences for failure to comply, individuals typically submit to such orders. Third in terms of levels of force are empty-hand submission techniques, including pressure point control tactics where police officers go hands-on with non-compliant individuals using a level of force that has a low probability of causing damage or bone fractures. The fourth level is hard control techniques where police officers use tactics including kicks, punches, and pepper spray to gain compliance.

Now we are nearing the high end of the threat continuum at Level 5, which is intermediate weapons whereby the amount of force is believed to have a high probability of causing soft connective tissue damage or bone fractures. These weapons include items such as batons, pepper spray, Taser, and beanbag rounds. The highest level of the threat continuum is deadly force, where an officer's actions carry a high probability of causing death or serious bodily injury.

Although we have the ability to assess this engagement without the stressors that individuals involved in such situations encounter, it is time to once again play armchair quarterback, where we ask ourselves if things were in fact handled in the most emotionally intelligent manner. Do you believe the councilman's refusal to obey the lawful orders of the police officers to position his hands at his back were grounds for the situation rising to Level 5 of the threat continuum, where the very next step in line would have been the use of deadly force if the stun gun was unsuccessful in gaining compliance? While you ponder that question, I would like to provide more information by noting that it is common for suspects to disobey the initial orders of police officers, which requires officers to go hands-on. What are your thoughts about the tactics noted in Level 3 of the threat continuum? Do you believe those tactics would have been sufficient in this case, where by the councilman being in a vulnerable position on his knees with both arms at his side, the officer could have easily taken his arm and, using pressure point control techniques, forced Miller to the ground and placed the handcuffs on him? This is something to consider when forming your opinions relative to the rightness or wrongness surrounding how the police officers handled this situation.

The last competency I would like to address within this scenario pertains to **political awareness**, which involves accurately reading situations and external realities. The realities of this situation are that the officers are employed by the same police department that made national news not too long before this incident, when Sandra Bland was discovered hanging in her jail cell. This in no way excuses the conduct of Councilman Miller, who was out of line and in clear violation of law by not backing away from the scene when ordered to do so by the police officers. The point I am making refers to the statement made earlier that "You can be right and still be wrong," particularly when operating in accordance with police protocol instead of weighing other options in light of external realities.

References

Cleaver, E. (n.d.). Eldridge Cleaver quotes. Retrieved from http://www.brainyquote.com/quotes/quotes/e/eldridgecl163 167.html

Cooper, A., & Smith, E. (2011). *Homicide trends in the United States, 1980–2008*. Washington, DC: Bureau of Justice Statistics.

Goff, P., Eberhardt, J., Williams, M., & Jackson, M. (2008). Not yet human: Implicit knowledge, historical dehumanization, and contemporary consequences. *Journal of Personality and Social Psychology, 94*(2), 292.

National Institute of Justice. (2009). The use-of-force continuum. Retrieved from http://www.nij.gov/topics/law-enforcement/officer-safety/use-of-force/pages/continuum.aspx

U.S. Department of Justice, Civil Rights Division. (2015). Department of Justice report on the Ferguson, Mo. Police Department. Retrieved from https://archive.org/details /ferguson-police-department-report-doj

5

Bridging The Gap Between Police And Communities

Alone we can do so little; together we can do so much

—*Helen Keller*

This section explores the need for change on several fronts connected with bridging the gap between police officers and local communities, and I highlight some of the previously mentioned EQ competencies by showing the role they play in effective communication. I begin this section by noting that an honest assessment of race relations in America shows that while things are significantly better than they were during the Jim Crow days, an undercurrent continues to permeate societal thought, where social class distinctions based on race routinely emerge during the assessment of crimes where African Americans are involved, regardless of whether they are the perpetrators or the victims. One example of this was the Trayvon Martin incident.

As I indicated in an earlier chapter, I responded to this incident by speaking with my son about the clothing he wore, out of fear that he would somehow give someone an excuse to cause him harm. Still, I recall engaging in conversations with several others who supported the taking of this young man's life as a justified shooting, and nothing would make them change their positions. After all, everyone has the right to defend him or herself, and there was evidence that Trayvon was shot only after he attempted to cause injury to the person who eventually became the assailant. That was their position, and evaluating this situation through a different perspective seemed out of the question until I proposed a scenario where an off-duty African American police officer living in an exclusive neighborhood situated in one of the stand-your-ground states observed a young man who just happened to be White walking down the street whom he did not recognize as someone living in the area. Bearing in mind that the officer is in plain clothes, what if the off-duty officer followed the young man, who after becoming tired of being what he considered antagonized, turned and confronted the off-duty officer in a threatening manner? Fearing for his life, the officer fired his pistol killing the young man. When things unfolded, it was learned that the young man had been estranged from his family and living on the streets for a while, which explained his tattered clothing. After tracking down where his parents had moved through an Internet search, the young man intended to surprise his parents by paying them a visit to let them know that he was trying to clean up his act and ask that he be allowed to move back home for a while.

There you have it, another sad case of mistaken identity and, similar to what occurred in the jury scene in the *A Time to Kill* film, it required a role reversal, or shall I say, race reversal, relative to both the person causing the harm and the victim, for many of the individuals I had spoken with to begin the process of gaining a better understanding of not only the frustrations felt by the African American community, but also the perceptions formed about the criminal justice system. The jury decision in the Trayvon Martin case, coupled with other similar judicial outcomes, appears to have awakened deep-seated feelings of unjust treatment within the African American community that has been played out in mass protests around the country, and the disparity that exists when comparing what takes place within African American communities to other communities is a phenomenon that must be addressed. When I contemplate the manner in which initiatives aimed at effecting meaningful change appear to fizzle out without much being accomplished, I can't help but associate the reason for change efforts failing with the following quote I stumbled across awhile back by Palmer (2014):

> A farmer is sitting on his porch in a chair, hanging out.
>
> A friend walks up to the porch to say hello, and hears an awful yelping, squealing sound coming from inside the house.
>
> "What's that terrifyin' sound?" asks the friend. "It's my dog," said the farmer.
>
> "He's sittin' on a nail."
>
> "Why doesn't he just sit up and get off it?" asks the friend.
>
> The farmer deliberates on this and replies, "Doesn't hurt enough yet."

The quote is an excellent example of how individuals might elect to do nothing as long as their circumstances are tolerable. Such a stance appears to be exactly what is taking place in many inner-city neighborhoods where efforts toward meaningful change are slow. Subscribing to the adage grin-and-bear-it makes sense in some situations; however, delaying the implementation of important change initiatives while the relationship between police officers and local neighborhoods approaches a point of disrepair does not seem to be a viable strategy.

Who Ever Said That All Lives Did Not Matter?

Similar to alcoholics taking the first step toward recovery by admitting that they have a drinking problem, acknowledgment on the part of the law enforcement community that monumental problems exist between police officers and the public would be an important step toward bridging the gap between police and citizen relations. Similarly, members of the public must accept that not all of the negative engagements between private citizens and police officers are the result of police officer misconduct. Rather than engaging in a staring game to see which side blinks first, any real closure of the gap between the two sides will necessitate a paradigm shift within the minds of the police officers and the manner in which the public treats police officers, particularly in light of the fact that the majority of police become law enforcement officers to protect and to serve communities.

To eliminate obstacles standing in the way of meaningful engagements between police officers and local communities, initiatives are taking place across the country to bring private citizens and the law enforcement community face-to-face to engage in honest dialogue with the purpose of developing a broader understanding of the perceptions each side holds of the other. A prevailing theme that appears to surface at these types of meetings involves the issue of respect, where community members, particularly in the inner city, have an overwhelming sense of being disrespected and, in some instances, devalued by police officers. One of the greatest positives coming out of the meetings however is willingness on the part of police officers to both listen to the expressed concerns of the community and provide clarity to issues wherever possible.

Okay, time to address another elephant that sits among us: the Black Lives Matter movement. Although activists sympathizing with the group insist their efforts are geared toward ensuring issues such as police reform remain part of the national conversation, at times the tactics used by the group are not strategic and detract from a very important message. This is particularly noticeable when opportunities for local community members to meet with city officials are adjourned without any meaningful dialogue ever taking place.

Such an incident occurred in South Los Angeles on October 19, 2015, when Mayor Eric Garcetti was confronted by approximately 50 of the group's supporters while at a town hall meeting, forcing him to be abruptly escorted out of the meeting by police officers. There have been a number of other occasions where group sympathizers have disrupted events around the country with the intent of being heard to the dismay of many, including some members of the African American community. Many fear that the group's tactics, while certainly capable of gaining public attention, at the same time lend themselves to being a barrier to meaningful change by continually disrupting speaking engagements featuring civic leaders who are in a position to facilitate improved relationships between police officers and local communities.

There are and have been a multitude of ways of responding to the Black Lives Matter movement. Sometimes the response comes in the form of a simple retort that "all lives matter," which on the surface actually makes plenty of sense when evaluating this assertion purely within the context of the value we all should place on human life; however, at the same time, such a retort merely dismisses the problem that brought about such a statement in the first place. At other times, activists are removed from venues, such as the 2016 March for the White House, when group members interrupted candidates who were speaking at rallies.

The Black Lives Matter movement has been successful in capturing national attention through pushing the issue of criminal justice. Consider the number of times actions on the part of activists have been covered in the media or how the topic of conversation during many of the 2016 presidential debates involved police treatment of African Americans. As successful as the group may have been in terms of ensuring police shootings remain in the public spotlight, their tactics continue to generate backlash that is often verbally and sometimes physically violent, which results in the message being lost. As a point of clarification, as we continue to advance through our conversation, the statement "Black lives matter" was never meant to insinuate that only Black lives are important, nor was it meant to insinuate that the lives of individuals who are not of African American descent are any less important. Perhaps the statement would have been more palatable, and met with less resistance, had it included just one more word, so that it read, "Black lives ALSO matter."

Although I am not trying to assemble a herd, it's time to discuss another elephant. In attempting to explain the backdrop of some of the discord between local communities and police officers, there is no getting around discussing police officers slain in the line of duty. I will first discuss the term *in the line of duty*, which speaks to the expectations associated with the job of policing among the law enforcement community. Beyond that, when an officer is killed in the line of duty, it means that the officer paid the ultimate sacrifice in the quest to protect our society.

Earlier in the book, I discussed how my former colleague Kim was killed in the line of duty, and now I would like to add to that discussion by briefly describing the unenviable responsibility, but honor nonetheless, of representing my agency at the funeral services of police officers during my time in law enforcement. Although the death of a police officer typically does not generate the attention given to alleged police abuses, at one time or another, you may have learned through the media about the gathering of police officers from around the country assembling to pay tribute to a fallen comrade. What is often lost in the enormity of the crowd is the hurt felt by the family, friends, and colleagues of the fallen officer who experience the same emotions of any other member of our society coping with the loss of a loved one.

Of the countless memorial services of fallen police officers I have attended, one in particular continues to weigh on my mind, although I never had the pleasure of meeting the officer. On February 7, 2008, a 27-year veteran of the Los Angeles Police Department (LAPD) named Randal David

266

Simmons lost his life during a shootout with a suspect in the Valley Community of Winnetka, becoming the first LAPD Special Weapons and Tactics (SWAT) officer to die in the line of duty. As I sat in silence among the thousands of people who filled the Crenshaw Christian Center's Faith Dome on February 15, 2008, to pay respect to the fallen officer, I was acutely mindful that SWAT officers are members of highly trained paramilitary units that tackle situations beyond the capability of conventional police forces. Still, the sobering thought that washed over me was that none of us is capable of escaping harm under the right conditions, not even an individual as highly trained as Officer Simmons was. While listening to the lyrical tribute by the Grammy-Award-winning American contemporary gospel duo Mary Mary, the reflections of a life lived well from the fallen officer's colleagues and family who referred to him as a good friend, loyal partner, and an exemplary officer revealed what it was about the officer that made him special and allowed him to rise above the crowd.

While Officer Simmons was a full-fledged SWAT officer, more than anything else, his character is what made him different. During his memorial service, I learned that he had a strong Christian faith that was central to his being. I learned that Officer Simmons was a minister known to his congregation as "Minister Randy," and that he was a humble person who shared an unconditional love of Christ. I also learned that in his capacity as minister, Officer Simmons led evangelism for 11 years, focusing much of his attention on children's outreach programs throughout South Los Angeles, Watts, Carson, Compton, and Long Beach, and while the depth of this officer's commitment to help others is without question very special, there are police officers all across the United States trying to make a difference in society in their own unique way, even though such valiant efforts often go unnoticed.

We will now further our attempt at better understanding the perspectives of police officers and private citizens by once again applying some of the EQ competencies; however, to get the most out of this discussion, it is important that we also recognize that many of the problems occurring in the African American community are isolated solely to those communities. Research studies have supported this for quite some time, but even without the backing of empirical evidence, we know what our eyes and hearts tell us and whether we are being honest with what is before us.

Where's The EQ?

Empathy, not to be confused with sympathy, relates to sensing another person's feelings and perspectives. Empathy refers to the ability to listen effectively and accurately enough to put yourself in another person's shoes. This is not to say that you agree with the other person, but that you can at least understand the situation from the other person's point of view. Using empathy as the foundation in which we assess what is taking place in the inner city, let's try to imagine the pain and frustration felt by individuals weighted down by a perception that they and everyone like them are being unfairly targeted by police officers and there is nothing they can do to stop it.

What does this have to do with the earlier discussion on the Black Lives Matter movement? Think back to when this group first began gaining media recognition following the death of young African American men, where in the vast majority of cases, individuals in the inner city were left with feelings of being let down by the judicial system. In response to such incidents, the mantra "Black lives matter" became somewhat of a rallying cry primarily within the African American community, but also by those not in the community who also sensed racial injustice when evaluating the treatment of African Americans by police officers when compared to other citizens.

On a side note, for years my wife collected refrigerator magnets, and there was one in particular that would always cause me to stop and try to figure out what it really meant. The magnet stated, "I holler because you don't listen to me when I talk normal," and although I had no idea if that message was meant for me or for our children, it was a powerful statement all the same. When I take stock of what I believe to be the real message the Black Lives Matter group is attempting to disseminate, disruptions and all, my thoughts drift back to the magnet that used to hang on our refrigerator, and that is where I find empathy for the group. I do not agree with some of their tactics, particularly when disruptions are carried out within a house of worship, but in a much broader sense, I understand where the group is coming from. The group is bringing to the forefront a legitimate issue that must be addressed, and pretending problems do not exist, or attempts at either wishing it away or kicking the can in hope that such issues will simply vanish with time, is not the answer, because the Black Lives Matter group will continue to "holler" if that is what they believe it will take for them to be heard.

The Bind Between Police Officers and Local Communities

The top reasons police officers and local communities need to find common ground relate to the common thread or symbiotic relationship linking the two together. A symbiotic relationship is a special type of interaction between species that is sometimes beneficial and sometimes harmful. These relationships are essential to many organisms and ecosystems, and they provide a balance that can only be achieved by working together. Service to the community is a major part of what police officers do; however, the ability to serve where it truly makes a difference often depends upon the cooperation police officers receive from those affected within the local community.

For example, because crimes are typically not committed in the presence of police officers, assistance from the community in developing leads used to identify those believed to have committed the criminal act often makes the difference between whether criminals are ever brought to justice. Without question, forensics represent a large portion of police work, however, as I am sure you are aware, what is typically portrayed on television is for entertainment and is not characteristic of how things actually work in the field. As such, without viable leads and the public's assistance, there is a chance a criminal case might become stale, leading to it being archived in a file cabinet until new information is developed by police officers warranting a renewed focus on the investigation. In illustrating the importance of fostering such a relationship, let's apply the systems thinking philosophy of systems scientist Peter

Senge to this equation, where the linkages and interactions between the components that comprise the entirety of a defined system are continually examined.

Where's The EQ?

In accordance with this concept, if we were to frame the relationship between the law enforcement community and the public as a system in which police officers and community members are critical elements, failure would occur anytime there was a breakdown between and within the system elements that must work together for overall success. These types of relationships also require that individuals possess two critical EQ competencies: **building bonds** and **trustworthiness**. The building bonds competency is where individuals build rapport with others through seeking mutually beneficial relationships, while trustworthiness relates to trust established through authenticity, where individuals not only admit when they have made a mistake, but also hold others accountable for unethical actions. As discussed throughout this book, many of the problems linked to the divide between police officers and community members appear to spin off from perceptions of unfairness where there is a belief that police officers are allowed to conduct themselves as if they are above the law, and only through addressing perceived inconsistencies will the public begin to view the law enforcement community as equal partners in fighting crime and begin to work with police officers to protect local communities.

Altering Publicly Held Paradigms of American Policing

Clearly, much work still needs to be done on the part of police organizations to improve relations with the neighborhoods they serve, from creating a dialogue with local communities where members have an opportunity to voice their concerns to ensuring hiring matrices in place are capable of identifying recruits who possess the soft skills rather than focusing solely on individuals accomplished in areas such as marksmanship, hand-to-hand combat, or interrogation. Questions that will likely be raised well into the future pertain to hiring practices of the Cleveland Police Department, and whether an inclusion of EQ competencies among the criteria used in deciding whether to hire the police officer involved in the shooting death of Tamir Rice, coupled with actually reading the officer's personnel file from his earlier employment with the Independence Police Department, would have made a difference in him making it onto the force, particularly in light of his reported emotional immaturity, where the officer was said to be incapable of maintaining composure under stressful situations, which lead to him being allowed to resign from his prior job as a police officer months earlier (Dewan & Oppel, 2015).

When it comes to creating harmony between the law enforcement community and the public, change geared exclusively toward policing will likely be insufficient in fully closing the gap that exists between police officers and local communities without change simultaneously taking place relative to the perceptions the public holds of police officers. Although they are often called in to clean up the mess, police officers are not to blame for all the bad that exists within our society. For example, a good share of the problems we encounter can just as easily be associated with things outside of the purview of policing, such as poor education, contempt for authority, disregard for human life, or the failure to hold individuals accountable for their actions.

For our next example, let's consider the incident that occurred on October 27, 2015, at a high school in South Carolina, where a deputy police officer serving as the school's resource officer was captured on video pulling a young girl from her seat and then tossing her across the classroom after she refused the officer's commands to stand up so that she could be removed from the classroom for disorderly conduct. The video is alarming, particularly when taking into account the sheer size and strength of the officer compared to the young girl who, although she was noncompliant and disruptive, was merely sitting in her classroom chair and not posing a threat at the time. The officer was fired within 72 hours after the incident for what the sheriff described as failure to follow proper procedures. The sheriff was likely referring to the many options police officers have at their disposal to gain compliance of uncooperative individuals, none of which include tossing someone across the room.

Before we dive into this situation further, let's bring into the discussion a somewhat similar incident that occurred the next day at Florin High School in California, leading to the arrest of two 15-year-old students and one 13-year-old student. During that incident, one of the students involved in the fight threw the school principal to the ground when the principal attempted to break up the skirmish. The video then showed the principal engaging one of the students, where he appears to be grabbing the student around his neck in an effort to separate the young man from the fight. We can now assess both situations from the perspective of whether having a police presence on school campus is a good idea, being that the subject has been largely debated following the South Carolina incident.

Many individuals I have spoken with about the South Carolina incident suggested that police officers have no business on school campuses, rationalizing that it is the responsibility of school administrators and not the police to bring order to chaotic situations where students are involved. Most would agree that the officer's actions when he threw the young girl across the room because she refused to get out of her classroom seat and leave the room were excessive. Some have even said that his actions were criminal. What is interesting however is when I ask those believing that the officer's actions warrant criminal sanctions what steps the officer should have taken to get the student to leave the room when she refused the instruction of her teacher and ignored the police officer when he also asked her to get out of her seat. The answer I am typically told is something like, "Just allow her to sit there among the other students while the school administrators contact her parents to come to the school and remove her."

When prodding for more information about why one student should be allowed to stand in the way of other students getting the education they came to class to receive, the usual response is that it has to be that way because no adult should put a hand on a student when in class. And then it comes out, a statement that police officers think that they are God and that people are just supposed to obey them when they speak. This is where we can interject EQ into this situation and perhaps better understand the feelings of some of the individuals looking at this from the outside, as well as how it might apply to the actions taken by the police officer.

Where's The EQ?

The officer was wrong in terms of the tactics he used. When police officers go hands-on with people they intend to arrest, the tactics do not involve hurling the individuals across a room. Had the police officer simply taken the student's arm and, using approved police tactics, forced her arm behind her back, she would have been more than amenable to standing up and following whatever orders the police officer had given her, and, more importantly, his actions would have likely fallen within departmental policy. Regardless of the officer's past record, in this particular incident, he fell short on the **emotional awareness** competency by not recognizing how his own feelings would affect his performance. In watching the video, the officer was clearly giving the student an opportunity to comply before he decided to force the issue, which was also likely the point where his patience waned and he lost his composure. Those actions are indicative of someone lacking in the area of **self-control**, when an individual is unable to remain composed, think clearly, and stay focused under pressure.

The **adaptability** and **innovativeness** EQ competencies would have been beneficial here. Think back to the suggestion made by some individuals that the student should have been allowed to stay in the classroom while school administrators called her parents to come and pick her up. While on the surface that sounds like a tremendous waste of time for the other students, what about allowing the disruptive student to stay in the classroom by herself? Why couldn't the other students be removed and placed in another classroom, the cafeteria, or the school auditorium, where they might have been able to continue with their learning?

Undoubtedly this would have challenged traditional thinking, but desperate times call for desperate measures, and similar to what would be considered appropriate actions when engaging noncompliant individuals during a sit-in, innovative thought is critical when those in an authoritative position must consider new perspectives to handle a problem at hand. The last emotionally intelligent way of possibly handling this situation would involve the **conflict management** EQ competency, where individuals possessing this skill are able to spot potential conflict and deescalate the situation before it gets out of hand. Again, the goal is to view this as we have viewed other volatile engagements between police officers and the public, which is through an EQ lens rather than allowing whatever biases that might dwell within us to thwart our ability to assess these types of situations.

Along those lines, we will spend a moment addressing the public outcry calling for the prosecution of the officer after the video was released that showed the aggressive nature in which the officer handled the student. We can use the EQ competencies in assessing the public's reaction to this event as well. Just as is typical with many other situations, not everyone sided with the student after reviewing the video. For instance, some individuals I have spoken with about this situation actually felt the police officer was placed in a no-win situation when he was called to the classroom to try to restore order and found himself face-to-face with a defiant student who demonstrated a lack of respect for authority, particularly when she was the cause of the conflict requiring the officer to be summoned in the first place.

The EQ competency that will be used for this example is **emotional awareness**. While some individuals focused primarily on the wrongdoing associated with the officer's conduct, the fact is the student was not blameless in this situation. As discussed during a few of the scenarios, emotional awareness is where individuals clearly understand which emotions they are experiencing and the reasons behind them, which brings us to the question were the reactions of those calling for the immediate firing of the police officer the result of perceived excessive force where some individuals have stated that nobody outside of parents have the right to put their hands on students within the school environment? Perhaps what is actually at play here are deep-seated emotions linked to an overwhelming perception of disparate treatment by police officers as it pertains to engaging African Americans. Again, none of this is meant to excuse the officer's actions, but it is equally important to at least consider how our emotions are capable of clouding our judgment, particularly in light of the varying conclusions drawn by those who viewed the video relative to where fault rests in what transpired between the police officer and the student.

A quick glance at social media makes it clear that some lines have been drawn in the sand representing a divide in thinking over this incident, where just like those who believe the officer's actions overshadow any behavior on the part of the student, some of those commenting on this issue believe that the officer did no wrong. Before brushing such opinions off as nonsensical, it is important to be mindful that individuals are guided by their own perceptions that stems from their respective environmental experiences, and as such, it is not uncommon to see different conclusions drawn from the same situation. For instance, many of those I have engaged in conversation about the South Carolina school incident are educators or have friends or family members who work within the educational system.

I found it interesting that while there appeared to be an overwhelming consensus that the police officer's actions were out of control, there was also consensus surrounding the difficulties faced by educators who seemingly have no authority when it comes to controlling unruly students. This brings us to the second school incident I spoke of earlier that occurred at Florin High School the day after the South Carolina school incident. The video showing the school principal affected many who work within the school system, as expressed in comments suggesting that while educators strive to maintain an environment conducive to student learning, the control they have within the classroom is severely hampered by uncooperative and disruptive students.

While some of the educators I spoke with admitted that they have personally experienced the same frustration the police officer must have felt in the South Carolina incident, particularly in light of what occurred the following day at

Florin High School when the school principal was thrown to the ground by a student, the majority believed that schools were better served by resource officers who possessed the skills to differentiate between administrative and criminal behavior. This would mean that the only time resource officers elevated beyond their role as mediator would be for situations truly warranting a law enforcement response. While a fair question at this point likely pertains to what exactly is meant by *warranting a law enforcement response*, the incident involving a school resource officer that occurred at Reach Partnership High in Baltimore, Maryland, on March 1, 2016, complicated things even further.

On the video that surfaced over the Internet, a resource officer is overheard using profanity and observed repeatedly slapping and kicking a young man. The initial media discussions of this incident focused on whether the young man was a student at the school or an unruly trespasser. That should have been a moot point when taking into account the conduct of the school resource officer when compared to what is widely considered acceptable treatment of private citizens.

In what might be perceived by some as a public relations move, an important first step in this investigation was the quick response by the head of the Baltimore school police force who placed two officers on administrative leave following the incident. Even though school resource officers and members of the Baltimore Police Department have separate reporting structures, because individuals who wear a uniform and badge are typically seen as the same, the conduct of the school resource officer further added to the distrust citizens already have of police officers. For example, Baltimore's mayor Stephanie Rawlings-Blake described the actions of the officer in the video as appalling in a statement that speaks to the net negative effect out-of-control police behavior has on the relationship between law enforcement and local communities.

An even larger problem may rest within the following statement made to the Baltimore media by a local citizen in response to the school incident: "He's lucky that wasn't my little brother because I would be in jail right now. He had no right doing that." For the moment, let's forget about the massive scrutiny the police profession has come under for questionable tactics in recent years and consider the implication of citizens becoming emboldened to the point of taking matters into their own hands in response to perceived police abuse as expressed by this individual. While the chaos resulting from such a backlash against police officers is something I do not believe any member of our society would truly want to experience, the way forward will likely include the implementation of processes within the police profession geared toward gaining the public's trust.

Restoring the Image of Law Enforcement

It is well known that bad news travels much faster than good news, and the law enforcement community is no exception to that rule. With all the negative publicity police officers have encountered throughout the media, it seems that anytime a news story involves encounters between police and the public, negative thoughts are typically the first to come to mind, as if police officers are bad guys. This is not to say that the less than ethical conduct on the part of a marginal percentage of police officers has not played a role in creating such an unfavorable perception of the police profession, but like everything else, there is another side of police work.

Because of the antipolicing sentiment that is lingering within our society, changing the minds of the public will not be easy. Think about how quickly negative images spread due to the enormous reach of social media, where seemingly every encounter between police officers and the public is captured on video and shown to the world audience well before the investigation into what actually occurred takes place. Because the commentary and images that appear to gain the most public attention are the ones that show police officers using questionable tactics, they further cement the negative images into the minds of those who do not hold police officers in high regard.

Earlier in the book, I asked for your response relative to being faced with an active-shooter situation, where the logical answer for most was assumed to be take cover or run. I also addressed the routine actions of police officers when faced with similar situations, where officers instinctively advance toward the threat rather than retreat. Although this does not apply to everyone, it often takes a traumatic incident or some other devastation such as the mass shooting on December 2, 2015, in San Bernardino, California, where 14 people were killed and 22 seriously injured in a terrorist attack, for some people to appreciate the sacrifices police officers make for the sake of protecting the public.

The good work on the part of police officers is not isolated to the type of horrific incident described in the above example, but is often present during routine encounters with the public. The Internet is flooded with good deeds done by police officers serving the public through helpful acts such as changing flat tires for motorists, mowing lawns for elderly persons, buying meals for the homeless, or helping children learn to read or ride a bicycle, all of which, aside from being indicative of the attributes described in the EQ competencies previously discussed, also demonstrate how rather than requiring any type of heroics on the part of police officers, compassion is often found among the simplest acts of kindness. Through my writing and blogging, I have attempted to accomplish a balanced perspective relative to the good and not-so-good side of American policing. Much of what I contemplate can be found on my Facebook page at B. Bernard Ferguson Ph.D.

With each of us having the ability to grow from being exposed to varying perspectives, it is important that we also supplement our thinking with positive aspects of policing, because just like the negative experiences we often hear about, there is a lot of good out there as well. I am fairly confident that each of us can recall at least one example either from the media, or knowledge acquired through other sources, where police officers have received praise for assisting with the birth of an infant on the side of the road or perhaps for using their training to perform CPR or the Heimlich maneuver to save someone's life. While the above acts are typically classified as valiant on the part of police officers, the following example of an encounter between a police officer and a youth, which, although it occurred a short time before the untimely death of the officer resulting from an event unrelated to the encounter that is about to be described, is not uncommon within routine police work.

In the encounter that was captured on surveillance video at a McDonald's restaurant in San Diego, California, in 2011, an African American boy approached police officer Jeremy Henwood and asked for 10 cents so that he could buy some cookies. After Officer Henwood purchased the cookies for the boy, he took the time to ask the young man what he wanted to be when he grew up, which is something that made an impression on the boy, as seen in a subsequent video following the death of the police officer, where the boy spoke about his positive encounter with Officer Henwood. This was the final act of kindness Officer Henwood performed, as he was fatally shot shortly after leaving the restaurant while sitting in his police vehicle at a stoplight.

Where's The EQ?

Officer Henwood demonstrated several EQ competencies during his conversation with the young man, starting with **adaptability**, where individuals possessing this competency are able to adapt their responses to fit fluid situations. It is doubtful that the officer entered the restaurant with the expectation of being approached by a child asking for money; however, his actions demonstrated that he was a quick thinker and able to switch gears on the spot. The next competency the officer demonstrated was **initiative**, which pertains to individuals being ready to seize the moment. After paying for the young man's order, Officer Henwood took the time to engage him in dialogue, which required him to project into the future about what he wanted to be when he grew up and demonstrated that the officer possessed excellent **communication** skills, which is a key EQ competency.

Another EQ competency that was present during the brief conversation between the officer and the young man was **leveraging diversity**, which involves respecting and relating well to people from varied backgrounds. An excessive amount of imagination is not necessary to envision a situation where someone being approached by another person asking for money while standing in line to purchase food tells the person to back away or just ignores them. Here, the officer looked beyond the many stereotypes regarding race and just saw a child who wanted a dime to purchase some cookies, and although it was only a request for 10 cents, we know that not everyone would have responded with the same compassion as Officer Henwood. These types of acts by police officers rarely if ever generate anywhere near the degree of attention on social media that we have come to expect from an allegation of police misconduct.

The reason might have something to do with such encounters being considered mundane, or perhaps the reason for paying more attention to negative encounters between police officers and the public is the result of people tending to have a negativity bias, where, according to Morewedge (2009), because bad news has a greater impact on our lives, individuals tend to focus more on negative information than on positive information. Although there have been numerous positive engagements between police officers and private citizens, in order to change public perception relative to the police profession, the law enforcement community must first change from within, such that police officers are not only held accountable but also rewarded through placement in positions of influence, where they can truly create workable relationships between themselves and the communities they serve. A good start would be for the law enforcement community to begin recruiting more police officers who possess the level of EQ demonstrated by Officer Jeremy Henwood, a fallen hero.

Epilogue

Given the negative publicity the law enforcement community has experienced, particularly following questionable shooting deaths of private citizens, examining engagements between police officers and the public has provided quite possibly the best platform for assessing the potential benefits of EQ when used in deescalating volatile situations and building goodwill within local communities.

Where's The EQ?

While this book was used primarily to assess some of the more high-profile engagements that have occurred between police officers and private citizens, the EQ competencies discussed throughout the chapters are without question applicable to everyone, regardless of their profession. Countless studies have shown that EQ skills can be separated into two categories: *intrapersonal*, which includes **self-awareness**, **self-regulation**, and **self-motivation**, and *interpersonal*, which pertain to skills such as **empathy** and **nurturing relationships**. It has become evident that the better developed a person's intrapersonal skills are, the easier it is for them to demonstrate their interpersonal skills, but more important, unlike an individual's IQ that is fixed early in life, EQ can be learned and enhanced through focusing on specific areas where an individual might be lacking.

Although the failure on the part of a select number of police officers to uphold the honor of the badge has tainted the trust many people have in the police profession, the gap representing the divide between police officers and civilians is not entirely the fault of the law enforcement community, but rather is symptomatic of a plethora of other forces at play within our society, including our perceptions, beliefs, and biases, all of which ultimately set the stage for how each of us thinks and acts. While we might be looking, we are not really seeing one another. If private citizens could really *see* police officers, they would come to know that the majority of officers do want to make a positive difference in our society and that these brave men and women have families and often experience similar frustrations about the state of American policing with regard to being able to bridge the gap between law enforcement and local communities.

If police organizations could *see* themselves, they would focus more attention on ensuring that individuals brought onto the force were adept at human relations skills and not just marksmanship or the physical skills needed to overpower suspects during arrest situations. If police officers could *see* private citizens, they would understand that the power they wield rests not with the firearms they carry, but instead within their ability to truly make a difference in society by upholding their oath, thereby garnering the respect of the communities they are sworn to protect and to serve. If we as a society could *see* one another, we would accept that although none of us was created the same, none of us has a greater right to freedom over another. Further, we would understand that each of us acts in accordance with our perceptions and that anytime we engage another person, be it positive or negative, even if only slightly, we are impacting the perceptions that person holds about the world.

From the time I began writing this book, I have deliberated about how I wanted to end it, and after a few sleepless nights following the deaths of Alton Sterling and Philando Castile at the hands of police officers, I knew that I had gone as far as I needed with my writing, and the time had come to make preparations for publishing my thoughts. A day later, another unthinkable act occurred when a sniper, in an apparent revenge plot, shot and killed Dallas police officers Brent Thompson, Patrick Zamarripa, Michael Krol, Lorne Ahrens, and Michael Smith. Seven additional police officers sustained injuries during the violent attack. Within 10 days of the Dallas shootings, while many mourned the loss of officers killed in the line of duty, tragedy once again struck the law enforcement community when a gunman fired shots at officers in Baton Rouge, Louisiana, injuring three and killing police officers Montrell Jackson, Matthew Gerald, and Sheriff Deputy Brad Garafola.

The hurtful truth is that racial policing does in fact exist. The question we must all contemplate is where do we go from here? I know for certain that subscribing to a notion of an eye for an eye will solve nothing, nor will spewing inflammatory comments such as the following tweet circulating on social media (before being deleted) : "3 Dallas Cops killed, 7 wounded. This is now war. Watch out Obama. Watch out black lives matter punks. Real America is coming after you" (Skiba & Crepeau, 2016).

Such hatred speaks to the crux of the dynamic I have attempted to address throughout my writing. In that, our life experiences create our perceptions, which often become our reality. Each of us is then guided by our belief system, which largely stems from the above-mentioned correlations. Empathy is one of the cornerstones of EQ and involves understanding why another person might feel a certain way, even if we do not agree with the particular position. Do I agree with the messaging of the tweet? Of course not. However, I do understand how the individual may have formed his or her frame of reference, which would then compel that individual to respond in such a manner based on the perception of where blame should be assigned for the shooting of police officers in Dallas.

This book has been about EQ, the ability to manage our own emotions, and the emotions of those with whom we engage. Studies have shown that individuals who possess higher levels of EQ are significantly better at navigating through difficult situations by being present in the moment and by clearly understanding what is taking place in the world around them. These are the skills police officers must possess in the 21st century, and while they are well beyond the type of competencies sometimes preferred in applicants seeking employment within law enforcement, such as being physically fit or possessing above-average marksmanship, what is important is that *EQ can be learned.*

There are many opportunities for the law enforcement community to improve, and while continuing to ignore the demands for change coming from communities across our nation might lead to a path of least resistance, bridging the gap between police officers and local communities necessitates that we begin to hold each other accountable and confront wrongdoing whenever and wherever it occurs. This means that everyone within our society must take a stand akin to the child in the fairy tale *The Emperor's New Clothes*, who rose above the crowd by having the courage to cry out that the emperor was not wearing anything at all, while others stood by silently, despite what they knew to be true. Demonstrators should, and must, continue exercising their constitutional rights, to petition the government peacefully regarding grievances pertaining to disparate treatment by police officers. The operative word here is *peacefully*, because while protests may bring attention to a problem, real change will likely occur from behind a desk.

What must not be diminished in all of this is the pivotal role the law enforcement community plays within our society and the selfless acts of bravery on the part of our men and women in blue, as the majority of police officers put their lives on the line daily to make all of us safe. At the beginning of this book, I talked about my time in Washington, DC, and the emotions I experienced while listening to the lyrics of "A Change is Gonna Come" during President Barack Obama's preinaugural ceremonies. I often reflect upon that occasion, still hopeful and knowing that change does not come without a struggle, and while change may be uncomfortable at times, it is often necessary. This is one of those times, and each of us has a unique opportunity to facilitate changes to the tone of engagements between police officers and the public. However, change will only occur by first understanding what and why we feel a particular way about that which we encounter and then challenging our own paradigms in such a way that we begin to *see* not only ourselves, but each other, through an EQ lens.

References

Dewan, S., & Oppel, R. (2015, January 23). In Tamir Rice case, many errors by Cleveland police, then a fatal one. *New York Times.* Retrieved from http://www.nytimes.com

Morewedge, C. K. (2009). Negativity bias in attribution of external agency. *Journal of Experimental Psychology: General, 138,* 535-545. doi:10.1037/a0016796

Palmer, A. (2014). *The art of asking: How I learned to stop worrying and let people help.* New York, NY: Grand Central Publishing.

Skiba, K., & Crepeau, M. (2016, July 8). Ex-Illinois Rep. Walsh says Twitter made him take down Dallas tweet 'Watch out Obama.' *Chicago Tribune.* Retrieved from http://www.chicagotribune.com

Bibliography

Akintayo, D. I. (2010). Influence of emotional intelligence on work-family role conflict management and reduction in withdrawal intentions of workers in private organizations. *International Business & Economics Research Journal, 9*(12), 131-140. Retrieved from http://journals.cluteonline.com/index.php/IBER/

Andreescu, V., & Vito, G. (2010). An exploratory study on ideal leadership behaviour: The opinions of American police managers. *International Journal of Police Science & Management, 12,* 567-583. doi:10.1350/ijps.2010.12.4.207

Antonakis, J., Ashkanasy, N., & Dasborough, M. (2009). Theoretical and practitioner letters: Does leadership need emotional intelligence? *Leadership Quarterly, 20,* 247-261. doi:10.1016/j.leaqua.2009.01.006

Avolio, B. J., & Bass, B. M. (2002). *Developing potential across a full range of leadership.* Mahwah, NJ: Erlbaum.

Avolio, B. J., Bass, B. M., & Jung, D. I. (1999). Re-examining the components of transformational and transactional leadership using the multifactor leadership questionnaire. *Journal of Occupational and Organizational Psychology, 72,* 441-462. doi:10.1348%2F096317999166789

Aycicegi-Dinn, A., & Caldwell-Harris, C. (2011). Individualism-collectivism among Americans, Turks and Turkish immigrants to the U.S. *International Journal of Intercultural Relations, 35,* 9-16. doi:10.1016/j.ijintrel.2010.11.006

Baker, D., & Hyde, M. (2011). Police have customers too. *Police Practice & Research, 12,* 148-162. doi:10.1080/15614263.2010.512131

Banner, D. K., & Tippins, S. (2011). Of anarchy, structure and organizational effectiveness. *Leadership & Organizational Management Journal,* 2011(3), 103. Retrieved from http://www.franklinpublishing.net/leadership.html

Bannon, B. (2014). America's Racial Divisions. U.S. News Digital Weekly, 6(34), 19.

Baran, B. E., & Scott, C. W. (2010). Organizing ambiguity: A grounded theory of leadership and sensemaking within dangerous contexts. *Military Psychology*, *22*(Suppl. 1), S42-S69. doi:10.1080/08995601003644262

Bar-On, R. (1988). *The development of a concept of psychological well-being* (Unpublished doctoral dissertation). Rhodes University, South Africa.

Bar-On, R. (1997). *The Emotional Quotient Inventory (EQ-i): A test of emotional intelligence.* Toronto, Canada: Multi-Health Systems.

Bar-On, R. (2010). Emotional intelligence: An integral part of positive psychology. *South African Journal of Psychology*, 40, 54-62. Retrieved from http://www.journals.co.za/ej/ejour_sapsyc.html

Bass, B. M. (1985). *Leadership and performance beyond expectations.* New York, NY: Free Press.

Bass, B. M., & Avolio, B. J. (1994). *Improving organizational effectiveness: Through transformational leadership.* Thousand Oaks, CA: Sage.

Bass, B. M., & Avolio, B. J. (2004). *Multifactor Leadership Questionnaire* (3rd ed.). Redwood City, CA: Mind Garden.

Batool, B. (2013). Emotional intelligence and effective leadership. *Journal of Business Studies Quarterly*, *4*(3), 84-94. Retrieved from http://jbsq.org/wp-content/uploads/2013/03/March_2013_8.pdf

Beschloss, M. (2009). The Jamestown Paradox. *Newsweek*, *153*(4-A), 56-59.

Boyatzis, R. E. (2009). Competencies as a behavioral approach to emotional intelligence. *Journal of Management Development, 28,* 749-770. doi:10.1108/02621710910987647

Bruinius, H. (2014, December 9). Eric Garner case 101: Why grand juries rarely indict police officers. Christian Science Monitor. p. N.PAG.

Bruns, G., & Shuman, I. (1988). Police managers' perception of organizational leadership styles. *Public Personnel Management, 17,* 145. Retrieved from http://ppm.sagepub.com/

Burke, W. W. (1994). *Organization development: A process of learning and changing* (2nd ed.). New York, NY: Addison-Wesley.

Burns, J. M. (1978). Leadership. New York, NY: Harper & Row.

298

Caillouet, B. A., Boccaccini, M. T., Varela, J. G., Davis, R. D., & Rostow, C. D. (2010). Predictive validity of the MMPI-2 Psy-5 scales and facets for law enforcement officer employment outcomes. *Criminal Justice and Behavior, 37,* 217-238. doi:10.1177/0093854809351948

Campbell, I., & Kodz, J. (2011). What makes great police leadership? What research can tell us about the effectiveness of different leadership styles, competencies and behaviours. A rapid evidence review. Retrieved from http://library.npia.police.uk/docs/npia/

Caruso, D. R., Mayer, J. D., & Salovey, P. (2002). Relation of an ability measure of emotional intelligence to personality. *Journal of Personality Assessment, 79,* 306-320.

Cengiz, A., Eren, E., & Erzengin, E. (2012). Determination of the relationship between leadership perceptions of blue collars and organizational outcomes by using MLQ analysis. *Procedia - Social and Behavioral Sciences, 41,* 196-208. doi:10.1016/j.sbspro.2012.04.024

Chaudhry, A., & Javed, H. (2012). Impact of transactional and laissez faire leadership style on motivation. *International Journal of Business & Social Science, 3*(7), 258-264. Retrieved from http://www.ijbssnet.com/

Chaudhry, M., & Shah, N. (2011). Impact of supportive leadership and organizational learning culture as a moderator on the relationship of psychological empowerment and organizational commitment. *Journal of Business Strategies, 5,* 39-50. Retrieved from http://www.sub.uni-hamburg.de/fr/recherche/elektronische-zeitschriften/fachgebiet//2700/J/K.html?libconnect%5Bnotation%5D=All

Cherniss, C. (2010b). Emotional intelligence: New insights and further clarifications. *Industrial and Organizational Psychology: Perspectives on Science and Practice, 3,* 183-191. doi:10.1111/j.1754-9434.2010.01222.x

Clarke, N. (2010). Emotional intelligence and its relationship to transformational leadership and key project manager competences. *Project Management Journal, 41*(2), 5-20. doi:10.1002/pmj.20162

Cohen, J. (1988). *Statistical power analysis for the behavioral sciences.* Hillsdale, NJ: Erlbaum.

Côté, S., Lopes, P. N., Salovey, P., & Miners, C. T. H. (2010). Emotional intelligence and leadership emergence in small groups. *Leadership Quarterly, 21,* 496-508. doi:10.1016/j.leaqua.2010.03.012

Creswell, J. W. (2009). *Research design qualitative, quantitative, and mixed methods approaches* (3rd ed.). Thousand Oaks, CA: Sage.

Darwin, C. R. (1872). *The expression of the emotions in man and animals*. London, England: John Murray.

Eagly, A. H., & Chin, J. (2010). Diversity and leadership in a changing world. *American Psychologist, 65,* 216-224. doi:10.1037/a0018957

Ellis, P., & Abbott, J. (2013). Leadership and management skills in health care. *British Journal of Cardiac Nursing, 8*(2), 96-99. Retrieved from http://www.cardiac-nursing.co.uk/cgi-bin/go.pl/library/article.html?uid=96522;article=cn_8_2_96

Emmerling, R. J., & Boyatzis, R. E. (2012). Emotional and social intelligence competencies: Cross cultural implications. *Cross Cultural Management, 19,* 4-18. doi:10.1108/13527601211195592

Engle, R., & Nehrt, C. (2011). Conceptual ability, emotional intelligence and relationship management: A multinational study. *Journal of Management Policy and Practice, 12*(4), 58-72. Retrieved from http://www.na-businesspress.com/jmppopen.html

Erdfelder, E., Faul, F., & Buchner, A. (1996). GPOWER: A general power analysis program. *Behavior Research Methods, Instruments, & Computers, 28,* 1-11. Retrieved from http://journalseek.net/cgi-bin/journalseek/journalsearch.cgi?field=issn&query=0743-3808

Esfahani, N., & Soflu, H. (2013). Emotional intelligence and transformational leadership in physical education managers. *Cypriot Journal of Educational Sciences, 8,* 105-120. Retrieved from http://www.awer-center.org/cjes/

Fan, H., Jackson, T., Yang, X., Tang, W., & Zhang, J. (2010). The factor structure of the Mayer-Salovey-Caruso emotional intelligence test V 2.0 (MSCEIT): A meta-analytic structural equation modeling approach. *Personality and Individual Differences, 48,* 781-785. doi:10.1016/j.paid.2010.02.004

Fazlani, T., Hassan Ansari, N., Nasar, A., Hashmi, P., & Mustafa, M. (2012). Influence of emotional intelligence and leadership performance on organizational development in the prospect of Pakistan's corporate culture. *Interdisciplinary Journal of Contemporary Research in Business, 3,* 1289-1311. Retrieved from http://ijcrb.webs.com/

Foltin, A., & Keller, R. (2012). Leading change with emotional intelligence. *Nursing Management, 43(11),* 20-25. doi:10.1097/01.NUMA.0000421675.33594.63

Gelder, J., & Vries, R. (2014). Rational Misbehavior? Evaluating an Integrated Dual-Process Model of Criminal Decision Making. *Journal Of Quantitative Criminology,* 30(1), 1-27. doi:10.1007/s10940-012-9192-8

300

Gottschalk, P., & Glomseth, R. (2012). Attitudes of police managers to different leadership roles in their jobs: An empirical study in Norway. *Journal of Leadership Studies, 6,* 23-29. doi:10.1002/jls.21225

Hahn, R., Sabou, S., Toader, R., & Rădulescu, C. (2012). About emotional intelligence and leadership. *Annals of the University of Oradea, Economic Science Series, 21,* 744-749. Retrieved from http://anale.steconomiceuoradea.ro/en/

Hargis, M. B., Watt, J. D., & Piotrowski, C. (2011). Developing leaders: Examining the role of transactional and transformational leadership across contexts business. *Organization Development Journal, 29*(3), 51-66. Retrieved from http://www.scimagojr.com/journalsearch.php?q=3900148507&tip=sid

Harms, P. D., & Credé, M. (2010). Emotional intelligence and transformational and transactional leadership: A meta-analysis. *Journal of Leadership & Organizational Studies, 17,* 5-17. doi:10.1177%2F1548051809350894

Hawkins, J., & Dulewicz, V. (2009). Relationships between leadership style, the degree of change experienced, performance and follower commitment in policing. *Journal of Change Management, 9,* 251-270. doi:10.1080/14697010903125498

Herkenhoff, L. (2010). Case study: Emotional intelligence as a differentiator in values-based healthcare communication. *Journal of Communication in Healthcare, 3,* 62-77. doi:10.1179/175380610792016428

Hersey, P., & Blanchard, K. H. (1977). *Management of organizational behavior: Utilizing human resources* (3rd ed.). Englewood Cliffs, NJ: Prentice Hall.

Hoffman, R. C., & Shipper, F. M. (2012). The impact of managerial skills on employee outcomes: a cross cultural study. *International Journal of Human Resource Management, 23,* 1414-1435. doi:10.1080/09585192.2011.581635

Hong, Y., Catano, V. M., & Liao, H. (2011). Leader emergence: The role of emotional intelligence and motivation to lead. *Leadership & Organization Development Journal, 32,* 320-343. doi:10.1108/01437731111134625

Humphrey, A. (2012). Transformational leadership and organizational citizenship behaviors: The role of organizational identification. *Psychologist-Manager Journal, 15*(4), 247-268. doi:10.1080/10887156.2012.731831

Hur, Y., van den Berg, P. T., & Wilderom, C. P. (2011). Transformational leadership as a mediator between emotional intelligence and team outcomes. *Leadership Quarterly, 22,* 591-603. doi:10.1016/j.leaqua.2011.05.002

Hwang, Y. (2012). Understanding moderating effects of collectivist cultural orientation on the knowledge sharing attitude by email. *Computers in Human Behavior,* 282169-2174. doi:10.1016/j.chb.2012.06.023

Hystad, S. W., Jarleeid, A. L., Tapia, M., & Matthews, M. (2010) An exploratory study of differences in emotional intelligence in U.S. and Norwegian undergraduate students. *Psychological Reports, 107,* 891-898. doi:10.2466/04.09.17.PRO.107.6.891.898

Ismail, A., Zainuddin, N., & Ibrahim, Z. (2010). Linking participative and consultative leadership styles to organizational commitment as an antecedent of job satisfaction. *UNITAR E-Journal, 6,* 11-26. Retrieved from http://journalseek.net/cgi-bin/journalseek/journalsearch.cgi?field=issn&query=1511-7219

Jain, A. K., Giga, S. I., & Cooper, C. L. (2009). Employee wellbeing, control and organizational commitment. *Leadership & Organization Development Journal, 30,* 256-273. doi:10.1108/01437730910949535

Jimoh, Y., Olayide, R., & Saheed, O. (2012). Influence of leadership styles and emotional intelligence on job performance of local government workers in Osun State, Nigeria. *Journal of Alternative Perspectives in the Social Sciences, 3,* 973-996. Retrieved from http://www.japss.org/

Jin, K. K., & Drozdenko, R. (2010). Relationships among perceived organizational core values, corporate social responsibility, ethics, and organizational performance outcomes: An empirical study of information technology professionals. *Journal of Business Ethics, 92,* 341-359. doi:10.1007/s10551-009-0158-1

Johnson, R. R. (2012). Police officer job satisfaction: A multidimensional analysis. *Police Quarterly, 15,* 157-176. doi:10.1177/1098611112442809

Jorfi, H., Fauzy Bin Yacco, H., & Md Shah, I. (2012). Role of gender in emotional intelligence: Relationship among emotional intelligence, communication effectiveness and job satisfaction. *International Journal of Management, 29,* 590-597. Retrieved from http://www.internationaljournalofmanagement.co.uk/

Jorfi, H., Jorfi, S., Yaccob, H., & Shah, I. (2011). Relationships among strategic management, strategic behaviors, emotional intelligence, IT-business strategic alignment, motivation, and communication effectiveness. *International Journal of Business and Management, 6*(9), 30-37. doi:10.5539/ijbm.v6n9p30

Jorfi, H., & Jorfi, M. (2012). Management: A study of organizational culture and the relationship between emotional intelligence and communication effectiveness. *Journal of Management Research, 4,* 1-14. doi:10.5296/jmr.v4i1.936

Joseph, D. L., & Newman, D. A. (2010). Emotional intelligence: An integrative meta-analysis and cascading model. *Journal of Applied Psychology, 95,* 54-78. doi:10.1037/a0017286

Khalili, A. (2012). The role of emotional intelligence in the workplace: A literature review. *International Journal of Management, 29,* 355-370. Retrieved from http://www.internationaljournalofmanagement.co.uk/

Khan, M., Aslam, N., & Riaz, M. (2012). Leadership styles as predictors of innovative work behavior. *Pakistan Journal of Social & Clinical Psychology, 9*(2), 18-23. Retrieved from http://www.gcu.edu.pk/Soc&ClinPsyJour.htm

Kiel, L., Bezboruah, K., & Oyun, G. (2009). Developing leaders in public affairs and administration: incorporating emotional intelligence training into the core doctoral leadership course. *Journal of Public Affairs Education, 15,* 87-105. Retrieved from http://www.naspaa.org/jpaemessenger/

Kotze, M., & Venter, I. (2011). Differences in emotional intelligence between effective and ineffective leaders in the public sector: an empirical study. *International Review of Administrative Sciences, 77,* 397-427. doi:10.1177/0020852311399857

Kun, B., Urban, R., Paksi, B., Csobor, L., Olah, A., & Demetrovics, Z. (2012). Psychometric characteristics of the Emotional Quotient Inventory, youth version, short-form, in Hungarian high school students. *Psychological Assessment, 24,* 518-523. doi:10.1037/a0026013

Laborde, S., You, M., Dosseville, F., & Salinas, A. (2012). Culture, individual differences, and situation: Influence on coping in French and Chinese table tennis players. *European Journal of Sport Science*, 12(3), 255-261. doi:10.1080/17461391.2011.566367

Lam, C., & O'Higgins, E. E. (2012). Enhancing employee outcomes: The interrelated influences of managers' emotional intelligence and leadership style. *Leadership & Organization Development Journal, 33,* 149-174. doi:10.1108/01437731211203465

Lassk, F. G., & Shepherd, C. (2013). Exploring the relationship between emotional intelligence and salesperson creativity. *Journal of Personal Selling & Sales Management, 33,* 25-38. Retrieved from http://www.jpssm.org/

303

Lee, C., & Yang, H. (2012). Organization structure, competition and performance measurement systems and their joint effects on performance. *Management Accounting Research, 22*(2), 84-104. Retrieved from http://www.journals.elsevier.com/management-accounting-research/

Lee, W., Koenigsberg, M. R., Davidson, C., & Beto, D. (2010). A pilot survey linking personality, leadership style, and leadership success among probation directors in the U.S. *Federal Probation, 74*(3), 34-42. Retrieved from http://www.uscourts.gov/FederalCourts/ProbationPretrialServices/FederalProbationJournal.aspx

Liang, S., & Chi, S. (2013). Transformational leadership and follower task performance: The role of susceptibility to positive emotions and follower positive emotions. *Journal of Business and Psychology, 28,* 17-29. doi:10.1007/s10869-012-9261-x

Lindebaum, D., & Cartwright, S. (2010). A critical examination of the relationship between emotional intelligence and transformational leadership. *Journal of Management Studies, 47,* 1317-1342. doi:10.1111/j.1467-6486.2010.00933.x

Lopez-Zafra, E., Garcia-Retamero, R., & Berrios Martos, M. (2012). The relationship between transformational leadership and emotional intelligence from a gendered approach. *Psychological Record, 62,* 97-114. Retrieved from http://thepsychologicalrecord.siu.edu/

Lorinkova, N. M., Pearsall, M. J., & Sims, H. P., Jr. (2013). Examining the differential longitudinal performance of directive versus empowering leadership in teams. *Academy of Management Journal, 56,* 573-596. doi:10.5465/amj.2011.0132

MacCann, C., Matthews, G., & Roberts, R. D. (2012). Casting the first stone of validity standards: A less critical perspective of the MSCEIT. *Emotion Review, 4,* 409-410. doi:10.1177/1754073912445817

Maloş, R. (2011). Emotional intelligence in leadership. *Annals of Eftimie Murgu University Resita, Fascicle II, Economic Studies*, 208-214. Retrieved from http://jml2012.indexcopernicus.com/Analele+Universitatii+Eftimie+Murgu+Resita+Fascicola+II+-+Studii+Economice,p1759,3.html

Martins, A., Ramalho, N., & Morin, E. (2010). A comprehensive meta-analysis of the relationship between emotional intelligence and health. *Personality and Individual Differences, 49,* 554-564. doi:10.1016/j.paid.2010.05.029

Mastrofski, S. D., Rosenbaum, D. P., & Fridell, L. (2011). Police supervision: A 360-degree view of eight police departments. Retrieved from http://www.nationalpoliceresearch.org

Maul, A. (2011). The factor structure and cross-test convergence of the Mayer–Salovey–Caruso model of emotional intelligence. *Personality and Individual Differences, 50,* 457-463. doi:10.1016/j.paid.2010.11.007

Maul, A. (2012). The validity of the Mayer–Salovey–Caruso Emotional Intelligence Test (MSCEIT) as a measure of emotional intelligence. *Emotion Review, 4,* 394-402. doi:10.1177/1754073912445811

Maulding, W. S., Peters, G. B., Roberts, J., Leonard, E., & Sparkman, L. (2012). Emotional intelligence and resilience as predictors of leadership in school administrators. *Journal of Leadership Studies, 5*(4), 20-29. doi:10.1002/jls.20240

Mayer, J. D., & Salovey, P. (1997). What is emotional intelligence? In P. Salovey & D. J. Sluyter (Eds.), *Emotional development and emotional intelligence: Educational implications* (pp. 3-5). New York, NY: Basic Books.

Mayer, J. D., Salovey, P., & Caruso, D. R. (2008). Emotional intelligence: New ability or eclectic traits? *American Psychologist, 63,* 503-517. doi:10.1037/0003-066X.63.6.503

Mayer, J. D., Salovey, P., & Caruso, D. R. (2012). The validity of the MSCEIT: Additional analyses and evidence. *Emotion Review, 4,* 403-408. doi:10.1177/1754073912445815

Moors, G. (2012). The effect of response style bias on the measurement of transformational, transactional, and laissez-faire leadership. *European Journal of Work & Organizational Psychology*, 21(2), 271-298. doi:10.1080/1359432X.2010.550680

Murphy, S. A. (2008). The role of emotions and transformational leadership on police culture: An autoethnographic account. *International Journal of Police Science & Management, 10,* 165-178. doi:10.1350/ijps.2008.10.2.72

Muyia, H. M. (2009). Approaches to and instruments for measuring emotional intelligence: A review of selected literature. *Advances in Developing Human Resources, 11,* 690-702. doi:10.1177/1523422309360843

Muyia, H. M., & Kacirek, K. (2009). An empirical study of a leadership development training program and its impact on emotional intelligence quotient (EQ) scores. *Advances in Developing Human Resources, 11,* 703-718. doi:10.1177/1523422309360844

305

Nafukho, F. M. (2009). Emotional intelligence and performance: Need for additional empirical evidence. *Advances in Developing Human Resources, 11,* 671-689. doi:10.1177/1523422309360838

Naseer, Z., Chishti, S., Rahman, F., & Jumani, N. (2011). Impact of emotional intelligence on team performance in higher education institutes. *Journal of Educational Sciences. 3,* 30-46. Retrieved from http://www.iojes.net/

National Organization of Black Law Enforcement Executives. (2012). Federal and Local government intelligence sharing: FDCH Congressional Testimony. Retrieved from http://homeland.house.gov/hearing/subcommittee-hearing-federal-government-intelligence-sharing-state-local-and-tribal-law

Nayyar, S., & Raja, N. (2012). The impact of impression management behavior on organizational politics among male and female employees in organic and mechanistic organizational systems of Pakistan Telecommunication Sector. *Interdisciplinary Journal of Contemporary Research in Business, 3,* 914-924. Retrieved from http://ijcrb.webs.com/

Newman, D. A., Joseph, D. L., & MacCann, C. (2010). Emotional intelligence and job performance: The importance of emotion regulation and emotional labor context. *Industrial and Organizational Psychology, 3,* 159-164. doi:10.1111/j.1754-9434.2010.01218.x

Nooshin, E., & Hamid Gheze, S. (2011). Relationship between emotional intelligence and transformational leadership in physical education managers. *Procedia - Social and Behavioral Sciences, 30,* 2384-2393. doi:10.1016/j.sbspro.2011.10.465

Ono, M., Sachau, D. A., Deal, W. P., Englert, D. R., & Taylor, M. D. (2011). Cognitive ability, emotional intelligence, and the big five personality dimensions as predictors of criminal investigator performance. *Criminal Justice and Behavior, 38,* 471-491. doi:10.1177/0093854811399406

Österlind, M., & Haake, U. (2010). The leadership discourse amongst female police leaders in Sweden. *Advancing Women in Leadership, 30*(16), 1-24. Retrieved from http://advancingwomen.com/awl/awl_wordpress/

Parker, J., Keefer, K., & Wood, L. (2011). Toward a brief multidimensional assessment of emotional intelligence: Psychometric properties of the emotional quotient inventory-short form. *Psychological Assessment, 23,* 762-777. doi:10.1037/a0023289

Peterson, S. J., Walumbwa, F. O., Avolio, B. J., & Hannah, S. T. (2011). The relationship between authentic leadership and follower job performance: The mediating role of follower positivity in extreme contexts. *Leadership Quarterly, 23,* 502-516. doi:10.1016/j.leaqua.2011.12.004

Petrides, K. V. (2001). *A psychometric investigation into the construct of emotional intelligence.* London, England: University of London.

Petrides, K. V. (2009). *Technical manual for the Trait Emotional Intelligence Questionnaires (TEIQue).* London, England: London Psychometric Laboratory.

Petrides, K. V. (2010). Trait emotional intelligence theory. *Industrial and Organizational Psychology: Perspectives on Science and Practice, 3,* 136-139. doi:10.1111/j.1754-9434.2010.01213.x

Petrides, K., & Furnham, A. (2006). The role of trait emotional intelligence in a gender-specific model of organizational variables. *Journal of Applied Social Psychology, 36,* 552-569. doi:10.1111/j.0021-9029.2006.00019.x

Petrides, K., Pita, R., & Kokkinaki, F. (2007). The location of trait emotional intelligence in personality factor space. *British Journal of Psychology, 98,* 273-289. doi:10.1348/000712606X120618

Petrides, K. V., Vernon, P. A., Schermer, J. A., Ligthart, L., Boomsma, D. I., & Veselka, L. (2010). Relationships between trait emotional intelligence and the Big Five in the Netherlands. *In Personality and Individual Differences, 48,* 906-910. doi:10.1016/j.paid.2010.02.019

Ponterotto, J. G., Ruckdeschel, D. E., Joseph, A. C., Tennenbaum, E. A., & Bruno, A. (2011). Multicultural personality dispositions and trait emotional intelligence: An exploratory study. *Journal of Social Psychology, 151,* 556-576. doi:10.1080/00224545.2010.503718

Quoidbach, J., & Hansenne, M. (2009). The impact of trait emotional intelligence on nursing team performance and cohesiveness. *Journal of Professional Nursing, 25,* 23-29. doi:10.1016/j.profnurs.2007.12.0002

Radhakrishnan, A., & UdayaSuriyan, G. G. (2010). Emotional intelligence and its relationship with leadership practices. *International Journal of Business & Management, 5*(2), 65-76. Retrieved from http://www.ccsenet.org/journal/index.php/ijbm/

Rahim, M., & Marvel, M. R. (2011). The role of emotional intelligence in environmental scanning behavior: A cross-cultural study. *Academy of Strategic Management Journal, 10*(2), 83-103. Retrieved from http://www.alliedacademies.org/public/journals/journaldetails.aspx?jid =13

Ransley, J., & Mazerolle, L. (2009). Policing in an era of uncertainty. *Police Practice & Research, 10,* 365-381. doi:10.1080/15614260802586335

Rehman, R. (2011). Role of emotional intelligence on the relationship among leadership styles, decision making styles and organizational performance: A review. *Interdisciplinary Journal of Contemporary Research in Business, 3,* 409-416. Retrieved from http://ijcrb.webs.com/

Riaz, A., & Haider, M. (2010). Role of transformational and transactional leadership on job satisfaction and career satisfaction. *Business & Economic Horizons, 1,* 29-38. Retrieved from http://ideas.repec.org/a/pdc/jrnbeh/

Riggio, R. E. (2010). Before emotional intelligence: Research on nonverbal, emotional, and social competences. *Industrial and Organizational Psychology, 3,* 178-182. doi:10.1111/j.1754-9434.2010.01221.x

Rowold, J., & Borgmann, L. (2013). Are leadership constructs really independent? *Leadership & Organization Development Journal, 34,* 20-43. doi:10.1108/01437731311289956

Rozčenkova, A., & Dimdiņš, Ģ. (2011). Emotional intelligence as a mediator between commanders' transformational leadership and soldiers' social identification with their unit in the military. *Baltic Journal of Psychology, 12,* 59-72. Retrieved from http://www.lu.lv/apgads/izdevumi/elektroniskie-izdevumi/zurnali-un-periodiskie-izdevumi/baltic-journal-of-psychology/

Sadri, G. (2012). Emotional intelligence and leadership development. *Public Personnel Management, 41,* 535-548. doi:10.1177/009102601204100308

Salovey, P., Mayer, J. D., Goldman, S., Turvey, C., & Palfai, T. (1995). Emotional attention, clarity, and repair: Exploring emotional intelligence using the trait meta-mood scale. In J. W. Pennebaker (Ed.), *Emotion, disclosure, and health* (pp. 125-154). Washington, DC: American Psychological Association. doi:10.1037/10182-006

Sanchez-Ruiz, M., Mavroveli, S., & Poullis, J. (2013). Trait emotional intelligence and its links to university performance: An examination. *Personality and individual differences, 54,* 658-662. doi:10.1016/j.paid.2012.11.013

Sayeed, O. B., & Shanker, M. (2009). Emotionally intelligent managers & transformational leadership styles. *Indian Journal of Industrial Relations, 44,* 593-610. Retrieved from http://www.srcirhr.com/ijir.php

Scaglion, R., & Condon, R. (1980). Determinants of attitudes toward city police. *Criminology 17*, 485-494.

Schlaerth, A., Ensari, N., Christian, J. (2013). A meta-analytical review of the relationship between emotional intelligence and leaders' constructive conflict management. *Group Processes & Intergroup Relations, 16 (1), 126-136.* doi:10.1177/1368430212439907

Schutte, N. S., Malouff, J. M., Hall, L. E., Haggerty, D. L., Cooper, J. T., Golden, C. J., & Dornheim, L. (1998). Development and validation of a measure of emotional intelligence. *Personality and Individual Differences, 25,* 167-177. doi:10.1016/S0191-8869(98)00001-4

Seal, C. R., & Andrews-Brown, A. (2010). An integrative model of emotional intelligence: Emotional ability as a moderator of the mediated relationship of emotional quotient and emotional competence. *Organization Management Journal, 7,* 143-152. doi:10.1057/omj.2010.22

Shahhosseini, M., Daud Silong, A., & Arif Ismaill, I. (2013). Relationship between transactional, transformational leadership styles, emotional intelligence and job performance. *Researchers World: Journal of Arts, Science & Commerce, 6,* 15-22. Retrieved from http://papers.ssrn.com/sol3/papers.cfm?abstract_id=2189291

Shih, H., & Susanto, E. (2010). Conflict management styles, emotional intelligence, and job performance in public organizations. *International Journal of Conflict Management, 21,* 147-168. doi:10.1108/10444061011037387

Shih, T., & Fan, X. (2009). Comparing response rates in E-mail and paper surveys: A meta-analysis. *Educational Research Review, 4,* 26-40. doi:10.1016%2Fj.edurev.2008.01.003

Shooshtarian, Z., Ameli, F., & Aminilari, M. (2013). The effect of labor's emotional intelligence on their job satisfaction, job performance and commitment. *Iranian Journal of Management Studies, 6,* 29-45. Retrieved from http://www.getcited.org/pub/103486573

Shuck, M. B., Tonette, S. R., & Albornoz, C. A. (2011). Exploring employee engagement from the employee perspective: Implications for HRD. *Journal of European Industrial Training, 35,* 300-325. doi:10.1108/03090591111128306

Siebert-Adzic, M. (2012). Emotions and leadership. Reasons and impact of emotions in organizational context. *Work, 41,* 5671-5673. doi:10.3233/WOR-2012-0915-5671

Singleton, R., & Straits, B. (2010). *Approaches to social research.* New York, NY: Oxford University Press.

309

Stanimirovic, R., & Hanrahan, S. (2012). Examining the dimensional structure and factorial validity of the Bar-On Emotional Quotient Inventory in a sample of male athletes. *Psychology of Sport & Exercise, 13,* 44-50. doi:10.1016/j.psychsport.2011.07.009

Stough, C., Saklofske, D. H., & Parker, J. D. A. (2009). *Assessing emotional intelligence: Theory, research, and application.* New York, NY: Springer.

Sung, H. Y. (2010). The influence of culture on parenting practices of East Asian families and emotional intelligence of older adolescents: A qualitative study. *School Psychology International, 31,* 199-214. doi:10.1177/0143034309352268

Talab, F., & Monfared, J. (2012). The relationship between emotional intelligence and organizational learning (Scope of research: Nation Iranian petroleum products distribution company (NIOPDC) in Sari City). *Interdisciplinary Journal of Contemporary Research in Business, 4*(8), 371-382. Retrieved from http://journal-archieves26.webs.com/dec12.pdf

Thiel, C., Connelly, S., & Griffith, J. (2012). Leadership and emotion management for complex tasks: Different emotions, different strategies. *Leadership Quarterly, 23,* 517-533. doi:10.1016/j.leaqua.2011.12.005

Torres, S., & Perri, L. (2009). The impact of culture on emotional intelligence: A comparison of French and German business students. Retrieved from http://www.nedsi.org/proc/2009/proc/p081019021.pdf

van Dusseldorp, L. C., van Meijel, B. G., & Derksen, J. L. (2011). Emotional intelligence of mental health nurses. *Journal of Clinical Nursing, 20,* 555-562. doi:10.1111/j.1365-2702.2009.03120.x

Van Rooy, D. L., Whitman, D. S., & Viswesvaran, C. (2010). Emotional intelligence: Additional questions still unanswered. *Industrial and Organizational Psychology: Perspectives on Science and Practice, 3*(2), 149-153. doi:10.1111/j.1754-9434.2010.01216.x

Volckmann, R. (2012). Integral leadership and diversity—definitions, distinctions and implications. *Integral Leadership Review, 12*(3), 1-21. Retrieved from http://integralleadershipreview.com/

Walter, F., Cole, M. S., & Humphrey, R. H. (2011). Emotional intelligence: Sine qua non of leadership or folderol. *Academy of Management Perspectives, 25,* 45-59. doi:10.5465/AMP.2011.59198449

Walter, F., Humphrey, R., & Cole, M. (2012). Unleashing leadership potential: Toward an evidence-based management of emotional intelligence. *Organizational Dynamics, 41,* 212-219. doi:10.1016/j.orgdyn.2012.03.002

Wang, J. (2011). Understanding managerial effectiveness: A Chinese perspective. *Journal of European Industrial Training, 35,* 6-23. doi:10.1108%2F03090591111095718

Weinberger, L. (2009). Emotional intelligence, leadership style, and perceived leadership effectiveness. *Advances in Developing Human Resources, 11,* 747-772. doi:10.1177/1523422309360811

Westerlaken, K. M., & Woods, P. R. (2012). The relationship between psychopathy and the full range leadership model. *Personality and Individual Differences, 5,* 441-446. doi:10.1016/j.paid.2012.08.026

Yunus, N. J., & Anuar, S. (2012). Trust as moderating effect between emotional intelligence and transformational leadership styles. *Interdisciplinary Journal of Contemporary Research in Business, 3*(10), 650-663. Retrieved from http://ijcrb.webs.com/

Index

"Black men and White cops don't mix", 185
"I feared for my life", 47, 65
"Kids for cash", 123
"Racism in the ranks", 185
2016 Presidential Debates, 265
A Time to Kill (film), 243, 260
Abuse of children, 122
Ahrens, Lorne, 293
Alexander, Michelle, 114
Amygdala hijack, 61, 63, 64
Ancestors, 64, 89
Anti-law enforcement, 227
Argyris, Chris, 24
Armored vehicles, 134, 232
Asch, Solomon, 19, 20
Aurelius, Marcus, 23
Autopsy, 43, 134, 245
Bailey, F. Lee, 34
Baldwin, James, 205
Baltimore Police Department, 191, 192, 283
Baltimore school police force, 282
Baton Rouge, 43, 293
Baum, Dan, 115-117
Baumeister, Roy, 18
BET Awards, 42
Bill of Rights, 233
Black Lives Matter, 263- 265, 269, 270, 293
Black Panthers, 42
Black teenagers, 103
Blackface, 80
Black-ish, 167
Blacks killed by other Blacks, 210
Bland, Sandra, 244, 256
Bodily-kinesthetic, 5, 54
Bon Jovi, Jon, ix
Bravery, 295
Bridge the gap, 220, 258, 262, 297
Bronco, 37, 38
Brown, Michael, 66, 77, 133, 134, 136, 192, 193, 205, 209, 216, 220, 223, 225, 227, 231, 234, 236
Buckwheats, 185

Building bonds, 235, 272
Bureaucracy, 139, 145
Carson, Ben, 40
Carter, Jimmy, 113
Castile, Philando, 45-47, 292
Caucasian, 70, 82, 88,103, 128
Charismatic, 2, 144
Chattel, 207
Child Protective Services, 73
Civil War, 88, 114
Civilian, 198, 291
Clark, Marcia, 35
Cleaver, Eldridge, 233
Clemency, 132
Cleveland Police Department, 273
Clinton, Bill, 113, 121
Clinton, Hillary, 121, 169
Cochran, Johnnie, 34, 35
Collectivist Society, 82
Colorblindness, 114
Command-and-control, 1, 143
Communication process, 150, 151
Community policing, 92, 93, 139, 140, 151, 219
Compliance, 30, 137, 138, 181, 183, 255, 256, 275
Composure, 119, 226, 231, 238, 239, 242, 247, 273, 277
Compton, 8, 40, 126, 268
Conflict management, 243, 278
Conscious awareness, 207
Contemporary organizations, 1, 143
Cooke, Sam, ix
Courage, 18, 295
Crack, 115, 215
Crash (film), 172, 174, 176, 179
Crime Bill, 121, 123-127, 129, 130
Crime control, 89, 91, 121
Crime legislation, 129, 131
Crime statistics, 104, 106, 108, 109, 210
Criminal behavior, 74, 76, 282
Criminal justice system, 39, 101, 104, 110, 115, 117, 120, 123, 127, 129, 260
Criminals, 91, 109, 118, 120, 129, 132, 146, 210, 271

Cross-cultural variations, 81
Cultural beliefs, 72, 79
Cultural differences, 151
Cultural norms, 82
Curfew, 10, 134
Dallas Police, 293, 294
Deadly force, 22, 44, 65, 156-160, 183, 189, 225, 255, 256
de Blasio, Bill, 166, 168
Deep Cover, 13
Deescalate, 45, 247, 278
DeGruy, Joy, 76, 77
Dehumanization, 70, 205, 207
Deindividuation, 20
Dershowitz, Alan, 34
Diplomatic relations, 142
Discrimination, 9, 27
Disparate treatment, 42, 49, 171, 230, 280, 295
Disproportionate, 62, 136, 162
DNA evidence, 34, 35
Douglas, Carl, 34
Drug dealers, 105, 110
Drug laws, 105, 113
Drug offenses, 107, 112, 115, 125
Durkheim, Emile, 74
Dysfunctional language, 118
Educators, 281
Ehrlichman, John, 116
Elephant in the room, 3, 263, 265
Emancipation, 89, 118, 119
Emotional awareness, 246, 256, 282, 285
Emotional commitment, 2, 144
Emotional immaturity, 273
Emotional-social intelligence, 55
Empathy, 17, 122, 223, 236, 239, 243, 253, 268, 269, 290, 294
Environmental, 14, 22, 55, 138, 184, 281
EQ assessment, 82, 83
EQ construct, 3, 6, 53, 55, 57, 82, 205
EQ traits, 145
Equality, 27, 28, 42, 101, 127, 130 170
Ethics, 183, 184, 194
Ethnic groups, 28, 82
Excessive force, 32, 157, 217, 242, 280
Existential intelligence, 5, 54
Facebook, 80, 286
FBI, 106-109, 112
Ferguson, Diane, 175-177, 179, 269
Ferguson, Don, 186, 187
Ferguson, JaNae, 175, 176
Ferguson, JaRon, 45, 130, 158, 169, 174, 259
Ferguson Police Department, 65, 162, 172, 230, 231, 233-236
Fight-or-flight, 60, 63, 64, 67
Fishburne, Laurence, 13

Florin High School, 275, 281, 282
Ford, Ezell, 217, 218, 220
Fox News, 40
Fuhrman, Mark, 35, 36
Gangs, 8, 9, 40, 122, 126, 218
Garafola, Brad, 293
Garcetti, Eric, 263
Garner, Eric, 133-136, 209, 217, 220
General factor of g, 50
General intelligence, 5, 50
Gerald, Matthew, 293
Globalization, 1, 143, 145, 146
Goldman, Ronald, 34, 36, 37
Goleman, Daniel, xx, xxvi, xxviii, 3, 17, 56, 57-59, 61, 221, 223
Goleman's EQ model, 56, 57, 58, 59, 221, 223
Google, 103
Government-sponsored slave patrols, 88
Gray, Freddie, 191, 193
Grey's Anatomy, 42
Group conformance, 19
Guilt, 33, 34, 36, 39, 128, 220
Gunfight, 126
Guns, 228
Haggis, Paul, 172
Hatred, 293
Henwood, Jeremy, 287, 288, 289
Hitler, Adolf, 35
Hogan, Hulk, 206
Homeland security, 94-96, 140-142
Howard, Terrence, 172
Human brain, 4, 49, 60, 67
Human intellect, 3
Human intelligence, 4, 5, 49, 52, 53
Humanness, 207
Incarcerated, 110, 113, 131, 132
Indentured servants, 87
Individualistic, 82, 145
Inflammatory, 14, 35, 293
Inmate, 107, 111, 124, 129, 131, 132, 187
Inner-city, 33, 40, 125, 126, 214, 261
Innocence, 34, 36, 39, 70, 71, 117, 132, 167, 220, 237
Innovative, 145, 146, 231, 278
Integrity, 18, 235
Intelligence quotient (IQ), 3, 4, 6, 49, 50, 57, 291
Intelligence test, 3-5, 50, 51, 54, 56
Internal investigation, 234
International Associations of Chiefs of Police (IACP), 96, 145
Interpersonal, 5, 18, 54, 55, 56, 290, 291
Interpersonal intelligence, 54
Interpersonal relationships, 18
Interrogation, 173, 273
Intrapersonal, 5, 54-56, 290, 291

2

Intrapersonal intelligence, 54
Jackson, Montrell, 293
Jackson, Samuel, L., 243
Jamestown, Virginia, 87, 88
Jigaboos, 185
Jim Crow, 77, 114, 258
Judicial system, 113, 157, 269
Juveniles, 68, 106, 123, 129
Kardashian, Robert, 34
Keller, Helen, 258
Kelly, Megyn, 40
King, Jr., Martin, 101
King, Rodney, 28, 33, 38
Knowles, Beyoncé, 2016 Super Bowl half-time performance, 42
Krol, Michael, 293
Ladder of inference, 24, 33, 39, 40, 165
Lamar, Kendrick, 2015 BET Awards performance of "Alright", 42
LaVette, Bettye, ix
Leary, Joy, xxvi
Leary, Mark, 18
LeDoux, Joseph, 61
Leveraging diversity, 235, 251, 288
Lincoln, Abraham, 88
Linguistic, 5, 54
Logical-mathematical, 5, 54
Long-term orientation, 79
Los Angeles Police Department (LAPD), 11, 28-29, 30, 36, 39, 172-173, 266, 267
Luzerne County judge, 122
Lynching, 77
Manage emotions, 6, 144
Marijuana, 107, 112, 113, 116
Marksmanship, 156, 273, 292, 294
Martin, Trayvon, 169, 259, 260
Mary Mary, 267
Masculinity versus femininity, 79
Mass incarceration, 77, 114, 121
McConaughey, Matthew, 244
McDonald, Laquan, 189
McKinney, Texas pool party incident, 240, 242-244
Mechanical intelligence, 5, 6, 52
Mechanistic work environments, 1, 143
Mental state, 3, 47, 144
Mental transactions, 26
Miller, Jonathan, 249-253, 255, 256
Minorities, 14, 15, 82, 107, 185, 212
Minority, 10, 80
Multiculturalism, 101
Multigenerational trauma, 77
Multiple intelligence, 5, 52, 53
Murders, 34, 36, 37, 39, 104, 106, 108, 190, 210
Musical, 5, 54
N.W.A.'s "Fuck Tha Police" (lyrics), 40

National Guard, 9, 10
Naturalistic, 5, 54
Navigating, 294
Neufeld, Peter, 34
New Mexico state police, 236
Newton, Thandie, 172
Nigger, 118-120, 185
Nixon, Richard, 112, 116, 117
Nurturing relationships, 235, 290
N-word, 35
Obama, Barack, 113, 132, 293, 295
Officer-involved shootings, 65, 80, 157, 158, 160, 173, 209, 216
Operant conditioning theory, 171
Oppression, 77
Orange County Sherriff's Department, 178, 181
Organizational effectiveness, 2, 4, 153
P = C = N, 118-120
Paradigm, 95, 139, 141, 149, 262, 273, 296
Paramilitary, 139, 148, 267
Peaceful protestors, 232, 233
Pell Grants, 129, 130
Penalties, 105, 110, 113, 115, 125
Personhood, 207
Physiological change, 3, 144
Police body cameras, 196-198
Police brutality, 21, 47, 48, 134, 157, 160, 207
Police corruption, 14, 90, 138, 235
Police militarization, 134, 141, 232
Policies, 109, 117, 149, 191
Policy, 94, 116, 136, 137, 159, 160, 184, 242, 254, 277
Political awareness, 256
Political era, 90
Politics, 94, 96, 116, 212, 242
Post Traumatic Slave Syndrome, 76
Postal Inspector, 137
Post-Civil War Jim Crow, 114
Postracial society, 78
Posttraumatic stress disorder, 77
Poverty, 75, 76
Power distance, 78, 145
Pre-Civil War slavery, 114
Preconceived, 22, 27, 108, 219
Prejudice, 27, 28, 70, 207
Presidential proclamation, 88
Protestors, 192
Protests, 47, 69, 77, 80, 134, 192, 209, 231, 241, 260, 295
Psychological process, 19
Public perception, 133, 134, 160, 190, 289
Public safety, 92, 95, 110, 162
Purge (film), 192
Questionable shootings, 149, 290
Questionable tactics, 34, 283, 285

Race control, 89
Race relations, 32, 41, 42, 167, 168, 211, 221, 229, 230, 231, 258
Racial bias, 103, 243
Racial caste system, 115
Racial group, 82, 109, 115
Racial injustice, 228, 242, 269
Racial profiling, 109, 161, 162, 164, 166, 170, 181, 182, 213, 221
Racial slurs, 14
Racial tensions, 32, 228
Racial undertones, 105, 117, 182
Racially motivated, 10, 77, 161
Racism, 14, 20, 28, 49, 77, 89, 185
Rawlings-Blake, Stephanie, 283
Recidivism, 74, 121, 131
Recruit, 14, 18, 96, 184, 273, 289
Reflexive loop, 25
Reform era, 90, 91
Relationship management, 6, 57, 59, 221, 231, 235
Researcher bias, 102, 108
Reynolds, Diamond, 47
Rialto, California, 198
Rice, Tamir, 68, 69, 273
Ruopp, Timothy, xvii, xviii
Sambos, 185
San Bernardino, California, 285
Scheck, Barry, 34, 35
School Resource Officer, 282, 283
Scott, Walter, 190
Seek and destroy, 232
Self-awareness, 20, 57-59, 72, 81, 83, 221, 223, 224, 290
Self-control, 233, 238, 242, 247, 278
Self-management, 57-59, 221, 223, 231, 232
Self-motivation, 290
Self-regulation, 290
Sentencing, 110, 111, 113, 116, 128, 129, 132
Shapiro, Robert, 34
Simmons, Randal, 267, 268
Simpson, Nicole, Brown, 34, 37, 38
Simpson, Orenthal, James, 33-39
Skinner, B.F., 171
Sky-writer, 10
Slager, Michael, 190, 191
Slave owners, 88, 208
Slave population, 88
Slave trade, 89
Slavery, 77-89, 114, 118, 207
Smith, Michael, 293
Snyder, Jimmy "The Greek", 208
Social awareness, 57-59, 221, 229, 230, 231
Social construct, 229

Social justice, 26, 154, 168
Social media, 44, 81, 192, 196, 280, 284, 288, 293
Social relationships, 5, 52
Social systems, 78
South Carolina School Incident, 274-276, 281
South Central Los Angeles, 10, 32
Spatial, 5, 54
Sportsman Park, 8
Stamper, Norm, 184-186
Standard intelligence tests, 5, 50, 54
Stanford Binet, 51
Stanford University, 128
Stephanopoulos, George, 65, 169, 224, 227-229, 231
Stereotype, 105, 219, 288
Stereotypical, 81
Sterling, Alton, 43, 44, 46, 47, 292
Straight Outta Compton, 40
Strain theory, 74
Strategic vision, 1, 2, 143, 144
SUNY Plattsburgh, 80
Superhumanization bias, 207
Super-predator, 121, 122
Sutherland, Edwin, 74
SWAT, 267
Systemic and structural racism, 77
Systems thinking, 271
Tased, 248, 249, 251, 253
Tear gas, 232
Tensions, 10, 32, 105, 228, 229
Terrorism, 94, 95, 146
Terrorist, 93-95, 133, 285
The Nigger in You, 118
The Prejudiced Discriminator, 28
The Prejudiced Nondiscriminatory, 27
The Unprejudiced Discriminator, 27
The Unprejudiced Nondiscriminatory, 27
Three-strikes law, 125, 127
Thompson, Brent, 293
To protect and to serve, 8, 92, 195, 219, 232, 236, 262, 292
Tonahill, Kim, xvi, xvii, xviii, xix, 266
Traffic stop, 165, 166, 173, 190, 238, 239, 240, 244, 245, 247, 248
Trustworthy, 154, 184, 196
Trustworthiness, 188, 231, 235, 272
Uelmen, Gerald, 34
Uncertainty avoidance, 78
Unreasonable searches and seizures, 142
Use of Force, 71, 160, 198, 220, 234
Van Dyke, Jason, 189
Vera Institute of Justice, 131
Victim, 111, 122, 123, 161, 210, 259, 260
Villaraigosa, Antonio, 87
Violent crime, 106

Violent Crime Control and Law Enforcement Act of 1994, 121-122
War on drugs, 110-113, 115-117
Warning shot, 237
Watts riots, 9
White drug offenders, 118
White House, 40, 116, 264
White teenagers, 103
Whites, 77, 78, 80, 107-109, 119, 207, 208, 210, 215

Whites killed by other Whites, 210
Wiley, J.W., 118-120
Williams, Jesse, 42
Wilson, Darren, 64-65, 80, 205, 206, 208, 223-231
Yahoe, John, 34
Zamarripa, Patrick, 293